Pointing at the Moon

Pointing at the Moon

Buddhism, Logic, Analytic Philosophy

EDITED BY MARIO D'AMATO, JAY L. GARFIELD,
AND TOM J. F. TILLEMANS

OXFORD
UNIVERSITY PRESS
2009

OXFORD
UNIVERSITY PRESS

Oxford University Press, Inc., publishes works that further
Oxford University's objective of excellence
in research, scholarship, and education.

Oxford New York
Auckland Cape Town Dar es Salaam Hong Kong Karachi
Kuala Lumpur Madrid Melbourne Mexico City Nairobi
New Delhi Shanghai Taipei Toronto

With offices in
Argentina Austria Brazil Chile Czech Republic France Greece
Guatemala Hungary Italy Japan Poland Portugal Singapore
South Korea Switzerland Thailand Turkey Ukraine Vietnam

Published by Oxford University Press, Inc.
198 Madison Avenue, New York, New York 10016

www.oup.com

Oxford is a registered trademark of Oxford University Press

Library of Congress Cataloging-in-Publication Data

Pointing at the moon : Buddhism, logic, analytic philosophy / edited by
Mario D'Amato, Jay L. Garfield, and Tom J. F. Tillemans
p. cm.
Includes bibliographical references and index.
ISBN 978-0-19-538155-9; 978-0-19-538156-6 (pbk.)
1. Philosophy, Buddhist. 2. Buddhism—Doctrines.
3. Philosophy, Comparative. I. D'Amato, Mario, 1969–
II. Garfield, Jay L., 1955– III. Tillemans, Tom J. F.
BL62.P65 2009
294.3'361—dc22 2008051544

9 8 7 6 5 4 3 2 1

Printed in the United States of America
on acid-free paper

Preface

In June 2001, I was returning to Cambridge from a stint as a visiting researcher of logic and philosophy of science at the University of California, Irvine; David Lake was returning to Cambridge from a holiday in Thailand; and we met on the bus from Gatwick. The journey to Cambridge was a long one, and by its end we had started a collaboration, some of the fruits of which you hold in your hand. Dr. Lake founded the St. Luke's Institute and invited me to be its conference director. In that capacity, I was able to organize the New Foundations seventieth anniversary meeting and a meeting on logic and rhetoric. Both of these meetings resulted in volumes which are in press as I write. The third meeting was called BILAP: Buddhism in Logic and Analytic Philosophy.

The reasons for BILAP are twofold. Dr. Lake had family connections in the Far East and had spent many years there, and he was pleased to think that his philanthropy should improve appreciation in the Occident of ideas that had their genesis in the part of the world that had supplied his fortune. My reasons for wishing to organize a meeting of this kind were quite different, and I hope to explore them one day in greater detail than we have space for here. I hoped—and still hope—that what I can learn from Buddhism will help me with two particular problems that arise in Western logic and which are usually hidden away, like the first Mrs. Rochester. I refer to the problem of *inexpressibility* and the problem of *haecceity*.

Philosophy students brought up in the Anglo-American tradition are likely, sooner or later, to encounter the *envoi* at the end of the *Tractatus*: *Wovon man nicht sprechen kann, darüber muss man schweigen.* And they will cherish Ramsey's summary: "the chief proposition of philosophy is that philosophy is nonsense. And again we must then take seriously that it is nonsense, and not pretend, as Wittgenstein does, that it is important nonsense!" (1931: 263). Therein lies the problem. We cannot explain how the nonsense comes to be important without giving it some semantics, and once it has semantics, it ceases to be nonsense.

Generally, the analytic tradition copes very poorly with the inexpressible, and it has a related problem with nonsense. Can we expect better from the Buddhist tradition? Buddhism—with its emphasis on practical wisdom—seems to point the way to a kind of radical instrumentalism that would defuse philosophical/religious conflicts by resisting the temptation to represent a divergence of practice as a difference of opinion about propositions. If we cease to maintain that the various internal states that mystics have (and this point is made particularly in connection with mystics) are to be construed as propositional attitudes, then much of the apparent disagreement evaporates.

Medieval Western philosophy isolated for our attention the concept of haecceity, an individual essence persisting throughout time, a bit like a soul, except that mere objects can have them—and, indeed, all do. Modern quantificational logic seems to follow the medieval tradition in this, in that it presents us with a picture of the world as inhabited by objects which then are allocated properties. To read a formula like "there is an x, such that Fx," one has to think something like "there is this chap x" and then append the reflection that this chap has property F. The chap seems to exist independently of the properties. I've always felt very uneasy about this, and the image I have always employed to parody it is that of objects-as-spikes on which one impales pieces of paper (at least in offices in the days before information technology).

I have long suspected that doing our thinking in terms of haecceities may be a dangerous error and wondered whether Buddhism might provide some needed light. Now, the editors of the present volume suggest to me that a haecceity compares interestingly to the Indian idea of a real individual entity (*bhāva*) or substance (*dravya*) that is the substratum for properties and exists independently of them. And I gather that such real individual entities or substances, be they things or selves, are rejected across the board in Mahāyāna Buddhism. Perhaps the insight that led to this particular aspect of Buddhist teaching could be profitably applied to, well, logic and analytic philosophy—hence the title of the conference and this volume.

Although the idea for BILAP was mine, it could never have happened without the ideas, enthusiasm, and contacts of my friend and colleague Graham Priest. When I told him of my plan, he knew immediately whom to invite, and the contributors to this volume were assembled largely because of him.

Dr. Thomas Forster
August 1, 2008

Acknowledgments

The editors would like to thank Dr. David Lake and the St. Luke's Institute for funding the conference on Buddhism in Logic and Analytic Philosophy (BILAP), held at Cambridge University in November 2005. Thanks also go to Dr. Thomas Forster for organizing the BILAP conference. Mario D'Amato would like to thank his undergraduate assistant, Alicia Florio, for her reliable assistance with numerous (numberless!) editorial tasks, especially in preparing the bibliography; and Rollins College for a travel grant to attend the BILAP conference. Jay L. Garfield would like to thank the Elisabeth de Boer Fund of the University of Lausanne and Smith College for a faculty development grant. Tom J. F. Tillemans would also like to thank the Elisabeth de Boer Fund of the University of Lausanne, which covered part of his travel expenses to attend the BILAP conference at Cambridge University.

Contents

Contributors

Dan Arnold is assistant professor of philosophy of religion at the University of Chicago Divinity School. He is the author of *Buddhists, Brahmins, and Belief: Epistemology in South Asian Philosophy of Religion* (2005), which won an American Academy of Religion Award for Excellence in the Study of Religion. His writings have appeared in the *Journal of Indian Philosophy*, the *Journal of the International Association of Buddhist Studies*, and *Philosophy East and West*.

Mario D'Amato is assistant professor in the Department of Philosophy and Religion at Rollins College in Winter Park, Florida. He specializes in the study of Mahāyāna philosophy, with a particular focus on the Yogācāra school, and has published papers on Yogācāra thought in the *Journal of the International Association of Buddhist Studies*, *Semiotica*, the *Journal of Indian Philosophy*, and the *Journal for Cultural and Religious Theory*. He is currently completing a book-length study and translation of a Yogācāra doctrinal treatise known as the *Madhyāntavibhāga* (Distinguishing the Middle from the Extremes).

Jay L. Garfield is Doris Silbert Professor in the Humanities, professor of philosophy, and director of the Logic Program and of the Five College Tibetan Studies in India Program at Smith College; professor in the Graduate Faculty of Philosophy at the University of Massachusetts; professor of philosophy at Melbourne University; and adjunct professor of philosophy at the Central Institute of Higher Tibetan Studies. He teaches and pursues research in the philosophy of mind, foundations of cognitive science, logic, philosophy of language, Buddhist philosophy, cross-cultural hermeneutics, theoretical and applied ethics, and epistemology.

Raymond Martin is Dwane W. Crichton Professor of Philosophy and chair of the Department of Philosophy at Union College in Schenectady, New York. Formerly, he taught at the University of Maryland, College Park. His publications on the self and personal identity include *Self-Concern: An Experiential Approach to What Matters in Survival* (1998), and "What Really Matters" (*Synthese*, 2008). He is also co-author (with John Barresi) of *Naturalization of the Soul: Self and Personal Identity in the Eighteenth Century* (2000) and *The Rise and Fall of Soul and Self: An Intellectual History of Personal Identity* (2006).

Chris Mortensen is emeritus professor of philosophy at the University of Adelaide and a fellow of the Academy of Humanities of Australia. His research interests are in logic, metaphysics, philosophy of science, and Buddhism. His publications include *Inconsistent Mathematics* (1995) and articles in the *Journal of Symbolic Logic*, the *Journal of Philosophical Logic, Synthese, Erkenntnis*, the *Australasian Journal of Philosophy, Philosophy East and West*, and other journals.

Graham Priest is Boyce Gibson Professor of Philosophy at the University of Melbourne and Arché Professorial Fellow at the University of St Andrews. He is well known for his work in logic and metaphysics. His nonphilosophical interests include Western opera and karatedo.

Rupert Read is reader in philosophy at the University of East Anglia, where he specializes in Wittgenstein, philosophy of the sciences, and environmental and political philosophy. His works include *Applying Wittgenstein* (2007) and *There Is No Such Thing as a Social Science* (2008). Perhaps his most famous book remains *The New Wittgenstein* (2000), an edited collection of essays.

Mark Siderits currently teaches Asian and comparative philosophy in the Philosophy Department of Seoul National University. His research interests lie in the intersection between classical Indian philosophy, on the one hand, and analytic metaphysics and philosophy of language, on the other. He is the author of *Buddhism as Philosophy* (2007) and *Personal Identity and Buddhist Philosophy: Empty Persons* (2003). He is presently working with Shoryu Katsura on a new translation of Nāgārjuna's *Mūlamadhyamakakārikā*s.

Koji Tanaka is lecturer in philosophy at the University of Auckland, New Zealand. He has published widely in leading journals and made contributions to logic, philosophy of logic, Chinese philosophy, and Buddhist philosophy. He has also served as reviews editor for *Studia Logica*, an international journal of symbolic logic.

Tom J. F. Tillemans is an expatriate Dutch Canadian, who since 1992 has occupied the chair of Buddhist studies at the University of Lausanne, Switzerland. His initial training was in analytic philosophy, with additional training in Sanskrit, Tibetan, and Chinese. His published work has been in Buddhist Madhyamaka and epistemology, with an increasing emphasis on issues of comparative philosophy. He has also made occasional forays into Tibetan grammar and poetry. Tillemans has edited the *Journal of the International Association of Buddhist Studies* (with C. Scherrer-Schaub) and is currently that association's general secretary; he also co-edits the series Studies in Indian and Tibetan Buddhism (Wisdom). His books include *Materials for the Study of Āryadeva, Dharmapāla, and Candrakīrti* (1990, reprinted in 2008); *Persons of Authority* (1993); *Scripture, Logic, Language: Essays on Dharmakīrti and His Tibetan Successors* (1999); *Dharmakīrti's Pramāṇavārttika: An Annotated Translation of the Fourth Chapter* (2000); and *Agents and Actions in Classical Tibetan* (1989, with D. Herforth).

Jan Westerhoff read philosophy and Oriental studies at Cambridge and London. He works mainly on systematic and historical issues in metaphysics and the philosophy of language. A particular interest of his is Indo-Tibetan Madhyamaka.

Introduction

The American Philosophical Association has an official position regarding the structure of the undergraduate philosophy major ("Statement on the Major," Proceedings and Addresses of the APA, Summer 2007) and a fortiori an official position regarding the scope of the discipline of philosophy. That position, perhaps surprisingly to some, follows Hegel and early Heidegger quite closely: philosophy, the APA informs us, began in Greece and was inherited by Europe. The principal philosophers, we are told, are Plato, Aristotle, Descartes, and Kant. Critique of the narrowness, arbitrariness, and ethnocentrism of this characterization is too easy and too boring to undertake here.

Fortunately, philosophical practice around the world—even in the United States, Europe, and Australia—has left this parochial definition behind. Philosophers originally trained narrowly in the Western tradition valorized by the APA are engaging happily with non-Western philosophical texts and traditions. This engagement has proven fecund indeed, enriching discourse in Western philosophy with insights and techniques from non-Western traditions and enriching those traditions with insights and techniques drawn from the West. Academic philosophy is globalizing, canons are merging, and borders are fast blurring. The distinction between Asian and Western philosophy, in particular, may soon become rather uninformative.

Certain Western philosophers are fond of another endangered distinction between forms of philosophy, this one typically drawn within the Western corpus: the distinction between "analytic" and "continental" philosophy. This distinction is hard to draw (a lot of philosophers typically denominated "analytic" live or write on the relevant continent; a lot of philosophers typically denominated "continental" do not, and indeed engage in a lot of analysis); and we think that the distinction is spurious, reflecting predilections for literary style rather than philosophical method or doctrine. Nonetheless, it has been surprisingly robust and is enshrined in the conference schedules and self-descriptions of philosophers and departments of philosophy.

Some have thought that the most natural meeting ground between Asian and Western philosophy would be with the so-called continental tradition. This is presumably because of the supposedly greater concern for phenomenology and "big questions" regarding the meaning of life among continental philosophers, which is taken to match the supposed special concern for phenomenology and big questions among Buddhist philosophers; or perhaps it is because self-described analytic philosophers profess to find both what they consider continental and everything written in Asia particularly obscure; or perhaps it is simply because Asian and continental philosophy share the essential property of being ignored by many of those who self-consciously self-ascribe the label analytic. And to be sure, there has been some notable meeting on this ground.

Nonetheless, a great deal of the most fruitful cross-cultural engagement has involved Western philosophers generally regarded as analytic in bent attending to Buddhist philosophy, and scholars of Buddhist philosophy finding much of use in contemporary Western philosophy written by those often denominated analysts. We will not speculate as to why this might be the case, but we do note that this engagement has been broad, encompassing work in logic, the philosophy of language, metaphysics, epistemology, and ethics. In each domain, philosophers grounded in Western philosophy or Buddhist philosophy have found much in the other tradition by way of insight and illumination. Moreover, this engagement has involved all of the major Buddhist philosophical traditions, including the Theravāda traditions that thrive in Sri Lanka and Southeast Asia, as well as the Mahāyāna traditions of Tibet, China, Korea, and Japan.

The chapters in this volume represent a sample of the fruits of such collaboration. Most, though not all, originated in a conference on Buddhism in Logic and Analytic Philosophy convened at Cambridge University in 2005. That conference brought together philosophers from the United States, the

United Kingdom, Australia, and Europe, some whose professional homes are in departments of philosophy, some whose homes are in Buddhist studies departments or programs. All share an interest in the interfaces among logic, the formal philosophy of language, recent Anglophone epistemology and philosophy of mind, and Buddhist philosophy. Some are serious textual scholars with great philological expertise, while some read Buddhist texts only in translation. But all engage primarily not with texts, but with ideas. This conference was exciting enough that its participants decided to collect the papers, to solicit a few more by like-minded philosophers, and to publish them in a single volume, making apparent to scholars within both academic philosophy and Buddhist studies that such collaboration is worthy of pursuit.

The chapters in this volume fall into three broad sections: discussions of ineffability and the limits of language; discussions of the two truths and the relation between conventional and ultimate reality; and discussions of epistemology and the philosophy of mind. The first and largest comprises works addressing the problems and paradoxes that arise in the context of discourse about the ineffable. This topic arises quite naturally in Buddhist philosophy, where there is a great deal of discussion about the limits of language and the relationship between language as a tool for describing the world of ordinary experience and as a tool for limning the domain of ultimate truth—the world as it is independent of any human conventions or cognition.

This topic provides a natural point of contact with Western philosophy, where this philosophical problem has a long history beginning with Heraclitus, Parmenides, and Cratylus and their worries about the descriptive adequacy of language—concerns that were raised to prominence in the modern period by Kant's project of limning the bounds of knowledge and expression, and brought to an apex in Wittgenstein's *Tractatus*. The question of the bounds of expression, and of the possibility of saying anything coherent about that boundary or about what lies beyond, has remained a hot topic in Western philosophy in the decades since the *Tractatus* and has important ramifications not only in the philosophy of language, but in philosophical logic as well, particularly in the theory of truth.

The first two chapters in this section address questions about ineffability as they arise within the Chan/Zen tradition of China and Japan. Mortensen explores the limits of the sayable in the context of Zen stories, arguing that the very fact that Zen addresses our mode of prereflective engagement with the world—a mode of engagement that is in important ways precognitive—means that much of what Zen has to teach us must be shown, and not said. This language, of course, is redolent of the *Tractatus*. Read picks up on this theme, addressing homologies between Wittgenstein's account of philosophical practice in both the *Tractatus* and the *Investigations* with accounts of practice in Zen, arguing that both Wittgenstein and such Zen thinkers as Shunryu Suzuki regard philosophy as, at one level, indicating that ordinary practice, ordinary language, and ordinary life are "in order" as they are—requiring neither critique nor validation by philosophy—while, at another, they regard philosophical insight as necessary to living ordinary life in an enlightened way. And the distinction between mere ordinary life and enlightened life is, on both accounts, profound but ineffable.

Westerhoff addresses a more specific and more pointed instance of paradox at the bounds of expression, considering Nāgārjuna's remarks in the *Vigrahavyāvartanī* and the *Mūlamadhyamakakārikā* to the effect that neither he nor the Buddha asserts any thesis, has any view, takes any philosophical position. This, of course, sounds suspiciously like a thesis, a view, a position. Hence the paradox. Westerhoff argues that the resolution to the apparent paradox is achieved by the Mādhyamika through adopting a semantic distinction between assertions made with or without ontological import. Nāgārjuna and his Mādhyamika followers, on this account, endorse a theory of linguistic meaning according to which their assertions do not implicate the reality of referents of apparently referring expressions. Nāgārjuna, Westerhoff argues, denies making assertions with ontological import, having views about entities that exist on their own, etc., but is able to say these things without being self-refuting because of a (surprisingly Wittgensteinian) view about language not shared by his non-Buddhist opponents.

D'Amato takes up this theme as well, arguing that there is indeed an important sense in which the Buddha never utters a word, that is, in which he never uses language in the way that language is ordinarily used. Drawing from the Yogācāra account of the awareness of a buddha, D'Amato, like Westerhoff, argues that the way to understand this apparently paradoxical statement is through drawing the distinction between a referential and a use semantics for natural language. If one takes it that to "utter a word"—to use language—just is to refer and to characterize, the Buddha fails to do that. But that is not the semiotic theory preferred by Buddhist philosophers of language. Instead, enlightened language use is precisely use, not reference. And the Buddha, D'Amato argues, can use words to undermine a natural semantics.

In the final chapter of this set, Siderits considers a paradox of expressibility not explicitly noted in Buddhist philosophical literature, nor indeed in the Western literature with which it makes most natural contact. Much Buddhist metaphysics, Siderits argues, is ontologically reductionist, reducing the apparent objects of conventional reality to entities that exist ultimately. Statements that are ultimately true, Siderits argues, are statements that correspond to how things are independently of minds or human conventions. Conventionally true statements, on the other hand, are just those that are useful, practically effective. Well, what about a statement to which a Buddhist reductionist might be committed, such as "This table is ultimately just a collection of partless atoms, not a real table"? If it is true, it must be true either conventionally or ultimately. Since it asserts the nonexistence of the table, it is not a conventional truth: conventionally, there are tables. Most plausibly, such a statement is a statement of ultimate truth: it presents the ultimate mode of existence of the table. But it refers to a table, and ultimately there are no tables, and hence no truths about them. If reductionism of this form is true, therefore, it is ineffable. Note that this is a problem not only for Buddhists but for popular Western reductionists as well.

Siderits's chapter raises questions about the two truths and their relation to one another, and he uses arguments, devices, and the rhetoric of contemporary Western debates about reductionism to address problems about Buddhism's two truths. Garfield and Priest address problems connected to the two truths as well, and they consider one standard Buddhist approach to resolving these problems, the use of the *catuṣkoṭi*, or four-cornered logic. They too adopt the techniques of contemporary logical theory to achieve greater clarity about ideas explored by Nāgārjuna and Zen thinkers such as Hakuin and Dōgen.

Using the Dunn four-valued semantics for relevant logics as a springboard, following a lead from Richard Sylvan, Garfield and Priest show that, indeed, the best account of the relation between the two truths is, as Nāgārjuna asserts, that they are both identical and different, and neither identical nor different. Garfield and Priest grant the inconsistency of this view, but argue that it is cogent inconsistency and of deep phenomenological and ontological significance. Their discussion connects directly to those of Mortensen and Read in their insistence that awakening is no different from ordinary experience, but is at the same time completely but ineffably different.

Tillemans offers a critical assessment of Garfield and Priest's willingness to read Nāgārjuna and other Mādhyamikas as deliberately, though cogently, inconsistent. While he rejects their view that Mādhyamika logic is paraconsistent in the strong sense that contradictions are literally acceptable, he endorses the view that at least early Mādhyamikas, and perhaps some of their commentators, accept a nonadjunctive logic in which assertions and their denials are each acceptable, but in which they do not conjoin. In his chapter, we see both nuanced textual scholarship and the judicious application of the techniques of modern logic in the reconstruction of a Buddhist philosophical position regarding the apparently inconsistent, but nonetheless true, conventional and ultimate truths.

The final three chapters in this volume address broader issues in Buddhist epistemology and philosophy of mind. Tanaka takes Garfield and Priest to task for reading Nāgārjuna as preoccupied with ontology and for ignoring Dharmakīrti's subsequent advances in semantics and logic. He argues that, by taking Nāgārjuna's project as the basis for forging links between Buddhist and contemporary Western philosophy, Garfield and Priest fail to engage with the most apposite strain of Indian thought, the logical project of Dharmakīrti. This work raises important metaphilosophical questions about just how such a dialogue is to proceed.

Martin considers the central Buddhist doctrine of *anātman*, or no-self, the view that there is nothing that corresponds to the notion of a soul or self. Philosophers in the West, including Sextus Empiricus, Hume, Wittgenstein, and Parfit, to name a few, defend positions akin to those defended by many Buddhist philosophers. This view raises certain interesting problems about agency, phenomenology, moral responsibility, etc., and requires some account of our sense of ourselves as individuals and of how we arrange social relations involving persons. In earlier work, Siderits had defended what he calls "ironic engagement" with a self that is in fact nonexistent and that reduces to impersonal processes. Martin takes issue with this account and also with the more general idea that the doctrine of anātman is important in the first place, arguing that, far from being the psychologically and morally profound and earthshaking view that Buddhists represent it as being, it is prosaic and has no real moral or phenomenological consequences. Making use of the interchange between Butler and Locke and of contemporary Western literature on the self, Martin argues that, once we reconstruct the self conventionally, we have all that the proponents of ātman want anyway. Here we find an instance of an interrogation of Buddhist metaphysics from the West that raises serious problems for a central Buddhist project.

Arnold draws surprising connections between the idea of *svasaṃvitti* or *svasaṃvedana* (reflexive awareness, apperception), a phenomenon very controversial in Indian and Tibetan Buddhist philosophy from the sixth through the nineteenth centuries, and the idea of methodological solipsism in the philosophy of mind and cognitive science, made popular by Fodor in the late twentieth century. In this rich chapter, he explores many interpretations in Indian Buddhist literature of the claim that cognition is always reflexive, but he extracts as a core of all of these views the commitment that the immediate content of consciousness is always a mental representation and never an external phenomenon; so, in order to understand consciousness and its contents, one must bracket the external world. Arnold explores the arguments for these positions and notes that they are strikingly similar in form and in detail to those offered by Fodor in defense of essentially the same thesis. His chapter suggests that even contemporary cognitive science can be in fruitful dialogue with Buddhist philosophy.

This collection is necessarily limited in scope. None of the papers addresses topics in ethics, political philosophy, or value theory. Many fascinating problems in metaphysics and epistemology that have attracted fusion philosophers, including discussions of the status of universals, mereology, foundationalism, etc., are omitted. That is all right. Readers already working at the borders between Western and Buddhist philosophy are aware of such work. Those who are discovering this terrain for the first time should know that there is vast room for exploration. Trails have been blazed and can be followed in the existing literature, but each foray leaves a lot of terrain unexplored, and each leaves a lot of difficult undergrowth, suggesting the need to reconsider. We do hope that, taken together, these works are philosophically interesting in their own right and provide evidence that, when Western philosophers explore Buddhist studies and when scholars of Buddhist studies engage with Western philosophy, good things happen.

Pointing at the Moon

I

Zen and the Unsayable

Chris Mortensen

This chapter tries to say something intelligible about a small number of Zen stories. I am well aware that I am attempting to do this with a tradition which emphasizes *unsayability*, though it is also true that Zen has said a lot. In proceeding, I will employ several versions of the common Buddhist distinction between the two truths: conventional truth and ultimate truth. My interest is in whether there are distinctions here which are philosophically and soteriologically significant. When I first encountered Zen stories (and even now), they seemed to have a curious rightness that defied verbal explanation. Thus, the present labor is somewhat in the nature of an attempt to put a ghost to rest.

The Conventional-Ultimate Distinction

The distinction between conventional truth and ultimate truth is often made by Buddhist thinkers. In the literature, at least the following three versions can be found. While there are other versions, here I wish to explicate and apply these three. One thing to note at the outset is that there is some blurring of the distinction between the things that are true (propositions) and the things that they are true of (referents).

(1) There is the distinction between the conventional as concealing, hiding, or obscuring, as opposed to the ultimate as that which is seen clearly and distinctly.

(2) There is the distinction between the conventional as a truth expressible in words or depending on conventions for its existence, contrasted with the ultimate as a truth which cannot be expressed in words, or which is beyond verbal conventions.

(3) We have a collection of distinctions which identify the conventional as somehow involving a relation, as opposed to the ultimate as being nonrelational or intrinsic. Thus, we have (a) the conventional as the identification of a thing in terms of the relations it bears to others, as opposed to the ultimate as the identification of a thing independent of its relations. There is also (b) the conventional as containing a perspective, as opposed to the ultimate as invariant of perspectives. Finally, there is (c) the conventional as a thing whose existence depends on the existence of other things, as opposed to the ultimate as intrinsically existent.[1]

Are these all equivalent? I do not think so. Do they reduce to a single core distinction? I doubt it. Does that matter? No. Are they all compatible? Perhaps, but they may not be equally significant soteriologically. In particular, I aim to argue here that sense can be made of a soteriologically important link between independence of convention and being beyond words.

Zen has been prominent in putting forward an escape from the verbal, but at the same time, Zen is certainly a verbal tradition. Interestingly, much of the Zen verbal tradition is composed of reports of conversations, i.e., *spoken words*. This has something to do with Zen having what I call the "need for speed." I will have something to say about that in the last section.

Occlusion, Illusion, and Delusion

There are two ways to be in knowledge failure. One can fail to have a belief (and hence knowledge) on a point, or one can have a false belief—i.e., one can fail to see something, or one can be wrong about it. The former is blindness, the latter error. In logicians' terminology, the former is incompleteness, or lacking a truth value, while the latter is completeness, but having the wrong truth value.

If an (opaque) thing A is in front of another thing B, then A occludes B. When something occludes something else, the latter is hidden: we fail to know something about it. Thus, *occlusion* falls into the former of the two kinds of knowledge failure. In contrast, *illusion* carries with it the implication of outright error, and I will use the term with this sense. It is perhaps because this implication is somewhat weak that we see the term "illusion" being used to cover both cases. An even stronger implication is seen in *delusion*, which clearly implies a false belief, and carries the further implication that the false belief is seriously unjustifiable, and even arises from epistemological pathology. It is therefore unfortunate when Buddhist theorists use such words in a blanket-like way, as this obscures (occludes) the distinctions that can be made in different examples.

A point to notice here, however, is that when one fails to know something, there is the possibility of a phenomenological slide into the illusion that there is nothing more to be known. More exactly, when one fails to perceive an existing thing or state of affairs B (because it is occluded), there can be a tendency to go on to complete the local theory by believing that B does not exist. The word "unaware" catches this, I think. One can fail to know about a thing, but to say that one is unaware of it is to carry some implication that one assumes or supposes that it does not exist. The belief mechanism fills in the occluded background with an absence. Prudent caution over one's ignorance is absent, and in its place there is the belief that the thing simply does not exist.

We can sum up these points by relating them to the conventional-ultimate distinction as embodied in our earlier definitions of it. There is a disputed issue of whether conventional truths are true. Some say yes, some say no. There is something to be said for both sides. But the prima facie problem for those who say no is to justify the use of the word "true" here at all. I would argue that some cases are true, some not. Conventional truth can arise in more than one way. If it arises by occlusion, then the conventional truth is true simpliciter. If it arises by illusion, there is falsehood somewhere. Either is less than optimal for knowledge, however, which accounts for why conventional truth is less desirable than ultimate truth. Moreover, the possibility or tendency for occlusion to slide into illusion—for deficit to slide into falsehood—must always be borne in mind. Finally, either occlusion or illusion may arise from attachments, in which case the situation is soteriologically significant.

The Verbal and the Nonverbal

One important place to look for examples of conventional and ultimate truths is in the distinction between verbal and nonverbal information or content. It will be argued that the latter satisfies one of the above versions of ultimate truth. While there are conventions involved in nonverbal truths, there are extra conventions involved in the verbal. It will also be seen that there is a sense in which verbal conventions occlude the ultimate nonverbal truth.

We begin then by noticing the difference between two sorts of information: verbal versus nonverbal (or sensory) information. It is obvious that police Identikit pictures are of much more use than verbal descriptions. What this shows is that there is information stored in us in ways that have no verbal equivalent. That is, sensory information is nonverbal. The opening bars of Beethoven's Fifth Symphony are phenomenologically distinct from the musical score. The *point* of the score is for it to be played and heard, not for it to be held up for the audience to see. If I hum it for you, you will know something important that you did not know before. If I try to tell you about it, I will fall absurdly short. In Wittgenstein's words, nonverbal information can be *shown, but not said.* Nelson Goodman (1968) had a useful term for this: *representation by exemplification.* While Goodman would not necessarily agree with what I say next, exemplification works by displaying something which exemplifies an identical property. In contrast, verbally expressed information works (in part) because of extra conventions which associate the representational vehicles (words, written or spoken) with sensory contents. Additionally, it is important that the same kind of representational vehicles (words) are used for multiple sensory modalities, as this makes verbal language a cross-modality unifier of information. We return to this point at the end of this section.[2]

At this point, it is appropriate to remind ourselves of the famous tale known as "The First Zen Story":

> Buddha held up a flower. Only Kāśyapa smiled.

What could this mean but that the Buddha was silently drawing attention to the nonverbal nature of reality, of minds, and of communication? It is a shame that only Kāśyapa intuitively grasped the point. His wordless response was a confirmation of the wordless content of the communication.

Both Goodman and Jerry Fodor point out that even nonverbal content requires a convention. A picture is not by itself true or false. It needs a convention that a certain act of exemplification is intended to assert something, rather than to deny it, or simply to tell a story. As Fodor puts it: "Having a thought *cannot* be simply a matter of entertaining an image, and this is true whether the image is motoric or iconic.... For thoughts are the sorts of things that can be true or false" (Fodor 1981: 65–66). Buddha held up a flower. He was showing something nonverbal. That is the conventional element. Kāśyapa grasped it. Perhaps the rest only saw the flower. But then Fodor goes too far: "They (i.e., thoughts) are thus the kinds of things that are expressed by *sentences* rather than words" (ibid.: 66). If this means "*wholly* expressed in sentences," which it seems to, then it is no more than an unsupported denial of all we have been arguing for here.

Still, it is important to see that there is a clear sense in which there is *one less* convention with the nonverbal. Representation by exemplification has one less convention because exemplification is natural and does not, to that extent, need another convention. Consequently, we can say that truths which *exemplify* are ultimate truths, relative to *verbally expressed* truths, which are merely conventional but true nonetheless. In this sense, in contrast with the case of illusions, conventional truths are indeed true.

In passing, we can recall the thesis that ultimate reality is indescribable, undefinable, and cannot be grasped by concepts. From the present viewpoint, one can say that what this should mean is that verbally expressed concepts do not exemplify reality. The totality of verbally expressed truths is far less than what is possible for human knowledge, since humans are natural sensory beings.

These matters connect with the so-called knowledge argument initiated by Frank Jackson (1982). Jackson set out to argue that physicalism is false. His argument runs as follows: suppose that Mary is born without color vision (or brought up solely in a room of black, white, and grey). Mary becomes a brilliant brain scientist and knows everything there is to know physiologically about color vision. Eventually, she gets color vision for the first time. Does she come to know something new after the experience of color for the first time? It seems so, but ex hypothesi Mary knew everything physical about vision. Hence, Mary must come to know a nonphysical fact about vision. Hence, physicalism is false.

I do not propose to add much to the extensive literature on this argument. I will remain neutral on the issue of the truth or falsity of physicalism, though I should express the view that it would be surprising if physicalism did not have reasonable defensive resources in response to the knowledge argument: physicalism is, one would think, compatible with color vision. The aim here is different, however. We want to know about the various possibilities for conventional and ultimate truths and knowledges, verbal and sensory. In that spirit, we can at least say the following about Mary after her gaining color vision:

> Mary is in a state in which she has never been before.
> Mary knows this.

How is this possible? The solution suggested here is that there is some nonverbal knowledge that Mary initially lacked. Later, she has that knowledge, and she knows it. What does she know now? That *this* color (exemplifying it) is red. This is nonverbal knowledge, and it goes along with other examples of sensory knowledge too numerous to mention, such as that the Fifth Symphony starts like *this* (hum it) and that square things look like *this*: □. I should emphasize here that there is no intention to buy into the "myth of the given," that is, that sensory experiences are incorrigible. In emphasizing the irreducible nature of our sensory states, there is lots of room for their being constructs in various ways.

One advantage of this suggestion is that, if we can agree that Mary comes to know something, then we can account for why she was in a deprived state beforehand. She was in an occluded state up to the change. As we have already seen, occlusion is a certain kind of deprivation and thus a defect, one of lack of knowledge rather than false belief. But the knowledge lacking in the case of Mary is nonverbal knowledge.

The application of this for Buddhism comes, as it inevitably must, from soteriology. Why is this soteriologically significant? Well, there is one important aspect of nonverbal information, namely, that it substantially comes from outside our bodies. Furthermore, following Fodor again, because it is modularized, it is not so cognitively penetrable. On these counts, it is thus less controllable by our verbal theories and stories. In this, it contrasts with the ability to construct those theories and to tell those stories themselves, which is readily under the control of the will. That is why observation is the test of theories: if a theory predicts that some sensory observation can be made, and some other observation is made despite strenuous attempts, then the theory is weakened, at least prima facie refuted. But the recalcitrance of sensory experience is also an assurance of the reality and recalcitrance of the external world. Thus, realism about the world requires detachment from one's theoretical constructs.

Where then is the illusion? The oft-noted tendency for expectations and attachments to affect one's perceptions is a source of illusion. As anyone who has observed tennis pros dispute a line call will agree, perception is cognitively penetrable to a degree (albeit a limited degree). Theoretical constructs are verbal, and they can occlude what the nonverbal world throws at us, if not actively distort it into illusion. The Second Noble Truth says that the cause of suffering is attachment. The failure to have one's attachments satisfied is a discomfort. So is being confronted by one's phobias. In each case, the suffering arises because of a mismatch between the attached expectations and reality. In short, it is a necessary aspect of liberation from suffering that our expectations be in accord with reality, as presented to us in no uncertain terms by nature.

For all this, the role of the verbal has to be acknowledged. It is all too easy to take too far the New Age mantra that the greatest truths are beyond words. In point of fact, our mental lives have the verbal and the nonverbal sewn together tightly. While they are distinguishable, each permeates the other. Thus, illiteracy is a terrible burden. Not understanding language at all is even more disempowering. Because of its extra element of conventionality, verbal representation has the extra capacity to unify multiple sensory modalities, to express abstract concepts which do not correspond closely to any sensory content, and to communicate these facts widely. A word can stand for anything and does not have to resemble it. That is why we are the only species on the planet to land members of our species on the moon, administer antibiotics, or invent Buddhism.

Relations and Perspectives

It is time to move on to take into account another version of the conventional-ultimate distinction, namely, that which involves *relationality* in some way or another. More exactly, one claim to conventionality is the presence of an occluded relation, particularly a relation to human interests and thus attachments. I call these *absolute-relative confusions*. The confusion arises by erecting a concept into an absolute (intrinsic, monadic, nonrelational property), when the truth is that there is relationality in the situation. It seems to me that this is one important idea that some Zen stories have addressed. At the risk of hubris, let me offer a diagnosis of two well-known Zen stories in an effort to illustrate the point.

> Ma-tsu and Pai-chang were walking one day when a flight of geese went overhead. Some time later Ma-tsu asked, "Where are the geese now?" Pai-chang replied, "They've flown away." Ma-tsu struck him, saying, "How could they ever have flown away?"

Ma-tsu sets a little trap. The geese are where they are, wherever that is, over the mountain or on the lake perhaps. Pai-chang makes the mistake of automatically and unthinkingly identifying position in terms that are relative to him: "The geese have flown away *from me*." Pai-chang is thinking of himself as at the center of the universe. He is committing an absolute-relative confusion, and it is habitual for him to do so. He is thus trapped in a conventional occlusion: he is failing to see position except from his perspective. This is soteriologically relevant to Buddhism because the habitual identification of position as relative to oneself indicates an attachment to one's own position before that of others.

Now for the second story:

> The Old Master died, and at the funeral the new abbot posed the following problem to the monks. "If any of you can say an appropriate word on the death of our master, then say it now. But if none of you can, then our Master must count as having failed. Speak now, quickly!" The monk Chao-chou replied, "What fault was there in our Master?"

The abbot poses a loaded question. The question falsely links the merit of the Old Master with something separate from it, something only in relation with it, namely, whether any of the monks have the wits to come up with an appropriate comment. The abbot's question thus contains a deliberate absolute-relative confusion. Moreover, it is a mistake which one who is overly attached to one's own enlightenment might well make: the Old Master's merit depends on *my* enlightenment. Chao-chou points this out quickly and succinctly. His is therefore an appropriate comment.

These stories raise the issue of the role of *perspective* in our knowledge, which is another aspect of the conventional-ultimate distinction. Perhaps the simplest model for perspective and the conventional-ultimate distinction is provided by reflecting on the linguistic phenomenon of *indexicality*. I can assert, "It is raining." The truth of such a claim is relative to the place and time of utterance and thus, in that sense, is conventional. But we can remove the conventionality by filling in the occluded place and time: "It is raining in Adelaide on April 1, 2009." This would be the ultimate truth.

Another simple model for a perspective is the perspective of vision. Perspectives vary with the viewpoints of the viewers. But they are not false, since they are projections of a nonperspectival reality, as viewed by a creature with an eye. A camera will photograph from a perspective too, and the images of the railway lines will converge and meet on the photo. So it can be said that perspectives represent a limited view of reality, but a true view nonetheless, an occlusion, as we have been using that word. Pai-chang spoke a truth, but it was a conventional truth. His error was to think that his perspective was the preferred one from which to describe reality. Other perspectives were occluded from him. If you habitually think like that, you will have difficulty grasping the perspectives of others, you will be firmly attached to your own perspective, and that way lies suffering for all of us.

The nonperspectival view, the ultimate truth, is often thought to be impossible ("the view from nowhere"), but that is also an error. One simple way that we deal with perspectives in our knowledge is by triangulation: change your perspective and look for constancies. As John le Carré would say, take a back-bearing.

The special theory of relativity in physics deals very neatly with perspectives, and thus affords us a (hopefully) soteriologically neutral, simple model of the conventional-ultimate distinction as applied to hidden relations. Reality can be described by frames, which can be thought of as supplying a collection of places-at-varying-times (sometimes called a *simultaneity convention*). Our ordinary (conventional) conception of space and time corresponds to a frame fixed relative to the earth. An older locution for frames was "observers," where it was supposed that observers made measurements, and that the measurements of different observers varied with their state of motion. This is correct but misleading, because the relationality of measured quantities persists as a geometrical fact, whether or not there is an actual observer making measurements. Thus, the more modern conception of frames sees quantities such as the mass and length of a body as relations to frames. Now we can see the occlusion: if we measure the mass of a body and we go on to conclude that it has that mass absolutely—the same mass no matter who measures it and what their state of motion is—then we slide from an occluded fact (the variable relation to different frames) to an illusion (mass is the same, that is, the same in all frames). We make no error, however, if we explicitly acknowledge the existence of the frame: its mass is m relative to the frame fixed on Earth.

Physics then goes on to an even more elegant description. Some quantities do have the same values (constancies) in all frames, for example, the speed of light. These are known as *invariants*. One can describe invariants in frame language, and that is not false talk, but one can go on to describe them in the language of space-time, which is frame neutral. A space-time description does not bother with collecting events into classes of mutually simultaneous events, for there is no such relation as simultaneity in reality. Space-time descriptions simply associate four numerical coordinates (x, y, z, t) with each point, with no presupposition that events with the same t coordinate are at absolutely the same time, i.e., simultaneous. This is a more economical way of asserting the ultimate truth.

The Need for Speed

I do not want to leave the false impression that I think that all Zen stories yield so readily to verbal explication. The great bulk of such stories continue to attract but baffle me. In that connection, the emphasis on speed and spontaneity in Zen is worth mentioning. Why the need to respond quickly and spontaneously? (Recall the word "quickly" in the last story.) Why not allow long reflection and careful diagnosis? An answer, I think, lies in the fact that liberation is not mere conviction; it requires character change. Assenting to the Four Noble Truths, taking refuge, and so on may make you a Buddhist, but these things will not make you a buddha (though they might help). The nexus between your perception of the significance of a situation and your emotional response to it needs to be conditioned appropriately. That is the importance of "doing Zen work." Naturalness of emotional response is the key, plainly. That is what gives it away in Pai-chang's case: the spontaneity of the reaction. He did not say something false: the geese really had flown away (from him). He was rather in the habit of identifying position as relative to him, and his automatic response gave it away.

We can see how, from this point of view, Zen training does not necessarily have to have much of a scholarly component. There are numerous Zen stories where the ignorant and uneducated best the scholar (perhaps the best known of which is that of the Sixth Patriarch, Hui-neng). Indeed, a scholarly component may even be a hindrance, if you come out with the "stink of Buddhism," vainly parading theological superiority for all to admire. There are stories about that, too. If you come across the Buddha on the road, kill him.

Conclusion

Let me not leave the impression that Buddhist scholarship is to be disparaged. There are important things to be said and reasoned about in Buddhism. This is hardly surprising, given that Buddhism is a tradition that uses words to get its message across. But some things have to be shown, not said, and this is the approach that Zen stresses. Zen is neither defined nor defiled by verbal explanations, but some mental contents have no verbal equivalents. Words are part of Zen, but words are not all there is to Zen.

NOTES

1. Versions of all of the above can be found, for example, in Priest and Garfield 2002: 253–270. The last three, a–c, can be found in Kalupahana 1976: 134–137 and Harvey 1990: 98–99.

2. For an extended defense of the distinction between verbal and nonverbal contents, see Mortensen 1989 and 2002.

2

Wittgenstein and Zen Buddhism: One Practice, No Dogma

Rupert Read

My propositions are elucidatory in this way: he who understands me finally recognizes them as nonsensical, when he has climbed out through them, on them, over them. (He must so to speak *throw away the ladder*, after he has climbed up on it.) / He must overcome these propositions.

—Wittgenstein, *Tractatus*

The most important point is to establish yourself in a true sense, without establishing yourself on delusion. And yet we cannot live or practice without delusion. Delusion is necessary, but delusion is not something on which you can establish yourself. It is like a stepladder. Without it you can't climb up, but *you don't stay on the stepladder.*

—Shunryu Suzuki, *Not Always So*

What is meditation? It is *not* blocking out or suppressing thinking. Mystics have long known that such strategies are absolutely ineffective, in all but the shortest of possible terms, at achieving the goals of meditation. But neither, obviously, is meditation simply *thinking*. That might have been what Descartes meant by the word, and even what passes for meditation much of the time in the West, but it is certainly not what contemplative traditions mean by the word.

I submit that meditation is this:[1] the paradoxical act of not trying to do anything, not even trying to think more intensely, nor even trying *not* to think. How do you not do anything, not even think (or not think)? Or, to put much the same question in other terms: how do you stop yourself from thinking, without acting and, in particular, without suppressing your thoughts? The answer surprisingly turns out to be: by giving up trying to stop yourself from thinking and by allowing yourself to think, if that's what happens.

"I want to think less," you say to yourself. Your ego works (and thinks) hard to fulfill the commandment. It works to satisfy your desires and to solve your problems or the problems you set for it. How does meditation work? By watching what happens. Thus, the ego is engaged in a wonderfully self-defeating task. That hard-working mental energy gradually—or suddenly[2]—transmutes into something else.

This is mindfulness. The energy of one's small mind is mobilized to produce, by an indirect route, the goal actually hoped for. The ego—the constant thinking that can be deep suffering—gives up, or becomes instead an indulgent grandmother watching children play, always with a half-smile.

This is Buddhism as what I understand it to be above all: a therapeutic spiritual practice, a psychology-in-action, a practice for working through the way we suffer from suffering. One example of the latter is that the ego loves to attach to answers, to problem solutions. But some difficulties, and indeed some attachments, are too profound to yield in that way. An indirect approach is necessary. You may need to be deluded/tricked into the right answer or, rather, into seeing that the idea that there is an answer may be the greatest delusion. If one tries to benefit oneself by meditating, one will not. The best way to benefit oneself and others is through endlessly not trying to benefit oneself and others.[3] This indirect approach is meditation.

What is Wittgenstein's method in philosophy? Throughout his writing, it is, I believe, to show the fly the way out of the fly bottle. Or, as I have put it previously: "Wittgenstein's primary aim in philosophy is . . . a *therapeutic* one" (Crary and Read 2000: 1). This way of understanding Wittgenstein's work is becoming increasingly popular but still remains controversial with regard to his early writing.

How can his celebrated *Tractatus* be read in this way? The *Tractatus* is usually taken, rather, as a metaphysical theory or account that cannot account for itself. But look at the epigraph above from Wittgenstein. The ladder is to be climbed up and *thrown away* (or *overcome*). The ladder—on the account Wittgenstein offers—is, moreover, nonsensical. What can be understood of nonsense? What can be deduced from nonsense? Nothing. Indeed, nonsense *is* nothing; it is nothing, however, that masquerades as something. It deludes you into thinking that it is something. You can establish nothing on such delusions.

The ladder, then, never was an account. And the "propositions," the *Sätze*, of which it appeared to consist? *They never really were*: the propositions of the book never really were such. To understand Wittgenstein's point in producing such a puzzling text, one must overcome those propositions, wrestle them down to the ground and realize that one was wrestling only specters. This is a ladderless ladder indeed. The preface to the *Tractatus* intimated that all this would be so:

> [This] book will . . . draw a limit to thinking, or rather—not to thinking, but to the expression of thoughts; for, in order to draw a limit to thinking we should have to be able to think both sides of this limit (we should therefore have to be able to think what cannot be thought). / The limit can, therefore, only be drawn in language and *what lies on the other side of the limit will be simply nonsense.* (Wittgenstein 1922: 3; italics added)

Only the *appearance* of a ladder will be generated. Wittgenstein is not gesturing at ineffable truths, nor speaking contradictory truths. He is simply returning us to ourselves, to the full power of our big—our nonfinite—minds. But one will not be returned if one attaches to Wittgenstein's words, to *any* of his words—including these framing remarks to his text.[4]

You haven't learned anything when you've read the text while understanding Wittgenstein's point in writing it. You haven't come away with any doctrines—not even ineffable ones. You haven't arrived anywhere new. You haven't come anywhere or gone anywhere. (In its full flowering in Wittgenstein, this is an unprecedented method of philosophy—at least in Western philosophy.)

Wittgenstein has deluded you into giving up your metaphysical delusions. The therapy of the *Tractatus* is *not* solving problems,[5] but enabling you to overcome the sense that you had any problems you needed to solve. And the method used to undertake this tricky task? Engaging that problem-solving energy in a self-defeating task. Mobilizing the ego energy of philosophy, including its long traditions (most notably Kantianism and empiricism, both of which find their demise in the *Tractatus*). Engaging you right here right now while you're trying to do philosophy. Deluding you for a while into thinking that you've been granted a workable philosophical theory, or at least a theory to end all theory. The delusion of a theory that the *Tractatus* generates as it returns you to yourself is a delusion that you don't stand upon, and that you don't stay upon. Rather, you find yourself standing on the earth and seeing the world aright.[6]

Shunryu Suzuki remarks, "Real enlightenment is always with you, so there is no need for you to stick to it or even to think about it. Because it is always with you, difficulty itself is enlightenment. Your busy life is enlightened activity. That is true enlightenment."[7] The remark that your life itself *is* enlightenment could be closely compared with a remark that the early Wittgenstein might have made, that our everyday language itself is *begriffsschrift* (1922: 5.5563), in a much-neglected passage clearly indicating how Wittgenstein's early philosophy closely anticipates his later work, a passage which actually reads, "All propositions of our colloquial language are actually, just as they are, logically completely in order. (Our problems are not abstract but perhaps the most concrete that there are.)"[8]

When you read this completely surprising book while understanding what turns out to be its author's purpose in writing it, you have learned nothing. And if you have really learned from the (experience of engaging with this kōan of a) book, you will not "stick" to it, nor even to the "enlightenment" it can yield. What you may have learned is something about yourself and perhaps others, namely, something about (y)our susceptibility to be systematically confused by certain thoughts. Or, better: something about the way we/you are inclined to be deluded by certain kinds of strings of words. This is what, according to Wittgenstein, philosophy *is*—at least, philosophy practiced according to what Wittgenstein would later call "*our* method."[9]

Philosophy, for Wittgenstein, is *not* trying to change the way that one thinks. Instead, it is letting oneself think the way one does; accepting that one is tempted to think in all these ways; noting it. Letting—watching—that same thinking come fully to consciousness, such that when one sees it all clearly, some of it will in turn no longer appeal to one and will wither away. Not telling you to shut up about anything. "Whereof we cannot speak, thereof we must remain silent" ends the *Tractatus*. Well, *of course*. When we are thus silent, we are not silent *about* anything. We are just not gassing any more. Rather, roughly: we use language as a skillful means, or not at all.

Nor is Wittgenstein telling you that you're not allowed to say certain things because they disobey the alleged "rules of our language." On the contrary: say what you'd like. It is a complete misunderstanding of Wittgenstein, early or late, to see him as a "language-policeman."[10] Wittgenstein was no positivist. Consider the following remark from *Culture and Value*: "Don't, for heaven's sake, be afraid of talking nonsense! Only don't fail to pay attention to your nonsense" (Wittgenstein 1998: 64).

Again: what Wittgenstein was aiming for was coming to know one's way about the temptations one suffers to say things that one will come to see as not saying anything at all. Coming to know, coming to terms with the temptations to which you are subject—and thus being liberated from them.

Thus, as anticipated by Jean-Jacques Rousseau and as in meditation, *the remedy is in the evil.* The change that Wittgenstein wants to bring about is a change that is brought about not by repressing or suppressing a part of yourself or some part of your thoughts, but by allowing it and them to full consciousness: by accepting that you really do have this inclination—and neither repressing it nor attaching to it. This is the real difficulty of philosophy: a difficulty of the will, not of the intellect. One must have the willpower to suspend one's will, to allow one's mind to cure itself.

It is a change that is not brought about by explaining anything, but simply by telling it/observing it as it is. As Wittgenstein famously puts it in his *Philosophical Investigations* (1958: 124): "Philosophy may in no way interfere with the actual use of language; it can in the end only describe it.... *It leaves everything as it is.*" Likewise, *Philosophical Investigations* 128 urges that philosophy, contra popular belief, has nothing to do with advancing controversial theses or dogmas. It is not by suppressing nonsense that one follows Wittgenstein but, to the contrary, by marshaling and above all allowing one's very inclinations to nonsense.

What is Zen Buddhism? It is not a doctrine nor a dogma. It is more of a practice, a way. Let's say: in Rinzai, it is the attainment of enlightenment through dwelling on kōans until the power of one's ego intellect is "broken" by them and the mind flows freely; in Sōtō, just sitting (*shikantaza*) until, through meditation, the same goal is attained. Why is it so hard? Because the overwhelming temptation is to try to achieve the goal. This will make one impatient with the present moment. Whereas, in truth, the "goal" is precisely to be at ease in and with the present moment. The skillful means of Zen are actually already the goal, surreptitiously. But this leads to the grave danger that one will attach to those means.

This also further explains why the route taken in Zen must be indirect, why the practitioner has to be deceived into the truth. There could not possibly be any such truth as one imagines there is in the direct route. For what one has to be cured of is exactly the temptation to think that there is anything, even anything unstateable/ineffable, which is the truth of Buddhism, the truth of life. The means *are* the end—but one must not attach to the means either.

The deep similarities to a vital minority tradition in Western philosophy, a tradition at whose culmination stands Wittgenstein, are evident. Why have they been so rarely seen, so rarely presented perspicuously? Why has the extreme closeness of Wittgenstein and Zen not been widely understood and practiced?

Wittgenstein's method is widely misunderstood, including by most of his so-called followers. The most famous and "loyal" scholar of Wittgenstein alive today is perhaps Peter Hacker. In his "celebrated" attack on the New Wittgensteinians—those who, as I do, wish to see Wittgenstein's method as therapeutic *throughout* his writing career—Hacker repeatedly ridicules the suggestion that Wittgenstein's method is akin to that of Zen, e.g., he says, "It is a mistake to suppose that [the *Tractatus*] is a work consisting of transitional nonsenses culminating in wholesale repudiation, or a work of Kierkegaardian irony or of a Zen-like dialectic" (2000: 370). Every claim in this sentence (and in others like it in Hacker's text) seems to me mistaken. James Conant has argued beautifully to the effect that the *Tractatus* (and, I would add, Wittgenstein's later writing, only in a more piecemeal fashion) is precisely a work of Kierkegaardian irony, which treats nothing so gently as the delusions in readers and in oneself that one is working to overcome.[11]

As for Zen: I think that just how extraordinarily close Wittgenstein is to Zen has not been sufficiently rendered. Wittgenstein *does*, I submit, as Hacker denies, write "in a spirit of Kierkegaardian irony [and] in the manner of a Zen master" (2000: 378). He is precisely a practitioner of a kind of "Zen pedagogy" (ibid.: 381). Zen and Wittgenstein may be different, but they are also deeply similar.

If Hacker knew Zen better, he would perhaps not fail to notice the extremely subtle, logical thought processes involved in examples such as the following, from Shunryu Suzuki: "You stick to naturalness too much. When you stick to it, it is not natural any more" (in Chadwick 1999: 382; one could quote any of a number of similar remarks—similar in terms of their deep rationality). Hacker would not then be so inclined to treat the category of "Zen" as a category of near-ridicule, as if Zen were merely a kind of irrationalism. If Hacker actually understood more of Zen, as presented here, he might not think it so risible to think of Zen as akin to Wittgenstein.

I would also argue that this is true of many Wittgensteinians' understandings of Zen. Some Wittgensteinians have tried to take the potential comparison more seriously, and have written thoughtfully and at greater length about the possible parallels, before (in most cases) coming down on the negative. But the fundamental problem remains the same: they tend not to understand Wittgenstein adequately and to have too narrow a diet of examples of Zen. For instance, D. Z. Phillips's acute piece "On Wanting to Compare Wittgenstein and Zen" (1977) rightly critiques Canfield (1975) for making Zen and Wittgenstein seem just a bit too much like theories. Phillips's own piece has as its "killer" blow against the aligning of Wittgenstein and Zen the claim that Zen, unlike Wittgenstein, wants to change our lives, our ways of being:

> [T]he distinction which has to be drawn between "just doing" in Zen and "just doing" in Wittgenstein [is that] "just being angry" or "just cursing" could not be instances of "just doing" in Zen, whereas that is precisely what they are in Wittgenstein. "Cursing" appears in Wittgenstein's list of language-games.... A confused language-game, given Wittgenstein's use of the term, is a self-contradiction. Yet the cursing boatman [in a Chuang Tzu story under discussion] is said to face occupancy which must be emptied, a confusion of soul, which he is exhorted to rid himself of. Zen would say the same of anger. Yet, in Wittgenstein, anger is an instance of "just doing." ... The lover does not smash the portrait of his beloved in order to express his anger. This is the form his anger takes. It is an instance of "just doing," but not one which Zen would recognise as "just doing." (Phillips 1977: 342)

There are a number of problems with this passage. Let me focus on just the following two (symmetrical) problems:

1. Phillips is trying to argue that Wittgenstein only contemplates and does not seek to change. But Wittgenstein was passionately interested in contributing—indirectly—to a *fundamental change in Western civilization*. He wanted us to overcome scientism and, deeper still, to find ways of overcoming delusional habits of mind that are to some large extent an inevitable consequence of the flowering of reason and language, of our whole deeply complicated form of life. Dis-eases of our humanity. Sure, Wittgenstein would not qua philosopher want us to suppress anger, but then, no more would Zen (see 2 below). But he would welcome an almost unimaginably huge change in form of life such that there were fewer occasions for anger, and such that anger when it still emerged would be neither dishonestly pretended away nor attached to. What he wanted above all was a change in way of life that would render his philosophy henceforth *superfluous*.[12]
2. Phillips does not seem to understand the extent to which Zen can allow such things as cursing and anger. If these are in some sense ideally to be eliminated, they are nevertheless not to be wished away or suppressed.[13] The method of taking care of them is fundamentally different from that: the method is contemplative, in much the same way that Wittgensteinian contemplation is intended to persuade one that where one is or wants to be in philosophy (e.g., Cantor's "paradise" of infinites) is not actually where one is or wants to be.

Consider the following Zen quotes, which are particularly hard to reconcile with Phillips's characterization:

i. Here is Shunryu Suzuki again: "The Buddhist way is to try hard to let go of... emotional discrimination of good and bad, to let go of our prejudices, and to see things-as-it-is. / When I say to see things-as-it-is, what I mean is to practice hard with our desires—*not to get rid of desires*, but to take them into account.... We must include our desires as one of the many factors in order to see things-as-it-is" (in Chadwick 1999: 30).

ii. And here is his great follower Katagiri Roshi:

> Zazen is not about destroying our thoughts or doing away with our subjective points of view.... / If you believe zazen is a means to an end, then it is easy for you to use zazen like a raft to reach the other shore. /... Sometimes people think they should carry their zazen around with them after reaching the other shore. But if you do that, you should know you haven't actually reached the other shore. You have just come up on a sandbar somewhere in the middle of the river. *Desires are endless*, and if you look carefully, you will see you are still caught by them. /... This is just how most of us are confused. We don't appreciate the fact that desires are endless. We have to come to realize that there is nothing to get into our hands, and that zazen is not a vehicle, not a means.[14]

These quotations seem to me to indicate clearly that Zen can perfectly well accept (and work with) desires, such as those that are expressed in/by anger, and does not compulsively need to deny or eliminate it/them; i.e., "just doing" *could* under some circumstances include (say) just cursing. So much, then, for Phillips.

Now, it might nevertheless be objected that, even if we leave aside the misunderstandings of a Phillips or a Hacker, nevertheless, Buddhism doesn't have the same positive orientation as Wittgenstein does toward "ordinary language." But I do not believe that even Wittgenstein has the special reverence for ordinary as opposed to other kinds of language that he is often alleged to have. (This is one respect in which the New Wittgensteinians—those who accept the therapeutic interpretation of Wittgenstein laid out above—move decisively beyond ordinary language philosophy, which in this respect is akin to Hackerian Wittgensteinianism, with its undue respect for grammar as a grid of rules which must be obeyed.)[15]

Let us stay a little longer with the objection, which might be continued as follows. An Indian Madhyamaka like Candrakīrti, for example, deeply values ordinary life and advocates "returning" to what the world accepts (*lokaprasiddha*), but he doesn't return to it via a diagnosis of how philosophers go astray through being bewitched by strange views on language. The culprit for him is not confusion about language usage, but "reification" (*satyābhimāna*, Tib. *bden 'dzin*), i.e., grasping things as being truly thus and so. This reification is *not* just a philosopher's problem. For Candrakīrti, the ordinary person falls into reification, too, and in a very important sense is even mixed up about the ordinary world. In short, the ordinary is to be understood/rediscovered; it is fundamentally fine as it is (when you get it right and don't reify it); but it is difficult for anyone to realize in this unreified way and is thus "uncanny" (to go with Cavell's formulation).

And it is, of course, the mention of the likes of Cavell that offers the key to an enlargement upon my response to this objection: Wittgenstein does not think that going astray is just a philosopher's problem either. See, for instance, my work on Wittgenstein and Marx,[16] and the close of my paper on consciousness:[17] these "philosophical" problems are problems of (our) culture, and more. Wittgenstein doesn't write for those self-identifying as philosophers. Far from it: Wittgenstein's writing is for whoever needs it, for whoever falls into or dwells in these kinds of delusions. Those who reify—those who Wittgenstein himself was particularly intent on de-deluding—include some scientists, mathematicians, psychologists, theologians, and indeed sometimes simply ordinary people going about their business, who are yet vulnerable to the siren call of delusional thinking of the kinds that Wittgenstein meant to show us. (Wittgenstein certainly did not think that *all* science, however, necessarily involves what Candrakīrti calls reification. Only science that gets out of its depth, or falls into scient*ism*.)

Rinzai and Sōtō, too, are (if pushed into explanations) much closer to targeting reification rather than language-game confusions. And what I am suggesting is that, in this respect, they are closely aligned with Wittgenstein. The New Wittgensteinians are fundamentally directed against the thought that Wittgenstein is interested in targeting language-game confusions in any narrow sense.[18] Wittgenstein and Zen are fundamentally aligned in thinking that philosophical error is by no means the preserve of academic philosophers or of academics of any kind, and in thinking that the task of overcoming one's own inclinations to delusions of a mythic nature or gravity is a task utterly bigger than and different from any policing of mere linguistic confusions.

To return now to Hacker, an exemplar of a reader of Wittgenstein who unfortunately takes him to be merely a tedious language policeman: Hacker gives no evidence of understanding much of anything about Zen, but neither does he understand *Wittgenstein*. Once one is a practitioner of both, one is in a position to see in Wittgenstein, as it were, a Western elective affinity with Zen, going in many respects further down the road that masters such as Shunryu Suzuki and Thich Nhat Hanh have laid out for their Western/worldwide audiences. Zen and Wittgenstein alike[19] find life and reality to be paradoxical, and they work intensely with that paradoxicality. It is absolutely central to their methods, for to truly find the remedy within the "evil" is necessarily paradoxical. Exposing nonsense (delusions) to the light is necessarily paradoxical (like exposing potatoes to the light to stop them from sprouting—but far stranger than that, because in this case what is exposed is only nothing, under the aspect of seeming as if it were something). For one necessarily practices by means of doing things that are absurd ("answering" absurd riddles, thinking so as not to think, engaging with one's temptations to speak what one is oneself inclined to judge as nonsense as if it were not).

In Zen and in Wittgensteinian practice, one does not believe that the truth can be said. But one does not believe either that there is an unsayable truth. For that would make the telos of one's practice sound much too like what one does not believe is available, in principle, full stop. Just as Descartes made mind and matter too alike to each other by making them both kinds of stuff/substance; just as talk of the actual infinite or of infinity as existing betrays infinity by making it too alike to the finite; just as talk of saying and showing is precisely what needs to be overcome, because it makes showing sound like just another kind of saying—Zen and Wittgenstein, when seeing the world aright, take care not to make it seem like they are seeing some thing, or some truth, that cannot be put into words. That that truly cannot be put into words is not something which if it *could* be put into words would say such and such.

And so we see, crucially, that unless the great Zen masters who have brought Zen to the West—and Dōgen and (I would add) Nāgārjuna—and Wittgenstein are less subtle thinkers than I take them to be, they cannot be ultimately saying that reality is contradictory, nor that there are true contradictions. For saying so makes the secret of their practice seem too like what is exactly the target of criticism in their practice. A "true contradiction" is something true that one can say about the meaning of life or some such topic. What Wittgensteinian psychology/therapy/"philosophy"/spiritual practice and Zen spiritual practice/psychology/therapy/thinking are interested in engendering is not *anything* that one can say. Not *any* kind of truth.

No. Zen and Wittgenstein simply show how to change your life, your practice, your way, while leaving everything as it is.[20]

NOTES

1. The paradox of meditation/practice that I am setting up here is not of course limited to Zen, let alone to Sōtō Zen. It very much figures, for instance, in Tibetan Mahāmudrā traditions and (especially) in the so-called Great Perfection teachings (Dzogchen). Let the cards fall as they may: what I say here applies only to some things called "meditation"; so then let it just apply to those things, to whatever it applies to. (If you like, you can call mine a "persuasive definition.")

2. Different traditions of Zen Buddhism were, of course, founded on this difference.

3. Compare Dōgen's "Guidelines for Studying the Way" (Dogen 1985: 4): "You should not practice Buddha's teaching with the idea of gain." "Clearly buddha-dharma is not practiced for one's own sake, and even less for the sake of fame and profit. Just for the sake of buddha-dharma you should practice it."

4. Compare the following remark from Wittgenstein's *Big Typescript*: "All that philosophy can do is to destroy idols. And that means not creating a new one—for instance as in 'absence of an idol'" (cited in the opening of Stone 2000).

5. In which enterprise, incidentally, Wittgenstein considered Ramsey to be quintessentially engaged: this is why Wittgenstein famously declared Ramsey to be a "bourgeois" philosopher.

6. For detailed argumentation in support of this understanding of the *Tractatus*, see Diamond 1991; Crary and Read 2000; and Read 2004, 2005, and 2006.

7. Cited as an epigraph for the chapter "Not Sticking to Enlightenment" (Suzuki 2002: 131).

8. Wittgenstein 1922: 117.

9. For explication, see Hutchinson and Read 2005.

10. For exposure of this misunderstanding, see Hutchinson and Read 2008.

11. See Conant 1989, 1992, 1995, and 1997.

12. I support claims along these lines in my "Marx and Wittgenstein on Vampires and Parasites" (Read 2002).

13. See, for instance, Thich Nhat Hanh 2002.

14. Katagiri 2000: 6 (italics added). Katagiri's words here demand comparison to Wittgenstein's late insistence that philosophy does not come to an end, that we practice it endlessly, most notably in his *Zettel*. One might call his (our) method a methodless method. Again: it does *not* seek seriously to eventuate in the goal of ending philosophy. On the futility of the latter project, with reference to Wittgenstein's philosophical method, see my "The *Real* Philosophical Discovery" (Read 1995).

15. Wittgenstein properly understood, and Austin too (properly understood and at his best), are *not* ordinary language philosophers. I argue for this conclusion in a forthcoming work.

16. Read 2002.

17. Read 2008.

18. See, for instance, Witherspoon's essay ("Conceptions of Nonsense in Wittgenstein and Carnap") in my collection with Crary (2000).

19. Isn't there something weird about comparing a vast set of traditions of many hundreds of years (Zen) with one man (Wittgenstein)? Yes, of course there is. But, one day, it might seem much less odd. That is the day of which I am thinking: a time, whose beginnings are perhaps here, in which Wittgenstein will be seen not as one man in the history of analytic philosophy, but as a major cultural figure who has helped to spawn a large set of long traditions, including some in close affinity with those spawned by another man, Śākyamuni Buddha.

20. Or, while leaving things-as-it-is. Many thanks to the editors, especially Garfield and Tillemans, for invaluable comments on earlier versions of this chapter. I hasten to add that they (especially Garfield) would nevertheless of course not agree with the final product! Thanks also to the many others who have offered helpful thoughts along the way, including my colleagues at the University of East Anglia, where I presented another version of this material.

3

The No-Thesis View: Making Sense of Verse 29 of Nāgārjuna's *Vigrahavyāvartanī*

Jan Westerhoff

The so-called no-thesis view is without a doubt one of the most immediately puzzling philosophical features of Nāgārjuna's thought and also is largely responsible for scholars ascribing to him either skeptical or mystical leanings (or, indeed, both). The locus classicus for this view is found in verse 29 of the *Vigrahavyāvartanī*:[1]

> If I had some thesis, the defect [just mentioned] would as a consequence attach to me. But I have no thesis, so this defect is not applicable to me.[2]

That this absence of a thesis is to be regarded as a positive feature is stressed in a passage from the *Yuktiṣaṣṭikā*, where Nāgārjuna remarks about the buddhas:

> For these great beings there is no position, no dispute. How could there be another's [opposing] position for those who have no position?[3]

It is important to observe that, when considered in isolation, it is hard to make any coherent sense of these passages. For even if we assume that the buddhas do not hold any philosophical position any more (having perhaps passed beyond all conceptual thinking), how are we to make sense of the first quotation which, in the middle of a work full of philosophical theses, claims that there is no such thesis asserted at all?

This first statement is even more difficult to interpret than the famous last sentence of Wittgenstein's *Tractatus*, which is preceded by the equally famous ladder metaphor.[4] Although Wittgenstein there denies that his preceding statements are of anything but instrumental value (they turn out to be nonsensical *after* they have fulfilled their instrumental role), at least he does not deny making any statements at all.

Verse 29 in Context

In order to get a clearer understanding of what these passages might mean, it is important to consider them in the argumentative context in which they occur. The *Vigrahavyāvartanī*, which contains the first passage given above, is a work of seventy verses accompanied by Nāgārjuna's autocommentary.[5] As its title (which translates as "dispelling of debates") suggests, its main aim is to answer objections which had been advanced concerning Nāgārjuna's theses. Its rather technical and specific nature makes it plausible to assume that the *Vigrahavyāvartanī* was written later than his main work, the *Mūlamadhyamakakārikā*, and was meant to deal with particular problems arising from the arguments set out there.[6] The first twenty verses and commentary contain criticisms of Nāgārjuna's position, which are answered in the remaining verses and commentary. Verse 29 specifically addresses the problem raised by the opponent in verse 4.

The principal point the opponent makes at the beginning of the *Vigrahavyāvartanī* concerns the status of Nāgārjuna's claim of universal emptiness. The opponent argues that Nāgārjuna faces a dilemma, the horns of which are *inconsistency* and *impotence*. If he assumes his claim not to be empty, he has contradicted his thesis of universal emptiness (because there is now at least one thing which is not empty). If, on the other hand, Nāgārjuna takes his claim to be empty too, the opponent argues, the claim is then unable to deny the existence of independently existing phenomena, which the opponent asserts. As becomes clear in verse 22, Nāgārjuna accepts the second horn of the dilemma: everything is empty, and his claim that everything is empty is also empty. As explained in the following verse, however, this does not entail that the claim cannot carry out its philosophical function. A key can open a door in a film even though it is only a key in the film, not a real key.[7] Verse 4 considers a specific comeback Nāgārjuna could make in reply to the difficulty arising from accepting this second alternative, i.e., the charge of argumentational impotence in his claim of universal emptiness. Nāgārjuna could argue that, if universal emptiness renders his own claim impotent, the opponent's claims, being also subsumed under the universal statement of everything being empty, are similarly impotent and therefore cannot act as a refutation of Nāgārjuna's claim either. But as the opponent is quick to point out, this involves a blatant petitio principii: only if we already accept that everything is empty will the opponent's arguments be rendered empty and impotent; but this is exactly the thesis the opponent denies. For him, at least, some things are not empty, and in particular his own statements are not subject to Nāgārjuna's claim of universal emptiness. The difficulty the opponent raises is a difficulty which arises because of the specific character (*lakṣaṇa*) of Nāgārjuna's system, namely, the claim that everything is empty. It does not apply to the arguments of someone who does not make that assumption.

Verse 29 is then made in reply to this supposed counterargument and its rejection as a petitio. There, Nāgārjuna claims that the particular defect (of his thesis of universal emptiness rendering his own philosophical assertions impotent) would indeed apply *if he had any position*. But given that he has no position, the difficulty therefore does not apply to him.

It may strike the reader that this is a rather curious reply to make. It is evident that the opponent's criticisms formulated in verse 4 and the preceding verses rest on a misunderstanding of the central term "emptiness." What exactly this misunderstanding amounts to is less clear. The above set of arguments would make sense if we assumed that the opponent understood *empty* to mean "false," or "meaningless," or even "nonexistent."[8] But as a reply to a criticism based on a misunderstanding of this kind, Nāgārjuna's reply in verse 29 seems a little extreme, given that it would have been perfectly sufficient and far less controversial for him to point out that emptiness entailed neither falsity, nor meaninglessness, nor nonexistence, and he thereby could both claim that his statements are empty *and* simultaneously refute his opponent's objections (he makes exactly these points in verses 21 and 22). Even if we agree with Mabbett that "it may be the case that the objection addressed by a given verse has already been essentially refuted, but in turning to each new objection Nāgārjuna seeks to make a fresh rebuttal in order to administer the *coup de grâce*,"[9] Nāgārjuna here seems to use a sledgehammer to crack a nut. Why deny holding any proposition whatsoever if it would have been perfectly sufficient to point out that, since empty does not mean nonexistent, it is completely unproblematic to claim that one's own position is as empty as everything else?

We can distinguish at least three different ways to interpret Nāgārjuna's crucial statement that he has no position. I will refer to these as the *semantic*, *argumentational*, and *transcendent* interpretations. According to the semantic interpretation, Nāgārjuna does not claim to hold no proposition whatsoever, but only claims to accept no statements which are taken to have a particular semantics. If we follow the argumentational interpretation, Nāgārjuna makes a claim about how one should proceed in debates, namely, by always refuting opponents via reductio arguments, without ever adopting any thesis oneself. The transcendent interpretation reads Nāgārjuna's statement as asserting the existence of an inexpressible reality beyond concepts and language.

All three of these interpretations have historical predecessors in the commentarial tradition. Semantic and argumentational interpretations can be found in works of the dGe lugs tradition, in particular those of Tsong kha pa[10] and mKhas grub rje;[11] while a variety of views which can all be regarded as transcendent interpretations can be found in the writings of scholars such as rNgog blo ldan shes rab,[12] Go rams pa,[13] and dGe 'dun chos 'phel.[14]

In the following, I will restrict myself to an exposition of the semantic interpretation because this gives us the clearest understanding of the role of verse 29 in the context of Nāgārjuna's arguments. The argumentational and transcendent interpretations tend to use Nāgārjuna's denial of theses as a textual peg on which to hang arguments concerned with quite different matters from those dealt with in the *Vigrahavyāvartanī*. Tsong kha pa, for example, refers to this verse in the context of expounding the distinction between Svātantrikas and Prāsaṅgikas;[15] Sa skya paṇḍita offers the transcendent interpretation in the context of a debating manual (advising the reader on how to debate with someone who does not put forward a position);[16] dGe 'dun chos 'phel's work, despite its title, is not a study of Nāgārjuna's thought in particular, but is mainly concerned with criticizing the then-prevalent dGe lugs' interpretation of Madhyamaka philosophy more generally.

This is, of course, not to say that the argumentational and transcendent interpretations are for this reason deficient or without interest in the contexts in which they are presented. However, it is important to be aware that these contexts were not Nāgārjuna's context. There is certainly no reason for suspicion toward later Indian or indeed non-Indian works as not giving valid interpretations of Nāgārjuna's thought. Nevertheless, the most interesting of these, for the present purposes of a philosophical analysis of Nāgārjuna's thought, are those which allow us to understand passages from his works in their argumentative context, rather than using them as starting points for presenting the interpreter's ideas on a particular topic.

The Semantic Interpretation

If we consider the major dGe lugs pa commentaries referring to verse 29, it becomes evident that these usually regard Nāgārjuna's statement as elliptical.

What Nāgārjuna *really* means when he says that he has no position, these commentaries claim, is that he has no positions which are nonempty.[17]

The key to understanding the point made in these commentaries lies, of course, in a precise understanding of what it means for a position or statement to be empty. An object is empty if it does not "exist from its own side" and is therefore dependent on other objects, so that its existence is not grounded in its "own nature" (*svabhāva*, Tib. *rang bzhin*). The Buddhist commentarial tradition considers a variety of dependence relations in which objects stand and which prevent them from existing in a nonempty way. These dependence relations include causal dependence, dependence of a whole on its parts, and dependence on a cognizing subject.[18] While in the case of certain objects, their independent existence seems at least a prima facie plausibility which the Mādhyamika then attempts to refute by appropriate arguments, in the case of statements, their emptiness appears to be entirely uncontroversial. Material objects might be considered to exist in causal and mereological dependence, but independent of a cognizing subject; abstract objects, Platonistically conceived, will be assumed to be independent in all three ways. Statements, however, can hardly be taken to exist from their own side in any of these three senses.

As even Nāgārjuna's opponent affirms in verse 1, *token* utterances are events which arise in dependence on causes and conditions, like all other events. When considering utterances as *types*, it is equally clear that, assuming a compositional semantics, these are mereologically dependent on their parts, since the meaning of the sentence type is a function of the meanings of its constituents or parts. Finally, considering a constituent like the expression "red," we realize that its referring to the color red is not a property the word "red" has independently of everything else: the connection of this particular phonetic or typographic object with the property is a convention which holds for speakers of English; for speakers of French, the same property is connected (by a different set of conventions) with "rouge," for speakers of Tibetan with "dmar po," and so forth. That *red* refers to the color red depends on a complex framework of conventions connecting a community of cognizing subjects who share a language. Unless we mistakenly consider *empty* to mean false or meaningless or nonexistent, the claim that utterances conceived of as either tokens or types are *not* empty seems to be a position that is hard to make sense of.

Despite the prima facie strangeness of their claims, theories of the nonemptiness of language have found their defenders. Perhaps the most extreme example is the view of language defended by the Mīmāṃsakas.[19] A primary motivation of the Mīmāṃsā theory of language is to provide a justification for the authoritative status of the Vedas. As opposed to the Naiyāyikas, who justify the Vedas by their divine authorship, the Mīmāṃsakas regard them as authorless (*apauruṣeya*). The elements of the Vedic language are assumed to exist eternally, without the need for a speaker. Any particular human utterance, of course, depends on a phonetic or typographical instantiation of a piece of language, but the types thus instantiated exist *ante rem*, without depending on the tokens instantiating them. The referents of expressions, which the Mīmāṃsakas take to be eternal and unchanging universals, are related to these expressions via a set of objective and necessary relations.[20]

While the Mīmāṃsā view of language attracted plenty of criticism from the Buddhist side (centered on Dignāga's *apoha* theory),[21] there is no good evidence that this is the view Nāgārjuna's opponent in the *Vigrahavyāvartanī* wants to defend.[22] There is, however, some interesting evidence that at least some of Nāgārjuna's Indian commentators saw him as opposed to similar conceptions of language. When commenting on *Mūlamadhyamakakārikā* 2:8 in his *Prajñāpradīpa*, Bhāvaviveka raises the question of why the verbal root *gam* ("to go") is used in its *ātmanepada* form, *gacchate*, rather than conjugated in the usual *parasmaipada* manner, as *gacchati*.[23] Bhāvaviveka lists a variety of quotations from Indian grammarians illustrating the perils of wrong grammar. When the god Tvaṣṭṛ created a serpent to destroy Indra, he exclaimed *indra-śatrur vardhasva*, intending to say "May you prosper, destroyer of Indra!" As he intended the compound to be a *tatpuruṣa*, he should have stressed the final syllable. Unfortunately, Tvaṣṭṛ stressed the first syllable, turning it into a *bahuvrīhi* meaning "having Indra as a destroyer." The words did what they meant, rather than what Tvaṣṭṛ intended them to mean, and Indra destroyed the snake, not the other way around.[24] Bhāvaviveka then observes that Nāgārjuna's irregular use of *gacchate* was not only intentional, but served a philosophical purpose. By demonstrating that no disaster will strike if we use the form *gacchate*, Nāgārjuna was aiming to convince his opponents to give up their attachment to mere words, together with the assumption that there is a substantial nature (*svarūpa*) of words which determine that they can only appear in certain grammatical forms.[25] Nevertheless, for the purposes of interpreting the *Vigrahavyāvartanī*, it makes better exegetical sense to ascribe a different (and less extreme) theory than that to Nāgārjuna's opponent.

According to this theory, whether a statement is empty or not does not depend on the mind-independent existence of language in some Platonic heaven, but focuses on the *semantics* we employ when interpreting the statement. Even if we accept that the link between "red" and the property of redness is conventional, this does not imply that we must also think that the property of redness only has conventional existence: redness can still be a property which exists in the world independent of human conventions and intentions.

Moreover, even if the linkage of *particular words* to their referents should prove to be conventional, the linkage of entire sentences to the world might not be. For example, we might suppose that the statement "the apple is red" is linked to the state of affairs to which it refers by a relation of structural similarity, by their sharing a common logical form, which in turn is not a product of convention. Once we have linked the simple signs of our language with the simple objects in the world, we then do not need a *further* set of conventions to link the complex signs (the sentences) with the complex objects (facts or states of affairs), in the same way as once we have settled by convention how the different chess pieces are to move, we do not have to bring in further conventions to decide whether a particular distribution of chess pieces on the board will allow white to mate in five moves. This can be decided just by reference to the initial conventions, in the same way the truth conditions of a sentence like "the apple is red" can be worked out by considering the simple signs of which it is made and how these are put together in the sentence.

Both of the assumptions behind this picture of the nonemptiness of statements—that there is a "ready-made world" (to borrow a phrase from Putnam [1982]) and that there is a structural link between language and the world—are extremely widespread, so widespread indeed that we might refer to them jointly as the "standard picture." It is evident that the standard picture does not sit well with the thesis of universal emptiness. Neither the existence of a world sliced up at the joints into particulars and properties, nor the existence of an objective structural similarity between sentences and the world would be acceptable for the Mādhyamika. A Mādhyamika-compatible semantics would deny the existence of a world differentiated objectively into different logical parts and would try to replace the structure-based picture of the language-world link by a different one, perhaps by a theory built on speaker conventions.

There is some historical evidence that the standard picture is indeed what Nāgārjuna's opponent presupposes. Garfield points out:

> [I]n the Nyāya-influenced logico-semantic context in which these debates [in the *Vigrahavyāvartanī*] originate, the dominant view of meaningful assertion (the one that Nāgārjuna calls into question) is one that from our vantage point can best be characterized as a version of Fregean realism: meaningful assertions are meaningful because they denote or express independently existent properties. A proposition is the pervasion of an individual entity or groups of entities by a real universal or sequence of universals.[26]

On this understanding of the emptiness of statements, we can read the opponent as claiming in verse 1 that, because of Nāgārjuna's thesis of universal emptiness, the Mādhyamika cannot accept the standard semantic picture for his utterances. For Nāgārjuna, questions of both ontology (how the world is sliced up) and semantics (how language and the world are linked) must be settled by appeal to conventions. The opponent, on the other hand, can assume that there is a ready-made world, as well as an objective, structural way of linking this to our language.[27] Now, the opponent argues that, on this picture, Nāgārjuna never gets out of his system of conventions to connect his claims with the things—and *that* is the reason that his claims are unable to refute the opponent's claims, which do manage to connect with the things: Nāgārjuna's arguments can no more refute the opponent than the rain in a meteorological simulation can moisten real soil.[28] Nāgārjuna's opponent thus considers the interesting case of a language where we have two kinds of statements: some are interpreted according to the standard semantics (referring via an objective-reference relation to objects which exist independently of us), and some are interpreted according to Nāgārjuna's semantics (which does not make these assumptions). The opponent argues that statements of the second kind could not possibly influence the first kind. To see this, consider a similarly structured case. Assume we recognize two kinds of norms, norms which are real, objective, out there, and norms which are the product of human convention. Moral realists take certain ethical norms to be of the first kind, while traffic rules are generally considered to be of the second kind. It is clear that, although the two kinds of norms could be in conflict, a norm of the second kind could never override one of the first kind, since the former are part of the objective, normative framework of the world, while the latter are only a supplement of human design.

Although he does not explicitly say so, Nāgārjuna seems to imply that he agrees that this situation would indeed be problematic. If there are two kinds of statements, the latter would be as impotent compared to the former as a film would be to reality: we could not escape the burning cinema by entering the scene projected onto the wall. Nāgārjuna counters the charge of impotence by denying that there are two kinds of statements, which differ like film and reality. All statements are to be interpreted in the same way, so that their interaction is not ontologically any more problematic than the interaction between two different characters in a film.[29]

Interpreting the emptiness of statements according to a nonstandard semantics, we can also give a more interesting rendering of the argument in verse 4. Remember that there the opponent claims that Nāgārjuna might want to say, "According to this very method, a negation of negation is also impossible; so your negation of the statement negating the intrinsic nature of all things is impossible." The opponent has just claimed that because Nāgārjuna's theory entails a nonstandard semantics, his assertions do not manage to connect with the world and are therefore meaningless. But if the opponent then sets out to refute the thesis of universal emptiness, this either means that he takes it to be meaningful after all (and therefore deserving refutation), or that the statement he wants to defend (which is the negation of Nāgārjuna's claim) is meaningless as well, since plugging in the word "not" will not help to turn nonsense into sense.

The opponent could reply to this charge by pointing out the difference between internal and external negation. While it is plausible to assume that the internal negation of a nonsensical statement is nonsensical too ("the number seven is *not* yellow [but rather some other color]" is as problematic as "the number seven is yellow"), this is not the case for external negation ("*it is not the case that* the number seven is yellow" is not just meaningful, but also generally taken to be necessarily true). Nāgārjuna's opponent could then claim that his negation of the claim of universal emptiness is external only and therefore not affected by the lack of meaning in the claim it negates.[30]

It is possible that the opponent did argue in this way, since a distinction between different scopes of negation, as well as the accompanying presuppositional and nonpresuppositional readings, was made in the philosophical literature of the time.[31] It must be noted, however, that the passage in question fails to make any direct reference to different kinds of negation being involved.[32]

A more abstract way of employing the distinction between the two kinds of negation in the opponent's reply consists in rejecting Nāgārjuna's peculiar semantics. Here, the opponent points out that he does not have to accept Nāgārjuna's semantics, as it is a particular characteristic (*lakṣaṇa*) of Nāgārjuna's system and nothing the opponent would be forced to take on board.[33] The opponent does not negate just Nāgārjuna's claim of universal emptiness, but the entire nonstandard semantics which comes with it. If *prasajya* negation is seen as a presupposition-canceling negation, which negates not just a proposition but also that proposition's presuppositions,[34] and if the semantics according to which a speaker wants the set of his utterances to be interpreted is included among these presuppositions, denying a claim together with the semantics it comes with can be regarded as an example of *prasajya* negation.

The Specific Role of Verse 29

It is interesting to note that verse 29, which is meant to be a reply to the opponent's argument given in verse 4, does not attempt a comeback in trying to argue that the opponent's negation of Nāgārjuna's claim of universal emptiness is somehow impossible after all. Instead, Nāgārjuna addresses a difficulty (*doṣa*) arising from the "specific character" of his system, which the opponent raises at the end of verse 4.

If we consider mKhas grub rje's *sTong thun chen mo*, an influential dGe lugs work which deals with the interpretation of this passage,[35] we realize that this difficulty is taken to be inconsistency. If Nāgārjuna assumed that his thesis of universal emptiness was nonempty itself (*rang bzhin gyis yod pa*) and, on our interpretation, would therefore have to be supplied with a semantics according to the standard picture, his position would be inconsistent (at least until he proposed a special reason that this statement should be excepted, which Nāgārjuna does not do). But, mKhas grub argues, since none of Nāgārjuna's claims of universal emptiness are taken to be nonempty, the difficulty of inconsistency does not arise.[36]

What is unsatisfactory about this interpretation is that Nāgārjuna has already made the point ascribed to him here in verse 22. There, he states that his claim of universal emptiness is also empty, and gives reasons that he thinks it can still have argumentative force, thus avoiding the charge of impotence. Unless we assume Nāgārjuna to be unnecessarily repetitive, it is not clear why we should assume that he makes the very same point once again a couple of verses later and also formulates it in a much more obscure manner than the first time.

It is important to note that verses 21–28, which deal with the objections raised in the first three verses of the *Vigrahavyāvartanī*, are primarily concerned with solving the dilemma of inconsistency and impotence which is faced by Nāgārjuna's claim of universal emptiness. Verse 29, however (pace mKhas grub and Tsong kha pa), is not again concerned with the thesis of universal emptiness. Nāgārjuna realizes that the twin problems of inconsistency and impotence are not just problems for his thesis of universal emptiness, but for *any other claim* he holds as well. Any other claim either will face the problem of being a counterexample to Nāgārjuna's assertion that all claims should be given a nonstandard semantics, or will fail to connect with the world in the way sentences with the standard semantics do and will therefore be meaningless. I want to argue that this is the difficulty arising from the specific character of Nāgārjuna's system to which the opponent refers in verse 4 and which Nāgārjuna takes up again at the beginning of verse 29. He is not interested in defending the claim (attributed to him by the opponent in verse 4) that his thesis of universal emptiness could not possibly be negated. Instead, he takes up the opponent's more important point that, apart from defending his claim of universal emptiness from the twin problems of inconsistency and impotence, he had better say something about the status of his *other* assertions as well. This is why he says in verse 29 that none of his other assertions should be regarded as propositions with standard semantics (*pratijñā*) either.[37]

The plausibility of this interpretation rests on there being two meanings of "thesis" (*pratijñā*) in play here, one which refers to theses with standard semantics (which Nāgārjuna rejects) and one which refers to theses with non-standard semantics (which Nāgārjuna does not reject). In fact, there appears to be good textual evidence that the notion of thesis is indeed used in two different ways in Mādhyamika literature.

Candrakīrti's commentary on Nāgārjuna uses one sense of thesis (*pratijñā*) to refer to statements with a clearly unproblematic status; indeed, some utterances by Nāgārjuna himself are regarded as theses in this way,[38] while theses in another sense are firmly rejected. We might want to refer to the first kind of theses as *propositions* and to the second as *views*. How are we to understand the distinction between them? It has been claimed that views are theses with philosophical or metaphysical commitments,[39] and more specifically that they postulate an independently existing entity (*bhāva*).[40] Propositions, on the other hand, do not make such commitments and are therefore philosophically unproblematic. It is important to note at this point, however, that what distinguishes a view from a proposition is not just that the former asserts the existence of objects existing from their own side while the latter does not. On this understanding, the statement "object *x* does not depend in any way on any other object" would be a view concerning *x*, while "object *x* stands in a variety of dependence relations with other objects and does not exist from its own side" would not be. Ontological commitment only comes into play at the level of semantics. Whether someone asserting that the average man has 2.4 children is committed to an object which acts as the reference of the expression "the average man" depends on the semantics given. If we interpret the statement in the way statements like "Paul has two children" are usually interpreted, such commitment to a strange man with partial children ensues; if, on the other hand, we read it (more plausibly) as a statement about ratios between the number of men and children in a certain set, there is no such commitment.

It therefore seems plausible to take the distinction between views and propositions and between theses with standard and nonstandard semantics as coinciding. The views the Mādhyamika rejects are theses which are interpreted as referring to a ready-made world and a structural link between this world and our language. The propositions he takes to be unproblematic, some of which he holds himself, are theses which are given a semantics which makes neither of these two assumptions. Some support for this semantic interpretation of the difference between the two senses of "thesis" can be gained from a verse from Nāgārjuna's *Mūlamadhyamakakārikā* (13:8):

> The Victorious Ones have announced that emptiness is the relinquishing of all views. Those who in turn hold emptiness as a view are said to be incurable.[41]

Although Nāgārjuna does not use the word *pratijñā* for "view" but rather talks of *dṛṣṭi*, it seems sensible to treat the two terms as synonymous in this context.[42] If the difference between propositions and views just depended on what the statement asserted, statements asserting the emptiness of some phenomenon (such as "each spatio-temporal object depends causally on some other object") ex hypothesi could not be views, contrary to what Nāgārjuna says in the verse just cited. If, however, we treat "view" as denoting a statement together with the standard semantics, this is indeed possible. For if we read "each spatio-temporal object depends causally on some other object" as asserting the existence of various objectively existing individuals in the world, linked by a relation of causation, about which we speak by exploiting an objectively obtaining structural similarity between language and the world, it would indeed be turned into a view.

That the point at issue here is a specific (and, as Nāgārjuna sees it, inappropriate) conception of semantics is supported by Candrakīrti's commentary on this verse. Candrakīrti argues that one taking emptiness to be a view is like one who, when being told by a shopkeeper that he has nothing to sell, asks the shopkeeper to sell him that nothing. The customer (like the White King in *Through the Looking-Glass and What Alice Found There*) treats "nothing" like a proper name and therefore expects it to denote a particular object, as proper names do. But though justified by the surface grammar of the sentence concerned, this does not lead to an understanding of what the merchant wants to say. Similarly, giving a standard semantic interpretation of statements asserting emptiness does not lead to an understanding of what Nāgārjuna wants to say.[43]

Conclusion

I hope to have convinced the reader that the semantic interpretation outlined above provides a good way of making sense of verse 29 within the argumentative structure of the *Vigrahavyāvartanī*. What Nāgārjuna means when he says that he "has no thesis" is that none of his theoretical statements (including the claim of universal emptiness) are to be interpreted according to a semantics based on the standard picture. For the Mādhyamika, no assertion is to be taken to refer to a ready-made world of mind-independent objects, nor can he assume that there is a structural similarity linking word and world which is independent of human conceptual imputation.

NOTES

1. Both the Sanskrit text and an English translation can be found in Johnston et al. 1978.

2. yadi kācana pratijñā syān me tata eṣa me bhaved doṣaḥ / nāsti ca mama pratijñā tasmān naivāsti me doṣaḥ // (Johnston et al. 1978: 61).

3. Verse 50: che ba'i bdag nyid can de dag / rnams la phyogs med rtsod pa med // gang rnams la ni phyogs med pa / de la gzhan phyogs ga la yod // (Lindtner 1982: 114).

4. *Tractatus Logico-Philosophicus* (Wittgenstein 1922: 7): "Whereof one cannot speak, thereof one must remain silent"; and 6.54: "My propositions are elucidatory in this way: he who understands me finally recognizes them as senseless, when he has climbed out through them, on them, over them. (He must so to speak throw away the ladder, after he has climbed up on it.)"

5. The traditional ascription of the *Vigrahavyāvartanī* to Nāgārjuna has been questioned by Tola and Dragonetti (1998) with arguments of varying strength; also see Ruegg 2000: 115n10.

6. See Mabbett 1996: 306–307 and Bhattacharya 1999: 124.

7. As Nāgārjuna points out in *Mūlamadhyamakakārikā* 1:10, this is a necessary condition for its being able to perform its function (only a cinematic key could open a cinematic door; a real key could not). See also the commentary on this verse in Garfield 1995: 119.

8. Indeed, we might think that the argumentative context makes it most likely that the opponent misunderstands "empty" as "nonexistent." In this case, the problem that nonexistent statements cannot really refute anything seems to be most pressing. But in the case of the other two alternatives, other problems become more serious. If Nāgārjuna means "meaningless" when he says "empty," his claim that everything is empty would obviously just be false, given that we perfectly well understand the claim he makes (in the same way as somebody saying "all statements, including this one, are not grammatically well formed" would utter a falsehood). If, however, "empty" means "false," Nāgārjuna's thesis of universal emptiness would reduce to the liar paradox, and there is no good textual evidence that *this* is the problem the opponent had in mind. On this last point, compare also the discussions in Mabbett 1996 and Sagal 1992.

9. Mabbett 1996: 307.

10. Tsong kha pa 2000–2004: 3:230 and 236–249.

11. Ruegg 2000: 173–187.

12. Ibid.: 32–33n59.

13. Ibid.: 194–195n135.

14. Lopez 1994; a translation of dGe 'dun chos 'phel's *kLu grub dgongs rgyan* can be found in Lopez 2005.

15. See Cabezón 1997.

16. In his *mKhas pa rnams 'jug pa'i sgo*, 3:37–39; see Jackson 1987: 1:271, for the Tibetan text, and 2:341–342, for an English translation. A summary with comments is in Ruegg 2000: 169–171.

17. "It is not being said that the Mādhyamika has no theses; he merely has no theses that inherently exist" (Hopkins 1983: 471). The same point is made in mKhas grub rje's commentary on this passage; see Ruegg 2000: 179.

18. See Gyatso 2005: 66–69.

19. The basic text of this school is the *Pūrva Mīmāṃsā Sūtra*; for the Mīmāṃsā theory of language, see especially Jaimini 1916: 1–22; see also D'Sa 1980: 113–140.

20. See Sharma 1960: 220–222.

21. See Dreyfus 1997: 213–215.

22. That Nāgārjuna's opponent was a Naiyāyika is claimed in Bhattacharya 1977: 265 and Johnston et al. 1978: 1; see Bhattacharya 1999: 124 for further references.

23. Ames 1995: 309. The form *gacchate* is not found in the editions prepared by La Vallée Poussin (1903–1913: 97, l. 14) and de Jong (1978). However, some paleographical research strongly suggests that *gacchate* is indeed the correct reading (MacDonald 2007: 32–33).

24. Ames 1995: 342n65; notes 64–70 provide very useful information for identifying some of the author's quotes.

25. Ibid.: 310.

26. Garfield 1996: 12. For discussion of the relation between the *Vigrahavyāvartanī* and the Nyāya school, see Meuthrath 1999, Bhattacharya 1977, and Oberhammer 1963. For some remarks on the realist background of the Navya-Nyāya, see Ingalls 1951: 1 and 33–35.

27. The opponent's conception of a harmonious word-world link goes so far as to deny the existence of empty names, thus arguing from the existence of a term like *svabhāva* to the existence of the referent (*Vigrahavyāvartanī* 9; Nāgārjuna replies in verse 57).

28. In *Vigrahavyāvartanī* 1, the opponent claims that "a fire that does not exist cannot burn, a weapon that does not exist cannot cut, water that does not exist cannot moisten; similarly a statement that does not exist cannot deny the intrinsic nature of all things" (na hy asatāgninā śakyaṃ dagdhum / na hy asatā śastreṇa śakyaṃ chettum / na hy asatībhir adbhiḥ śakyaṃ kledayitum / evam asatā vacanena na śakyaḥ sarva-bhāva-svabhāva-pratiṣedhaḥ kartum) (Johnston et al. 1978: 43).

29. See particularly verses 23 and 27 of the *Vigrahavyāvartanī*, as well as *Mūlamadhyamakakārikā* 17:31–33.

30. Garfield (1996: 12) reads the argument in this way and argues that the opponent just wants to negate Nāgārjuna's position, without asserting the contrary.

31. For the present purposes, we can assume a (simplifying) identification of *paryudāsa* with internal negation and *prasajya-pratiṣedha* with external negation. For further differentiation, see Ruegg 2002: 19–24n6.

32. Compare also the discussion in Ruegg 2000: 117.

33. "The objection applies only to the specific character of your proposition, not to that of mine. It is you who say all things are void, not I. The initial thesis is not mine" (tava hi pratijñā-lakṣaṇa-prāptaṃ na mama / bhavān bravīti śūnyāḥ sarva-bhāvā iti nāham / pūrvakaḥ pakṣo na mama) (Johnston et al. 1978: 45–46).

34. As, e.g., in Shaw 1978: 63–64.

35. See Ruegg 2000: 173–187 for a summary and analysis of the relevant part of the commentary.

36. See ibid.: 179 (150a1–3). The same point is made by Tsong kha pa (2000–2004: 3:241):

> Therefore, the issue as to having or not having theses is not an argument about whether Nāgārjuna has them *in general*. It is instead an argument as to whether the words of the thesis "all things lack intrinsic nature" have intrinsic nature. Hence the meaning of the lines from the *Vigrahavyāvartanī* is this: If I accepted that the words of such a thesis had an intrinsic nature, then I could be faulted for contradicting the thesis that all things lack intrinsic nature, but because I do not accept that I cannot be faulted.

37. Oetke (2003: 468–471) reconstructs Nāgārjuna's argument differently and suggests an alternative reading of verse 29; he argues that, here, Nāgārjuna claims that, for the Mādhyamika, there is no thesis to be made at the absolute level (*paramārtha*)—a reading entirely consistent with Nāgārjuna's other statements (e.g., *Mūlamadhyamakakārikā* 18:9).

38. See, for example, *Mūlamadhyamakakārikā* 1:1 in the *Prasannapadā* (La Vallée Poussin 1903–1913: 13, l. 3). See Ruegg 1983: 213–214 for further examples. Oetke (2003: 458–459), however, argues that the distinction between the two senses of *pratijñā* only arises in later Prāsaṅgika literature and should not be read back into Nāgārjuna's works.

39. Sagal 1992: 83.

40. Ruegg 1983: 213.

41. Śūnyatā sarva-dṛṣṭīnāṃ proktā niḥsaraṇaṃ jinaiḥ / yeṣāṃ tu śūnyatā-dṛṣṭis tān asādhyān babhāṣire (La Vallée Poussin 1903–1913: 247, ll. 1–2).

42. As in Ruegg 1986: 232–233 and Mabbett 1996: 301. For more details on the relation between the two terms *pratijñā* and *dṛṣṭi*, see Ruegg 2000: 129–136.

43. This interpretation does, of course, not imply that one could hold "any position at all" as long as one gives it the required nonstandard semantics, as Galloway (1989: 27n5) asserts. A statement like "things arise from what is other than themselves" will be regarded as false by Nāgārjuna, independently of whether it is interpreted according to the standard or nonstandard semantics.

4

Why the Buddha Never Uttered a Word

Mario D'Amato

Words are not the ultimate, nor is what is expressed by words the ultimate.

—*Laṅkāvatāra-sūtra*[1]

In the *Laṅkāvatāra-sūtra*, the claim is made that the Buddha never taught anything at all, that he never uttered a word.[2] On the face of it, this is certainly an odd claim for the text to make, especially since the *Laṅkāvatāra* is itself a sūtra, a discourse of the Buddha; not to mention the fact that this text is found in both the Chinese and Tibetan canons, collections which contain hundreds of such extended utterances attributed to the Buddha. And the *Laṅkāvatāra* is not alone in making such a remark: similar claims are made in other Mahāyāna sūtras, such as the *Tathāgataguhya-sūtra*[3] and the *Vajracchedikā-sūtra*,[4] and in Mahāyāna treatises, such as the *Mahāyānasūtrālaṃkāra*.[5] In fact, no less a luminary than Nāgārjuna in his magnum opus, the *Mūlamadhyamakakārikā*, states that "no teaching has been taught anywhere by the Buddha to anyone" (25.24).[6] What is to be made of all this talk about not talking? How are we to understand the Buddhist claim that Buddhist teaching itself is just so many illusory fingers pointing to nonexistent moons?[7] A clue may be found in considering Buddhist reflections on the role of language and conceptualization.

A dominant theme in Mahāyāna soteriological thought is that language and conceptualization are at the root of the problem with sentient existence, that language and conceptualization are the fundamental afflictions (*kleśas*) leading to the suffering of sentient beings. And insofar as language itself is understood to involve conceptualization, we might simplify the previous statement by saying that conceptualization is *the* fundamental affliction.[8] Indeed, the *Mahāyānasūtrālaṃkāra-bhāṣya* states that conceptualization (*vikalpa*) is the only affliction of concern to bodhisattvas, beings on the path to the unsurpassed, complete awakening of a buddha.[9] And in the *Vimalakīrti-nirdeśa*, the claim is made that the root of desire and greed—which are basic afflictions—is "unreal conceptual construction" (*abhūta-parikalpa*).[10] As Gomez (1976) has shown, the focus on conceptualization as the fundamental problem is a tendency in Buddhist thought which may be traced back to some of the earliest extant canonical sources. In elucidating the tension in Buddhist thought between having no views and having right view, Gomez points out that some of the earliest strata of the Pāli canon favor the position of having no views.[11] We might understand this tension, and the tendency toward emphasizing the efficacy of removing all views whatsoever, as an extension of the fundamental Buddhist doctrine of anātman—the absence of self. And the tendency toward no views is given perhaps its fullest expression in Mahāyāna texts, where the fundamental cause of suffering is often considered to be conceptualization (or conceptual identification, conceptual discrimination, imaginative construction, conceptual proliferation, etc.),[12] and the ultimate goal of buddhahood is often described in terms of a nonconceptual awareness (*nirvikalpa-jñāna*), an awareness that does not engage in conceptual thought.

But if buddhahood is described in terms of a nonconceptual awareness, and if conceptualization is understood to be a condition for the use of language, then how is it possible that a buddha can teach, or say anything at all? After all, it is part of the standard description of a buddha that he is one who has discovered the way things really are on his own and has established the dharma (i.e., Buddhist teaching) in the world for others to follow. As Dunne puts the problem, "as an immanent teacher, a buddha must speak, but the use of concepts and language would imply a spiritual ignorance (*avidyā*) that a buddha as transcendent must not have" (1996: 525–526). Indeed, as Dunne points out, Buddhist philosophers are themselves aware of this doctrinal problem and have attempted to address it in different ways. In this chapter, I will discuss one possible response to this problem. First, I will discuss aspects of the doctrine of buddhahood according to certain Yogācāra texts—primarily the *Mahāyānasūtrālaṃkāra*[13]—focusing on accounts of the awareness of a buddha. I will highlight how, according to these accounts, a buddha is said to possess both a nonconceptual and a conceptual awareness. Finally, I will offer a few brief reflections on what I take to be the implications of such a model of buddhahood, especially with respect to a buddha's use of language.

Buddhahood in Terms of Forms of Awareness

Before turning to accounts of the awareness of a buddha, it is worth pointing out that various descriptions of buddhahood are found in Yogācāra texts. Primary among these are (1) defining buddhahood in terms of its constituent components, or in terms of its various virtues, powers, and other characteristics; (2) specifying buddhahood in terms of the three embodiments of a buddha: the real or true body of buddhahood (*dharma-kāya*), the enjoyment body (*saṃbhoga-kāya*), and the emanation body (*nirmāṇa-kāya*); and (3) describing buddhahood in terms of the various forms of awareness of a buddha. There are two models of the awareness of a buddha, one twofold and one fourfold. According to the twofold model, a buddha has a nonconceptual awareness (*nirvikalpa-jñāna*) and a subsequently attained awareness (*pṛṣṭha-labdha-jñāna*). According to the fourfold model, a buddha has mirror awareness (*ādarśa-jñāna*), equality awareness (*samatā-jñāna*), analytical awareness (*pratyavekṣā-jñāna*), and accomplishing awareness (*kṛtyānuṣṭhāna-jñāna*).[14]

I begin with an account of the twofold model. To get a sense of what the MSA/Bh states about these forms of awareness, we turn to a discussion of the nature of the "realm of the real" (*dharma-dhātu*, a term which is synonymous with "reality" understood in its broadest sense). MSA 9.56 discusses the nature of reality:

> sarva-dharma-dvayāvāra-tathatā-śuddhi-lakṣaṇaḥ / vastu-jñāna-tad-ālamba-vaśitākṣaya-lakṣaṇaḥ //
>
> The characteristic [of reality] is the thusness of all phenomena, purified of the two obstructions. Its characteristic is the imperishable sovereignty of the awareness of objects and [the awareness] which is the support of that [awareness of objects].

From this verse, we may note two things about the nature of reality: it is apprehended as thusness, purified of afflictive and cognitive obstructions—obstructions which keep sentient beings in saṃsāra and prevent them from knowing the way things really are; and it is understood in terms of two forms of awareness, the awareness of objects and the awareness which is its support. Here the text is referring to two standard types of awareness of a buddha: nonconceptual awareness (*nirvikalpa-jñāna*; here, the "awareness which is the support") and the subsequently attained awareness (*pṛṣṭha-labdha-jñāna*; here, the "awareness of objects," or *vastu-jñāna*).[15] Nonconceptual awareness is the basic awareness of a buddha: it does not distinguish between subject and object and does not construct experience into individuated objects with characteristic properties. However, it should be emphasized that nonconceptual awareness is understood to be a form of awareness, and as Griffiths points out, it "has both an object (*dmigs/ālambana*) and some content (*rnam pa/ākāra*)" (1990: 87). Its object, according to Asaṅga's *Mahāyānasaṃgraha* (c. fourth to fifth century C.E.), is the "'indescribability of things' (*chos rnams brjod du med/dharma-nirabhilāpyatā*) which is, in turn, identified with the 'Thusness of absence of self' (*bdag med de bzhin nyid/nairātmya-tathatā*)" (ibid.).[16] The subsequently attained awareness is based on nonconceptual awareness, but is itself understood to engage in some form of conceptual construction: according to the *Buddhabhūmyupadeśa*, "the conventional wisdom that is subsequently attained (*pṛṣṭha-labdha-saṃvṛti-jñāna*), although it is not apart from *tathatā* [thusness], because it is discriminative, does not realize the essence of *tathatā*" (Keenan 1980: 742). Furthermore, the subsequently attained awareness is a "worldly" (*laukika*) awareness, allowing for buddhas to act in the world on behalf of sentient beings, especially through teaching the dharma.[17] So, according to the twofold model, a buddha has both a nonconceptual and a conceptual awareness.

Turning to the fourfold model, MSA/Bh 9.67–76 discusses mirror awareness, equality awareness, analytical awareness, and accomplishing awareness. In the MSAVBh, Sthiramati states that buddhahood is encompassed by five topics—the "purity of the realm of the real" and the four awarenesses[18]—which indicates that these four awarenesses are central to the Yogācāra account of buddhahood. Beginning with (1) mirror awareness (*ādarśa-jñāna*), MSA 9.67–68 states:

> ādarśa-jñānam acalaṃ traya-jñānaṃ tad-āśritaṃ / samatā pratyavekṣāyāṃ kṛtyānuṣṭhāna eva ca // ādarśa-jñānam amamāparicchinnaṃ sadānugaṃ / sarva-jñeyeṣv asaṃmūḍhaṃ na ca teṣv āmukhaṃ sadā //
>
> Mirror awareness is unmoving. Three awarenesses—equality, analytical, and accomplishing—are based on it. Mirror awareness is without ego, without limit, always occurring, without confusion regarding any object of knowledge, and it never faces them.

From the first verse, we see that mirror awareness is the basis of the other three awarenesses, thus it is understood to be a foundational or fundamental form of awareness.[19] While it is unmoving, the other three awarenesses are fluctuating.[20] Furthermore, mirror awareness is without any sense of self and without spatial or temporal limits—capable of ranging over all knowable objects at all times. Since it is free from all obstructions,[21] it has no confusion or error with respect to objects of knowledge. But it should also be understood that mirror awareness does not confront objects of knowledge; that is to say, mirror awareness does not stand in a subject-object relation with respect to objects of knowledge, since "it never faces them"—which might be understood in terms of the absence of ego or any sense of self in mirror awareness. So, while all objects of knowledge are perfectly reflected in mirror awareness, mirror awareness does not function to discriminate these reflections into distinct objects in opposition to itself as an apprehending subject. And insofar as it does not engage in conceptual discrimination, mirror awareness should be understood as equivalent to nonconceptual awareness (*nirvikalpa-jñāna*), a point which Sthiramati explicitly makes in his subcommentary to the MSA, as does Bandhuprabha in his *Buddhabhūmyupadeśa*.[22]

In our consideration of mirror awareness, it should be noted that the MSA/Bh also identifies buddhahood with omniscience. A clear statement of this may be seen at MSA 9.2:

> sarvākāra-jñatāvāptiḥ sarvāvaraṇa-nirmalā / vivṛtā ratna-peṭeva buddhatvaṃ samudāhṛtaṃ //
>
> Obtaining the awareness of all modes of appearance, purified of all obstructions, buddhahood is said to be like an uncovered basket of jewels.

Here, the text identifies buddhahood with the attainment of an awareness of all modes of appearance. In commenting on MSA 20–21.58, the MSABh identifies the "awakening which has all modes of appearance" with an "awareness of all objects of knowledge and all modes of appearance" (*sarva-jneya-sarvākāra-jñāna*), emphasizing that buddhahood entails an awareness of all knowable objects in all their aspects. Also recall that mirror awareness is defined as "without limit" and "without confusion regarding any object of knowledge." So, from this, we can see that the MSA/Bh understands buddhahood in terms of omniscience and that mirror awareness itself is equivalent to omniscience. As the *Buddhabhūmyupadeśa* states, "It is because this mirror wisdom at all times has all dharmas as its object that we say that the Tathāgata is omniscient (*sarva-jñāna*)" (Keenan 1980: 563).

Next is (2) equality awareness (*samatā-jñāna*). At MSA/Bh 9.70, the text states:

> sattveṣu samatā-jñānaṃ bhāvanā-śuddhito mataṃ[23] / apratiṣṭha-samāviṣṭaṃ samatā-jñānam iṣyate //

> yad bodhisattvenābhisamaya-kāle sattveṣu[24] samatā-jñānaṃ pratilabdhaṃ tad bhāvanā-śuddhito bodhi-prāptasyāpratiṣṭhita-nirvāṇe niviṣṭaṃ samatā-jñānam iṣyate /
>
> The awareness of equality among sentient beings is properly thought to be purified through cultivation. It is known as equality awareness because it has entered the equality which is non-abiding.
>
> The awareness of equality among sentient beings, obtained by the bodhisattva at the moment of realization, is purified through cultivation. When awakening is attained, it is known as equality awareness because it has entered non-abiding nirvāṇa.

Here, we see that equality awareness is so called because of its understanding of the equality of all sentient beings—whereby self and other are seen as equal—and because it has entered into non-abiding nirvāṇa—wherein saṃsāra and nirvāṇa are viewed as without distinction. Since non-abiding nirvāṇa is interpreted as a form of nirvāṇa through which a buddha continues to engage with the world for the spiritual benefit of sentient beings, we see that equality awareness is closely associated with a buddha's activity in conditioned existence. MSA 9.71 makes this association more explicit:

> mahāmaitrī-kṛpābhyāṃ ca sarva-kālānugaṃ mataṃ / yathādhimokṣaṃ sattvānāṃ buddha-bimba-nidarśakaṃ //
>
> [Equality awareness] should be properly thought of as always having great benevolence and compassion; it shows buddha-forms to sentient beings in accordance with their inclinations.

Equality awareness, then, is a form of awareness that allows a buddha to see self and other, saṃsāra and nirvāṇa, indeed to see all forms whatsoever, as equal to one another. This point is emphasized in the *Buddhabhūmi-sūtra*, which states that equality awareness is "far removed from all differentiating marks" (Keenan 1980: 700). In elucidating this passage, the *Buddhabhūmyupadeśa* cites the *Prajñāpāramitā*'s claim that the "dharma nature has only one mark, and that is no mark," adding the comment, "This no-mark is precisely the equality of the dharma nature (*dharmatā-samatā*)" (ibid.: 701). Hence, through equality awareness, all phenomena are understood to be equal, in that all phenomena are without any distinguishing mark, characteristic, or essence whatsoever (i.e., all phenomena are empty).

The next form is (3) analytical awareness (*pratyavekṣā-jñāna*), which is the topic of MSA 9.72:

> pratyavekṣaṇakaṃ jñāne jñeyeṣv avyāhataṃ sadā / dhāraṇīnāṃ samādhīnāṃ nidhānopamam eva ca //

> Analytical awareness is always unimpeded with respect to objects of knowledge; it is like a treasure of retentive powers and concentrations.

Analytical awareness, then, is able to apprehend all knowable objects and is the basis of the numerous powers of memory and concentration of a buddha. Furthermore, analytical awareness allows a buddha to identify the particular and general characteristics of all phenomena,[25] and allows a buddha to understand "the unlimited causes and results of the three realms" (Keenan 1980: 736)—the manifold causal relations among the phenomena comprising conventional reality. Bandhuprabha in the *Buddhabhūmyupadeśa* states that, although mirror awareness reflects all objects of knowledge, "because it is non-discriminative, it is unable to enunciate the dharma.... But this [analytical awareness] is able to know [all these marks], and, because it is discriminative, it can enunciate the dharma teaching for all" (ibid.: 749). Or, as the MSA itself states (9.73), analytical awareness "rains down the great dharma" (*mahādharma-pravarṣakaṃ*). So, while mirror awareness is nonconceptual, analytical awareness is conceptual, and as such it can engage in speech in order to teach the dharma.

The last form of awareness in the fourfold account is (4) accomplishing awareness (*kṛtyānuṣṭhāna-jñāna*). The previous two forms of awareness may be understood as theoretical in orientation: equality awareness identifies the ultimate absence of characteristics of all conventional phenomena, while analytical awareness identifies their particular and general characteristics from a conventional point of view. Accomplishing awareness, on the other hand, is practical in orientation. At MSA 9.74, accomplishing awareness is directly related to the emanation body of a buddha:

> kṛtyānuṣṭhānatā-jñānaṃ nirmāṇaiḥ sarva-dhātuṣu / citrāprameyācintyaiś ca sarva-sattvārtha-kārakaṃ //
>
> Accomplishing awareness brings about the benefit of all sentient beings in all realms through emanations that are varied, innumerable, and inconceivable.

An emanation body is a form by which a buddha manifests in the realms of conditioned existence in order to aid sentient beings. Here, it is pointed out that such emanations are a function of accomplishing awareness, highlighting the practical dimension of this form of awareness. The *Buddhabhūmi-sūtra* explicitly interprets this awareness as a form of skillful means (*upāya-kauśalya*) and considers it in terms of an analogy to "efficacious, physical actions," such as farming (Keenan 1980: 758). Hence, we might understand accomplishing awareness, in Ryle's terms, as a form of "knowing *how*" rather than "knowing *that*" (Ryle 1984: 27–32).

I would suggest that the fourfold model of a buddha's awareness might be interpreted in the following way: mirror awareness directly and immediately apprehends thusness, the fundamental nature of reality; equality awareness conceptually apprehends the equality of all entities in all conventional domains or universes of discourse, through apprehending their emptiness; analytical awareness conceptually apprehends the distinct entities of every specific conventional domain or universe of discourse, and the relations that conventionally obtain among those entities; and accomplishing awareness makes pragmatic determinations regarding the contextually appropriate conventional domain or universe of discourse to adopt and the system of logical syntax or grammar to employ (i.e., which universe of discourse and syntax to utilize in a particular context, or what to say and how to say it).[26] And on the account offered here, a buddha's nonconceptual, mirror awareness could be understood as a buddha's fundamental form of awareness insofar as it directly apprehends thusness or emptiness, implying that every conventional domain or universe of discourse is empty. And the emptiness implied by nonconceptual, mirror awareness serves as the basis for the other three awarenesses' nonreferential use of language.

Finally, it should be noted that the two models of the awareness of a buddha may be correlated with one another. As indicated above, mirror awareness is a nonconceptual awareness and is described as unmoving. The other three awarenesses—equality, analytical, and accomplishing—are said to be fluctuating and are described as engaging in some form of conceptual discrimination; as Bandhuprabha states in the *Buddhabhūmyupadeśa*, "The other three wisdoms . . . do have a kind of non-clinging and non-purposeful discrimination" (Keenan 1980: 657). And insofar as these three awarenesses do engage in conceptualization, they may be understood as equivalent to the subsequently attained awareness (which was specified as a conceptual form of awareness).[27] So the fundamental awareness of a buddha, according to both the twofold and the fourfold models, is a nonconceptual awareness (*nirvikalpa-jñāna*), an awareness that does not engage in any form of conceptualization (*vikalpa*) but rather reflects all things the way they really are, in their radically ineffable nature.[28] Through this mode of awareness, it would be neither possible nor desirable to engage in speech; as Griffiths points out in his study of buddhahood, Buddhist texts "claim that construction-free awareness [*nirvikalpa-jñāna*] is not implicated with language because deployment of words is taken by them to be among the more important functions of *vikalpa*" (1994: 160). However, a buddha is also understood to have a "specific or analytical understanding of the intensional meanings and grammatical forms of words (*nirukti*)" (ibid.: 116), which would be a function of a conceptual form of awareness. And, according to the account offered here, it is a buddha's conceptual awareness which allows a buddha to speak.

Mindful Buddha versus Mindless Buddha

Since the very goal of the Mahāyāna is understood to be buddhahood, Mahāyānist thinkers have paid significant attention to accounts of just what buddhahood is supposed to be, and while various accounts agree in some fundamental respects, they often differ in many others. For example, as indicated above, according to one dominant stream of Mahāyāna thought, conceptualization is the fundamental affliction binding beings to saṃsāra. Buddhahood, therefore, must entail the eradication of this fundamental affliction. Certain accounts of buddhahood, however, allow for a buddha to reengage with conceptualization in some way, thereby accounting for a buddha's ability to teach. And, as we have seen here, the MSA offers one such account, through developing models of the awarenesses of a buddha: while the fundamental awareness of a buddha is nonconceptual, a buddha also attains a subsequent awareness which does engage in conceptualization, allowing for a buddha's use of language. We might refer to such a model of buddhahood as a "mindful buddha" account, since a buddha is interpreted as reengaging with conceptual thought, although in a way that has somehow been fundamentally transformed through the attainment of a nonconceptual awareness: a buddha engages in conceptual thought but is mindfully aware of the baselessness of conceptualization through having attained a nonconceptual gnosis of thusness.[29]

In order to better bring into relief the MSA's account of the awarenesses of a buddha, we may juxtapose such an account with what might be referred to as a "mindless buddha" account, according to which a buddha does not engage in any form of conceptualization or thought at all. As Dunne points out, for example, "Candrakīrti [c. 600–650 C.E.] holds strong views on the impossibility of a buddha having conceptual knowledge" (1996: 540). While, according to certain Buddhist thinkers, such as Dignāga (c. 480–540 C.E.) and Dharmakīrti (c. 600–660), perception is without conceptual construction, according to Candrakīrti's view, "even raw sense data are in some sense conceptual," so "at the highest state of understanding where one's knowledge is completely nonconceptual, nothing appears at all" (ibid.: 544). Dunne goes on to specify that, according to Candrakīrti's account of buddhahood, for buddhas "the fluctuations of mind and mental functions" have "completely ceased" (ibid.). Jayānanda (c. 1100), the only known Indian commentator on any of Candrakīrti's works, affirms Candrakīrti's account and "explains that enlightenment is a process of 'not knowing' and is characterized by the elimination of the knowing instrument, the mind" (Vose 2005: 191–192).[30] But how can a mindless buddha teach the dharma? Dunne states that, according to Candrakīrti, "the *dharma-kāya* causes a didactic sound to emit from a buddha . . . [but] the production of this sound does not at all mean that a buddha is cognitively active" (1996: 549). Being mindless, a buddha is unable to use language in any ordinary sense; on this view, a buddha only appears to use language—what is actually occurring is that certain sounds emanating from a buddha are interpreted by unenlightened beings as words and language.[31] So, on a mindless buddha account, it is literally true that the Buddha never uttered a word.

According to a mindful buddha account, however, it is only metaphorically the case that buddhas do not use language. On the model of the awarenesses of a buddha considered here, a buddha possesses both a nonconceptual and a conceptual awareness, and it is a buddha's possession of some form of conceptual awareness that allows for the use of words and language. However, through the attainment of nonconceptual awareness—through directly apprehending thusness, the fundamental, ineffable nature of things—a buddha's relation to conceptualization and language has been radically altered. In any occurrence of language use, a buddha would remain aware that putative linguistic referents do not actually exist. A buddha would employ language without falling under the spell of words and objects—employing concepts and language in perfect accordance with conventional usage, while remaining aware that ultimately there are no referential objects. We might describe a buddha's mindful awareness in terms of what some contemporary philosophers have referred to as fictionalism.[32] Stanley states: "On a fictionalist view, engaging in discourse that involves apparent reference to a realm of problematic entities is best viewed as engaging in a *pretense*. Although in reality, the problematic entities do not exist, according to the pretense we engage in when using the discourse, they do exist" (2001: 36). According to such a fictionalist view, one might engage in conventional discourse without positing that the entities referred to in such discourse ultimately exist, for example, through adding an operator "in fiction *f*" (or "according to the conventional domain") to any truth claim. Hence, on a mindful buddha account, a buddha may be said to use language "under erasure," employing words while remaining mindful that words do not actually refer in the way they purport to—mindfully aware that referents are nothing more than fictions. And insofar as a buddha uses language without subscribing to the reality which language purports to describe, it might be said in metaphorical terms that the Buddha never uttered a word.

Semiosis Transformed

In conclusion, I would like to offer some reflections on just what is at stake in deciding between a mindful buddha and a mindless buddha account. One way to understand what is at stake would be to view the question from a semiotic perspective: what does each account imply about the possibility of a buddha engaging in some form of semiosis?[33] According to one thread of Buddhist thought, the highest goal is to be understood in terms of signlessness (*animitta*), but how is signlessness to be interpreted? Is it the end of all forms of semiosis, or does it represent semiosis transformed in some fundamental way? Does it mean becoming mindless or, rather, transforming the mind? While, according to a mindless buddha account, the highest goal means reaching a state wherein signs and language have no place, a mindful buddha account allows for a buddha to use signs while realizing the emptiness of all signs. Although a mindless buddha account, through denying the possibility of any form of semiosis for a buddha, emphasizes a buddha's complete disengagement from the root problem of conceptualization, it does so at the cost of constructing a buddha who is utterly unlike ordinary sentient beings (he is, after all, mindless), creating a rift between what it means to be an ordinary sentient being and what it means to be a buddha.[34] Alternatively, on a mindful buddha account, a buddha reengages with semiosis in some fundamentally transformed way; and while such an account implies that a buddha can reengage with the root affliction of conceptualization through a mode that is not afflictive, it allows for the more human aspects of buddhahood to be emphasized. And in allowing for the human dimensions of a buddha to be emphasized, a mindful buddha account preserves buddhahood as a projected idealized possibility, something that could stand as a meaningful ideal toward which one might strive. So, on a mindful buddha account, a buddha's engagement with conceptualization and language has not ceased, but has been fundamentally transformed through the attainment of a nonconceptual awareness of thusness. And, according to this reading, insofar as a buddha has attained a realization of the baselessness of words and language while still remaining capable of using them, it may be said that the Buddha never uttered a word.

NOTES

1. Nanjio 1923: 87: na... vacanaṃ paramārthaḥ na ca yad vacanenābhilapyate sa paramārthaḥ.

2. Nanjio 1923: 142: yāṃ ca rātriṃ tathāgato 'bhisaṃbuddho yāṃ ca rātriṃ parinirvāsyati atrāntara ekam apy akṣaraṃ tathāgatena nodāhṛtaṃ na pravyāhariṣyati (From the night that the Tathāgata was fully awakened till the night that he attained parinirvāṇa, the Tathāgata never uttered a single word, nor will he ever speak). This passage, from an important Mahāyāna sūtra, might be understood as a commentary on the Hīnayāna claim that "whatever the Tathāgata speaks, utters and proclaims from the day of his perfect enlightenment up to the day when he utterly passes away into the Nibbāna-element without residue left—all that is just so and not otherwise" (*Aṅguttara-nikāya* 4.23; trans. Thera and Bodhi 1999: 83).

3. Cited in Candrakīrti's *Prasannapadā* (La Vallée Poussin 1903–1913: 366): yāṃ ca... rātriṃ tathāgato 'nuttarāṃ samyak saṃbodhim abhisaṃbuddho yāṃ ca rātrim upādāya parinirvāsyati asminn antare tathāgatenaikākṣaram api nodāhṛtaṃ na pravyāhṛtaṃ nāpi pravyāhariṣyati.

4. Conze 1957: 38 (13b): tat kiṃ manyase Subhūte api nv asti sa kaścid dharmo yas Tathāgatena bhāṣitaḥ? Subhūtir āha: no hīdaṃ Bhagavan, na- asti sa kaścid dharmo yas Tathāgatena bhāṣitaḥ ("What do you think, Subhūti, is there any teaching which was taught by the Tathāgata?" Subhūti replied, "No, indeed, Blessed One, there is no teaching which was taught by the Tathāgata").

5. Lévi 1907: 77: dharmo naiva ca deśito bhagavatā (No teaching was taught by the Blessed One).

6. de Jong 1977: 82: na kvacit kasyacit kaścid dharmo buddhena deśitaḥ.

7. See the *Laṅkāvatāra* for the trope of an ignorant person looking at a pointing finger rather than the object pointed to (Nanjio 1923: 196), and the trope of all phenomena being like reflections of the moon in water (ibid.: 72).

8. The *Laṅkāvatāra* states that words arise from conceptual thought (*vikalpa*; Nanjio 1923: 87). I take it to be a relatively uncontroversial claim that the use of language requires conceptual thought, unlike the much more controversial claim that thought is determined by language (a strong version of the Sapir-Whorf hypothesis), which these Buddhist texts do not endorse; the *Laṅkāvatāra*, for example, indicates that, in other world realms, communication is conducted by means of nonlinguistic signs (ibid.: 105). These texts do, however, endorse something like the claim of C. S. Peirce, "All thought... must necessarily be in signs" (1992: 24).

9. Lévi 1907: 5: vikalpa-kleśā hi bodhisattvāḥ. Also see ibid.: 3, which states that the Mahāyāna is an antidote to all forms of affliction (*kleśa*), since it is the basis of nonconceptual awareness (*nirvikalpa-jñāna*).

10. See Takahashi et al. 2006: 68 (6.5).

11. "Contrary to the customary insistence on 'right views' the *Aṭṭhakavagga* speaks of giving up *all* views" (Gomez 1976: 140).

12. For an excellent study of the Sanskrit terms *saṃjñā, vikalpa, parikalpa, prapañca,* etc., in Buddhist literature—and the relations among these terms—see Williams 1980.

13. I date the final redaction of the *Mahāyānasūtrālaṃkāra* (MSA) and its commentary, the *Mahāyānasūtrālaṃkāra-bhāṣya* (MSABh), to approximately the fourth century C.E.; see D'Amato 2000, chapter 2. When referring to both the MSA and the MSABh together, I will use the abbreviation MSA/Bh. All further references to this text, by chapter and verse, are drawn from the Sanskrit edition of Lévi. I will also draw from a subcommentary, the *Mahāyānasūtrālaṃkāra-vṛtti-bhāṣya* (MSAVBh) by Sthiramati (c. sixth century C.E.); another subcommentary, the *Mahāyānasūtrālaṃkāra-ṭīkā* (MSAT) by Asvabhāva (c. sixth century C.E.); a sūtra related to the MSA, the *Buddhabhūmi-sūtra* (c. 400 C.E.); and a commentary to this sūtra, the *Buddhabhūmyupadeśa* by Bandhuprabha (sometime after the mid-seventh century C.E.).

14. Wayman states, "Of the two main philosophical schools of the Mahāyāna, it is the Yogācāra rather than the Mādhyamika that is mainly responsible for this terminology [i.e., of the four forms of awareness], because the mirror usually symbolizes the mind and this fact especially suits the idealistic Yogācāra school" (1971: 353). For a discussion of the metaphor of the mirror as mind in Buddhist literature, see Demiéville 1987.

15. Sthiramati and Asvabhāva explicitly equate the term *vastu-jñāna* with *pṛṣṭha-labdha-jñāna.* Sthiramati, MSAVBh ad 9.56 (DT [Derge Tanjur] sems tsam MI 134a3): dngos po shes pa [*vastu-jñāna*] ni de'i rgyab nas thob pa dag pa 'jig rten pa'i ye shes [*pṛṣṭha-labdha-śuddha-laukika-jñāna*] la bya ste. Asvabhāva, MSAT ad 9.56 (DT sems tsam BI 72b5): dngos po shes pa [*vastu-jñāna*] ni rjes la thob pa'i ye shes [*pṛṣṭha-labdha-jñāna*] so.

16. Asaṅga's *Mahāyānasaṃgraha* is a Yogācāra treatise which often quotes the MSA; see D'Amato 2000, chapter 2.

17. The *pṛṣṭha-labdha-jñāna* is sometimes referred to as *laukika-jñāna* (worldly awareness), while *nirvikalpa-jñāna* is sometimes called *lokottara-jñāna* (supramundane awareness); see, for example, MSABh ad 14.42–46.

18. MSAVBh intro ad 9.1–3 (DT sems tsam MI 106a6–7). These five topics also comprise a central part of the *Buddhabhūmi-sūtra* (Keenan 1980: 541).

19. This is further supported by the fact that, according to Sthiramati, mirror awareness is the result of the transformation of the store consciousness (*ālaya-vijñāna*), which is understood to be the foundational form of consciousness for nonawakened sentient beings; see MSAVBh intro ad 9.12 (DT sems tsam MI 113b4–5).

20. According to Bandhuprabha's *Buddhabhūmyupadeśa,* "The other three wisdoms... are realized in a temporal sequence. They may be active or not. For these reasons they are not unshakeable" (Keenan 1980: 657).

21. Sthiramati's MSAVBh ad 9.68c (DT sems tsam MI 139b2) states that mirror awareness is without afflictive and cognitive obstructions. And the *Buddhabhūmi-sūtra* states, "[J]ust as when a mirror is shined to a luster, its mirror surface is pure and free from dust... just so is the Tathāgata's mirror-wisdom,

because, being Buddha wisdom, it is eternally separated from the obstacles of passion and knowledge" (Keenan 1980: 664).

22 MSAVBh ad 9.69d (DT sems tsam MI 140a6) states that mirror awareness is a nonconceptual awareness. In fact, as Hakamaya points out (1971: 467–466), both Sthiramati and Asvabhāva interpret mirror awareness as nonconceptual. Bandhuprabha's *Buddhabhūmyupadeśa* indicates that "mirror wisdom is non-discriminative [*nirvikalpa*]" (Keenan 1980: 562), that "mirror wisdom is eternally separated from the oscillations of discrimination" (ibid.: 657).

23. Lévi's edition (1907: 47) reads *'malaṃ*. Here, I am following Funahashi (1985: 39) and the Tibetan (*'dod*).

24. Following Funahashi (1985: 39) and the Tibetan (*dus na sems can rnams*), I am reading *kāle sattveṣu* for *kāleṣu*.

25. This point is made in a passage from the *Buddhabhūmi-sūtra* quoted in Sthiramati's MSAVBh ad 9.72ab: "the Analytical Wisdom of the Tathāgatas is girded with non-delusion regarding both the particular and general characteristics [of all phenomena]" (Nguyen 1990: 448; cf. Keenan 1980: 747).

26. We might describe a buddha's approach to logical systems as instrumentalist:

> The *instrumentalist* position results from a rejection of the idea of the "correctness" of a logical system.... On the instrumentalist view, there is no sense in speaking of a logical system's being "correct" or "incorrect," though it might be conceded that it is appropriate to speak of one system's being more fruitful, useful, convenient...etc. than another (perhaps: for certain purposes). (Haack 1978: 224)

27. Makransky makes the point that the "other three gnoses, as 'moving,' correspond to different aspects of a Buddha's subsequent gnosis (*pṛṣṭha-labdha-jñāna*). They 'move' in that they are cognizant of and operative within the conditioned world of changing phenomena" (1997: 100–101).

28. As Makransky states, "A Buddha's fundamental awareness, whether described as nonconceptual gnosis (*nirvikalpa-jñāna*) or mirror gnosis (*ādarśa-jñāna*), is perfect realization of universal thusness" (1997: 103).

29. The contents of such a mindful awareness might be characterized in terms of the limit paradoxes described by Garfield and Priest, especially the paradox of expressibility: "linguistic expression and conceptualization can express only conventional truth; the ultimate truth is that which is inexpressible and that which transcends these limits. So it cannot be expressed or characterized. But we have just done so" (Garfield and Priest 2003: 16).

30. Jayānanda writes, "Since enlightenment is by way of not knowing (*anadhigama*) at all, we assert that the activities of mind and mental factors—feeling and so forth—[all] having the character of experiencing, have ceased their engagement" (Vose 2005: 191). Vose (ibid.: 188–208) offers an excellent discussion of Jayānanda's account of buddhahood, including the way he incorporates the fourfold model of awareness into his interpretation.

31. Such an account might be interpreted in terms of Griffiths' proposed distinction between buddhahood as it is in itself, and buddhahood as it appears to ordinary beings. Griffiths states: "I suggested...that Buddha's actions in the world...can be interpreted in terms of properties of the kind *seems to S to be P at t*, where *S* is some non-Buddha, *P* some mode of appearance, and *t* some time.... I shall show that all properties of Buddha *svabhāvataḥ* [in terms of its own nature] are nonrelational" (1994: 147). Thus, on this account, *in reality* a buddha does not use language, but it *appears* to other sentient beings that a buddha does.

32. See Yablo 2001 for an account of different forms of fictionalism.

33. See D'Amato 2003 for an overview of various scholars' approaches to Buddhist thought in terms of semiotics.

34. Similarly, Dunne states that Candrakīrti's account of buddhahood "is one of a completely detached buddha who is so far removed from our life-world that all his volition has long since ceased.... In short, Candrakīrti's buddha appears to be more a volitionless, transcendental force than a speaking, feeling human" (1996: 550). And Vose states that Jayānanda's account of buddhahood "presents fundamental disjunctions between ordinary mind and enlightenment" (2005: 192).

5

Is Reductionism Expressible?

Mark Siderits

Buddhists hold that there is no self. Their view is, I claim, best represented as a form of ontological reductionism. Ontological reductionism about things of kind K is typically described as the view that Ks *just consist in* things of some other kind (that a K is *nothing but* things of some distinct kind). So a reductionist about chariots might say that a chariot just consists in wheels, spokes, felly, axle, etc., all arranged in a certain way. And a reductionist about persons might hold that a person is nothing but a causal series of psychophysical elements, none of which is at all person-like. The Buddhist non-self view is, I have claimed, a kind of reductionism about persons.[1] But this claim is controversial, since Buddhists do not typically put theirs as the view that a person just consists in certain other things. Instead, they explain their view by employing the notion that there are two kinds of truth. They say that, while it is conventionally true that there are persons, the ultimate truth is that there are impersonal psychophysical elements in causal connection. I have called the Buddhist view *reductionist* because I think the device of the two truths represents a better way of formulating ontological reductionism. I shall say something in defense of that choice. But my main concern is to explore the objection that, if this is the correct formulation of reductionism, then reductionism will turn out to be inexpressible. To see how this objection might arise, we must first consider why the Buddhist way of putting their non-self view could be said to represent a better way of saying what reductionists wish to say. So I shall start by defending my decision to call the Buddhist view a reductionist position.

Buddhist Reductionism

The Buddhist position on persons follows from a more general view concerning wholes and parts, the view I call *mereological reductionism*. Thus, Buddhists say the same sorts of things concerning a pot and its constituent atoms as they say about a person and a causal series of psychophysical elements. There are special problems that beset any formulation of reductionism about persons, and these are mostly extraneous to the issues I want to address. So, I propose that we consider the case of reductionism about pots instead. According to the usual understanding, a reductionist about pots would be someone who holds something like the following:

> While pots exist, a pot just consists in a large number of atoms arranged in a particular way.

Someone who says this is prima facie committed to the existence of both pots and atoms. But then the question arises of what is meant by "*just* consists in" (or "is *nothing* but"). Suppose there are n atoms arranged pot-wise. Are there then n objects in the region where we say the pot is, or are there $n + 1$? In saying that pots exist, the reductionist seems committed to the latter answer, but the "just" suggests the former answer. In fact, there are deep difficulties with both. If the reductionist holds that there are $n + 1$ objects, the position becomes indistinguishable from that of the mereological realist, someone who holds that the whole exists distinct from the parts. But if they say there are just n objects, they seem to be saying that the pot doesn't count, which would be inconsistent with their claim that pots exist. Perhaps the view is that the pot is identical with its parts; in that case, once the atoms have been counted, there would be no need to count the pot as well. But this would make one thing identical with many things, which seems absurd. Can the view be coherently stated?

The Buddhist approach to pots suggests a way out: they would say that it is conventionally true that there are pots, but it is ultimately true that there are atoms arranged in a certain way. Buddhists often put this point not in terms of two kinds of truth, but in terms of two ways of existing: *conventionally* and *ultimately*. The pot, they say, is conventionally real, while the atoms so arranged are ultimately real. What makes this a reductionist claim is the fact that it invokes a two-tier ontology with an essential asymmetry: only those things that properly belong in our final ontology are ultimately real, while conventional reals may be said to exist only by virtue of their supervening on the ultimate reals. This suggests a way out of the dilemma we just saw the reductionist facing, the dilemma that, if they say the pot exists, they cannot say it *just* consists in the atoms, while if they say it does not exist, then what is it that undergoes reduction?[2] The Buddhist approach resolves this dilemma by saying that both the pot and the atoms exist, but the pot has a lesser kind of existence than do the atoms.

This immediately raises the question of how something might be said to have a lesser kind of existence than something else. One thing this decidedly does not mean is that it possesses a lesser degree of reality. So what does it mean? Consider the notion of a folk ontology: the set of entities that the use of our folk theory commits us to the existence of. And suppose we agree that there are certain things in our folk ontology (e.g., sunrises and sunsets) that do not belong in the final ontology, that are not among the things that must be mentioned in a completed account of the nature of mind-independent reality. Now, it may be that some of these things are missing from the final ontology for the simple reason that they are unreal, like witches, or the disease-causing demons that occurred in the folk ontology of our ancestors. But there may be others whose absence stems not from the fact that they are posits of a theory that is straightforwardly false in the way that the demonic-possession theory of disease is. Their absence may instead derive from their being posited by a theory that turns out to be superfluous when viewed in the light of the final theory. Because the final ontology is meant to contain only those things that are mind-independently real, the standpoint of the final theory prescinds from our interests and cognitive limitations. Our folk theory, on the other hand, is shaped in part by our interests and cognitive limitations. Thus, it may happen that a given arrangement of entities might show up twice: as a many in the final ontology, and as a one in our folk ontology. It might be that atoms arranged in a certain way appear in our final ontology as atoms, but in our folk ontology they show up in the guise of a pot. Pots would then be in our folk ontology because, given our interests and cognitive limitations, the theory that there are pots turns out to be a suitable way to treat such arrangements of atoms. We might then say that pots have the lesser, "merely conventional" kind of existence.

We are now in a better position to understand what is meant by "ultimately true" and "conventionally true." Ultimate truth may be defined in terms of correspondence with mind-independent reality. Statements are ultimately true by virtue of their correctly stating of things in our final ontology how those things are. But the form the definition takes will depend on how we conceive of correspondence. It seems natural to think of correspondence as a relation that holds between a statement and a state of affairs when the referents of the terms in the statement stand to one another as the statement asserts. But then we may ask whether a given term must map onto a single object, or if instead correspondence might hold when a single term is taken as referring to a multiplicity of objects. If not—if correspondence can only involve a one-to-one mapping—then the following will suffice:

> A statement is ultimately true if and only if it corresponds to mind-independent reality.

But if correspondence can involve a one-to-many mapping (e.g., from "the pot" onto many atoms arranged pot-wise), then a given statement might express commitment to things that are not in our final ontology and yet be made true by corresponding to how things in the final ontology are. Then, a definition like the following will be required:

> A statement is ultimately true iff it corresponds to mind-independent reality and neither asserts nor presupposes the existence of anything not in the final ontology.

Thus, for the Buddhist who embraces a wholesale form of mereological reductionism, a statement will be ultimately true just in case it employs only referring expressions that map in a one-to-one fashion onto impartite entities and what it asserts of those entities in fact obtains mind-independently.

So much for ultimate truth. What is conventional truth? In the past, I have explained this in terms of utility: conventional truths are those statements the acceptance of which invariably leads to successful practice. But this approach may be criticized on two grounds. First, successful practice seems to require persons, which are the chief targets of Buddhist reductionism. Second, conventional truth is meant to capture the semantic practices of the folk, and the folk do not think of truth as the property of being conducive to successful practice. The first criticism can, I think, be answered. I believe it is possible to explain the notion of successful practice in a thoroughly impersonal way. But I shall not seek to do that here.[3] The second criticism is more serious. Considerations of utility may play an important role in explaining why the folk come to accept statements about pots, given that there ultimately are no pots. But to define conventional truth in terms of utility is to leave unexplained why it should be thought of as a kind of truth. It would be better if we could offer an account that came closer to the pretheoretic notion of truths as statements that "tell it like it is." The challenge is to do so in a way that avoids commitment to entities that are not in our final ontology. But this is a common problem, one that is also faced, e.g., by those wishing to explain how statements about fictional characters might be true. There is a variety of proposed "fictionalist" solutions to the general problem. I want to explore how a version of fictionalism developed in Sider (1999) might work here.

The general problem that all fictionalisms seek to solve might be put as follows. Suppose there is a body of statements widely accepted as true, but alleged by some to generate problematic ontological commitments. Then those who allege this must say that those statements are false. But, given the statements' widespread acceptance, those who allege this may need to pay the statements some sort of alethic compliment. Sider's candidate for this role is "quasi-truth." Suppose S is among the widely accepted statements generated by acceptance of folk theory T. And suppose that T involves ontological commitments sufficiently problematic that S must be deemed false.[4] Then S is quasi-true if there is some true statement P such that, had T been true, P would have been true and would have entailed S. P then counts as an underlying truth, since the quasi-truth of S supervenes on the truth of P. Take, for instance, the folk theory that there are pots and the statement "This pot has peas in it." Further suppose that, while this statement would be accepted by the folk under its conditions of utterance, pots are not in our final ontology, so that the statement could not be ultimately true. Then, it might still be quasi-true, provided there were some true statement—presumably, a statement concerning peas[5] and atoms arranged pot-wise—which, had it been true that there are pots, would have been true and would have entailed that this pot has peas in it.

An important difference between this and other fictionalist approaches is that, on Sider's account, S and P need not be sufficiently similar that S might readily be confused for P. Sider's approach differs in this regard from paraphrase approaches (such as metaphoricalism), which seek to give S an alethic commendation by claiming that, while S is, strictly speaking, false, there is some near semantic neighbor S′ that is strictly true and that, for ordinary purposes, S can serve as an acceptable abbreviated paraphrase of S′.[6] The difficulty Sider sees with this approach is that, once our ontological scruples have been accommodated, the resulting S′ may bear no obvious semantic relation to S. It may not be evident to everyone that a statement about the spatial relations obtaining among certain atoms and certain peas is at all close in meaning to a statement about peas in a pot. He thus claims it is better to require of an underlying truth only that its truth would make true the false statement in question had the folk theory been true. Those who believe that this pot has peas in it need not even understand what it would mean to say that these atoms bear these spatial relations to these peas. We can nonetheless understand how their false belief arose, given the relations among the atoms and the peas, plus the casual Meinongianism of ordinary discourse. And this in turn makes it evident why their false belief should be close enough to true for most ordinary purposes.[7]

The notion of quasi-truth seems to capture much of what Buddhist reductionists have in mind when they speak of conventional truth. They hold, for instance, that for every statement that is conventionally true, there is some ultimate truth that helps to explain why acceptance of the statement in question would lead to successful practice. But it is also clear that the ultimately true statement is not to be thought of as a translation of the conventional truth; there is no synonymy between a conventionally true statement and the ultimate truth that serves as an underlying statement. We are also told that the erroneousness of conventional truths stems from the fact that they involve commitment to things that are not in our ultimate ontology. Given all this, it seems natural to express the notion of conventional truth in terms of the idea that, given the relevant ultimate facts, these are statements that would have been true had those things that are conventionally real been ultimately real. And this is what quasi-truth amounts to. Reductionism about pots may then be expressed as follows:

> While it is conventionally true (i.e., quasi-true) that there are pots, it is ultimately true (i.e., true) that there are atoms arranged pot-wise; the quasi-truth of statements about pots supervenes on the ultimate truth of statements about atoms arranged pot-wise.

The Expressibility Problem

Suppose we agree that this represents a suitable way of formulating ontological reductionism. A new question will now arise: is reductionism expressible? Notice that the supervenience claim rests on a counterfactual conditional: if the folk theory had been true, i.e., if there were pots, then the truth of the statement about the atoms would have entailed the statement about pots. According to the Buddhist reductionist, the counterfactual is actually a counterpossible: given that pots are partite, such things cannot possibly exist. So the antecedent of the conditional is false in every possible world. In that case, the conditional would seem to be vacuously true. Now, some would claim that counterpossible conditionals are nonetheless perfectly intelligible. After all, they say, even those who believe they have conclusively refuted some metaphysical thesis will say that they can understand what it would mean for it to have been true. One way to make sense of this would be to distinguish between *metaphysical* impossibility and *logical* impossibility. One could then say that the antecedent is metaphysically impossible but logically possible, so that the conditional is not vacuously true.[8] But even if this is right, there is another problem. Is this conditional supposed to be ultimately true or conventionally true? It cannot be ultimately true, for it contains an expression that refers to pots. But neither can it be conventionally true, for it contains an expression that refers to atoms. No ultimately true statement can contain expressions that refer to pots, and no conventionally true statement can contain expressions that refer to atoms. So the conditional can be neither ultimately true nor conventionally true.

This last claim requires some defense. It is based on the idea that there is a kind of semantic insulation between ultimate truth and conventional truth, that statements referring to conventionally real things lack ultimate truth value, and statements referring to ultimately real things lack conventional truth value. Why might this be? The brief answer is that the insulation prevents bivalence failure. Suppose we allow that statements that are about both pots and atoms can be true. We will then be able to ask about the atoms that are arranged pot-wise in the region where a pot is located: is the aggregate of atoms identical with the pot, or is it distinct? The aggregate is a many, while the pot is a one, so identity seems ruled out. But their distinctness leads to systematic causal overdetermination: everything the pot is thought of as causing can be accounted for by the causal powers of the atoms. What's more (though no Buddhist reductionist ever put it in these terms), there are sorites difficulties lurking when we allow statements with mixed vocabulary. For then the most plausible thing to say about the relation between the atoms and the pot is that the atoms compose the pot. And suppose we remove randomly chosen atoms from the aggregate. At what point in this process will the pot cease to exist?

There are, of course, various approaches to resolving these difficulties. One might, for instance, resist the question of whether pot and atoms are identical or distinct on the grounds that identity and distinctness are always sortal relative. One might seek to block the sorites difficulties by claiming that there are many distinct aggregates of atoms arranged pot-wise, each with slightly different persistence conditions, and that all of them are equally good candidates for being the pot. Or one might claim that the identity conditions for pots are inherently vague. But such resolutions always come at a price. The relative identity solution leads to co-location and, consequently, to systematic overdetermination. The vague identity solution requires that we either accept true contradictions or else place ad hoc restrictions on the abstraction operator. And so on. The Buddhist reductionist solution—two truths with semantic insulation between them—is far more conservative. It allows us to preserve classical logic and a bivalent truth-predicate. And it coheres with all our intuitions about pots. It accomplishes all this through the feature of semantic insulation. And that feature is not ad hoc; it is motivated. We can see why there would be a mismatch between the predicates of conventional discourse and those of ultimate discourse. The former must be *tolerant* in Wright's sense: there is a degree of change (in the case of sortals for partite entities, change in composition) too small to make a difference in their application (Wright 1997: 156). This means that there is the possibility of bivalence failure wherever the two vocabularies appear jointly.

Perhaps it will be objected that the conditional does not contain a use of the expression "pot"; it merely mentions the expression. Bivalence failure might result from statements involving commitment to both pots and atoms. But if the conditional is merely asserting something about the folk's use of the expression "pot," there need not be commitment to the existence of pots. So the conditional can be ultimately true.

The difficulty with this attempt at resolving the difficulty is that the reductionist will need to make the conditional plausible. And if the conditional is to be understood as a claim concerning the linguistic dispositions of the folk, something will need to be said concerning relations between aggregates of atoms and dispositions to use "pot." So the reductionist incurs the obligation to say just which aggregates of atoms will trigger this disposition. And here we have the makings of sorites difficulties. Indeed, we have the makings of a hierarchy of nested sorites difficulties. Not only are there aggregates of atoms where it is indeterminate whether they would be called a pot by the folk, it is indeterminate just where this begins to be the case.

One might wonder whether the semantic insulation must be impermeable in both directions. We are used to the idea that the terms of conventional discourse must be kept out of the vocabulary of an ultimate discourse. Frege was making this sort of claim when he said that a "scientifically respectable language" would contain none of the vague expressions found in ordinary language. But it might be thought that conventional discourse need not be kept free of terms taken from the domain of ultimate truth. Why could it not be conventionally true, for instance, that pots are composed of atoms? There are three answers that might be given here. The first is that the truth-predicate of ordinary language seems to be bivalent. This is in any event what Saṃghabhadra is saying when he claims that a proposition's being indeterminate (*avyākṛta*) is evidence of its illegitimately attempting to employ vocabulary from the two distinct domains of conventional and ultimate truth (La Vallée Poussin

1937: 175). That he takes indeterminacy or lack of truth-value to indicate a difficulty shows that he takes both kinds of truth to be bivalent. At one time, I was nonetheless inclined to think that the conventional truth-predicate is degree-theoretic.[9] In that case, one could say that, after a certain number of the atoms have been removed, the statement that there is a pot on the table is less than fully true. But I am no longer sure that this would reflect the ordinary understanding of "true."[10]

A second reason to reject this way of resolving the difficulty is that it is in any event unclear that it would be acceptable to the reductionist. The proposal is to allow that conventional truths may contain terms from the ultimate discourse, so that the reductionist thesis may be formulated as a conventional truth. But if the reductionist thesis is true, surely it must be more than merely conventionally true. And third, there are certain advantages to having full-blown semantic insulation between the two domains. For instance, reductionism about persons would then give us a way to reconcile the libertarian view of agency with the fact of psychological determinism.[11] It likewise yields a solution to the problem of too many subjects.[12] So, even if permeability were an option, there would still be reasons to prefer saying that the insulation is impermeable in both directions. In that case, we cannot speak of pots and atoms in the same breath. So while the two-truths approach looks like the right one for the reductionist to take, it seems to have the consequence that the reductionist claim can be neither ultimately true nor conventionally true. On the best possible formulation of reductionism, the reductionist thesis cannot be expressed.

Solving the Problem

What can reductionists say in response? One thing they might say is that, even if their thesis is strictly inexpressible, it may still be true. If we are semantic realists, then we agree that there are truths that will never be expressed. Couldn't there likewise be truths that can never be expressed? The difficulty with this response is that it is then unclear to what truth is to be attributed. There might well be those states of affairs that the reductionist claims make reductionism true. But what is said to be true here is the representation of those states of affairs. And to say that reductionism is inexpressible is to say that there can be no such representation. Of course, it may make sense to speak of truths that are inexpressible in practice (i.e., for beings like us). Enumerating the present position of every atom in a building would simply take too long, yet we would still say there is some such truth concerning those atoms. But the inexpressibility in the present case looks to be the in-principle kind. So this response won't help.

Let us try to be clearer about the source of the difficulty here. The reductionist holds that, strictly speaking, there are no pots. But the problem they confront is not that of how to deny the existence of something unreal. There is a clear path around Meinongianism here: view the entity in question as a fabrication constructed out of reals. What the reductionist wants to say is that, while there are only atoms, the belief that there are pots turns out to be a useful construction for creatures like us. The difficulty comes in trying to make this claim precise. Given that there are no pots and only atoms, the assertibility conditions associated with the conventional predicate "pot" must be somehow tied to facts about atoms. It is at this point that the possibility of bivalence failure enters in. If the truth of our statement about the pot is to supervene on some statement about atoms, the truth-predicate in play here will have to be degree-theoretic. And this appears to be an anomaly, given that the ultimate truth-predicate is bivalent.

There is, though, a way of mitigating the anomaly. The reductionist might explain it as the result of facts about creatures like us. They might say that, given our interests and cognitive limitations, we will have a use for predicates like "pot," and that these must be tolerant in Wright's sense. Thus, it will prove impossible to say in any more than an approximate way how the assertibility conditions for such predicates supervene on facts about atoms. In this case, bivalence failure is safely contained within the realm of discourse usage; it does not infect the world.

Here is one place where it may seem to make a difference whether our reductionism is to extend beyond pots to persons. This metalinguistic strategy requires that we bring in facts about "creatures like us." If there ultimately are no such creatures, then no ultimately true statement can invoke facts about their interests and cognitive limitations and their resulting speech habits. This is widely taken to constitute an insuperable difficulty for reductionism about persons.[13] If this problem cannot be overcome, then reductionism about persons will be at best inexpressible and perhaps incoherent. But I think this conclusion is over-hasty. If the metalinguistic strategy for containing bivalence failure works for reductionism about pots, then I think it can be made to work for persons as well. But saying how that might go involves a long and complicated story, which I won't try to tell here.[14]

Instead, I shall finish by raising one last point about the intelligibility of reductionism. I think it is best expressed in terms of two kinds of truth that are sealed off from one another. But suppose we agree with Asaṅga that the ultimate reals are inexpressible in nature.[15] In that case, given that atoms can be described, atoms would not be ultimately real. Nothing mentioned in any discourse would be. We then wind up with something like Jñānaśrī's "pan-fictionalism," the view that anything expressible is a conceptual fiction.[16] The question is whether this would still count as a kind of reductionism. If reductionism is best understood in terms of the notion of quasi-truth, then it would seem not. For if the ultimate truth is inexpressible, then there can be no underlying truths. The only way a statement could then be true is conventionally, and underlying truths must be ultimately true. Perhaps, though, it will be said that the statement about the atoms, while only conventionally true, is still closer to being ultimately true than is the statement about the pot. For the supervenience relation still holds between the two statements, and the asymmetry involved in supervenience could be taken as evidence of the kind of dependency that characterizes the relation between the reduced and its reduction base. The move from talk of pots to talk of atoms might then be described as a partial reduction of pots; it is only a partial reduction because atoms, being partite, are themselves reducible. We can then imagine there being a series of partial reductions; but this series has no final step, since that would require an expressible ultimate truth. Still, the series is moving in the right direction, so the view does count as a kind of reductionism. Or so it might be argued.

There is a difficulty with this way of construing things, though: it is not clear how we are to tell that the series is moving in the "right" direction. To fix a direction, we need to be able to say something about the nature of the ultimate. For instance, we might say that going from talk of pots to talk of atoms is taking us closer to the ultimate truth, if we knew that the ultimate reals were truly impartite in nature. But if the nature of ultimate reality is inexpressible, we can know no such thing. Indeed, we would be equally justified in saying that the ultimately real is just pure being, one only without a second. In that case, the "right" direction would be just the opposite—from parts to ever more inclusive wholes. Since there can be no reason to prefer one direction over the other, perhaps this view could not be called reductionism. Perhaps we should say instead that there is just a single truth-predicate and a contextualist semantics. The argument for this would be that the different "levels" are really just distinct contexts determined by different interests, none of which can be said to better represent the nature of mind-independent reality. If this alternative is the right way of looking at things, does this mean that the Yogācāra formulation of Abhidharma reductionism turns it into the minimalism of Madhyamaka?[17]

NOTES

1. See Siderits 1997. Also see chapter 1 of Siderits 2003.

2. Alternatively, one might ask what would then distinguish the reductionist about pots from the eliminativist. While Merricks 2002 calls a view quite like the Buddhist view "eliminativism," this terminological choice strikes me as unfortunate. For it would then be unclear how the above view concerning pots differs from the view we now take toward phlogiston or toward the disease-causing demons in which our ancestors believed.

3. Much of my response to this objection may be found in chapter 3 of Siderits 2003.

4. Buddhist reductionists do not say that conventionally true statements are ultimately false. They say instead that such statements are indeterminate with respect to ultimate truth value: they are semantically ill formed. We should note, though, that there is some tension between this claim and the claim that those who accept conventional truth are "deluded," that conventional truth is massively in error (as Candrakīrti claims in his debate with Bhāvaviveka).

5. Here, we are assuming that, while pots are not in our final ontology, peas are there along with atoms. Note also that, by "atom," we here mean atoms properly so called, i.e., genuinely impartite material particles.

6. See, for instance, Walton 1990. Goodman 2005 explicates the two-truths doctrine as a kind of metaphoricalism.

7. See Sider 1999: 333ff. for an account of how this might all go.

8. In ibid.: 339–340, Sider adopts this approach. Buddhist reductionists might be reluctant to go this route, however. Buddhist philosophers generally follow their orthodox Indian colleagues in denying that *tarka* or *prasaṅga* inferences (i.e., reductio arguments) count as a means of knowledge, for the reason that the antecedent of the conditional that is employed in such an inference lacks a real-world truth maker. *Tarka* may be employed to get the opponent to withdraw some claim, but it cannot be used to support any thesis.

9. So I claimed in chapter 4 of Siderits 2003.

10. For one thing, this would leave unexplained the fact that so many people are convinced by slippery-slope arguments. The reasoning in such arguments depends on the truth-predicate being bivalent.

11. The idea, roughly, is that libertarian agent causation would represent the conventional truth about persons, while psychological determinism represents the ultimate truth about the causal series of psychophysical elements. Semantic insulation would mean that facts about the causal ancestry of an action could not be incompatible with the action's being attributed to a responsible agent. This is spelled out in greater detail in Siderits 2008.

12. I am referring to the puzzle of whether both I and my brain are currently thinking a certain thought. See Merricks 2002: 47–53. The puzzle was originally formulated by Chisholm as a problem for Lockean sortal-relative identity theories, in chapter 3 of Chisholm 1976. See also Noonan 2003: 209–214. Semantic insulation

would resolve the difficulty by ruling out any talk of both me (a whole) and my brain (a part) in the same breath.

13. See, e.g., Merricks 2002: 121.

14. I tell a good bit of the story in chapter 3 of Siderits 2003.

15. Asaṅga argues for the conclusion that nothing can be said about the nature of the ultimate reals at Dutt 1978: 30–31.

16. See chapter 4 of Siderits 1991.

17. I argue for reading Madhyamaka as a variety of minimalism about truth in chapter 8 of Siderits 2003.

6

Mountains Are Just Mountains

Jay L. Garfield and Graham Priest

Before I studied Zen, mountains were mountains, and water was water. After studying Zen for some time, mountains were no longer mountains, and water was no longer water. But now, after studying Zen longer, mountains are just mountains, and water is just water.[1]

Nāgārjuna and the Catuṣkoṭi

The standard view in Western philosophy, dating back to Aristotle, is that every proposition is either true or false—not neither, and not both. There are just two possibilities. A traditional view in Buddhism, of equally ancient ancestry, is that there are four. A proposition may be true (and true only), false (and false only), both true and false, or neither true nor false—*t*, *f*, *b*, *n*. This is the *catuṣkoṭi*.

In the *Mūlamadhyamakakārikā* (MMK), Nāgārjuna famously deployed the catuṣkoṭi in two different ways. The first of these is *positive*: he says that, for certain propositions, all four of the possibilities may hold. Thus:

> Everything is real and is not real,
> Both real and not real,
> Neither unreal nor real.
> This is the Lord Buddha's teaching.[2]

The second is *negative*. In such cases, he argues that none of the four hold. Thus, he argues that none of the four possibilities applies to the proposition that the Buddha exists:

> We do not assert "empty."
> We do not assert "non-empty."
> We neither assert both nor neither.
> They are asserted only for the purpose of designation.[3]

Both of these applications of the catuṣkoṭi have an air of paradox about them—if only because, standardly, exactly one of the four possibilities is supposed to apply.

A common view is to the effect that Nāgārjuna's use of the positive catuṣkoṭi showed that he took conventional reality to be contradictory. It seems to us, however,[4] that, as applied to conventional reality, the contradictions are mainly prima facie. The various possibilities need to be disambiguated with respect to the two notions of truth operative for Nāgārjuna and quite generally in Buddhism. When this is done, things are perfectly consistent. Thus, something may be true (conventionally), false (ultimately), true and false (conventionally and ultimately, respectively), and neither true nor false (ultimately and conventionally, respectively). All this is said, of course, from the conventional perspective.

Again, a common view is that Nāgārjuna's use of the negative catuṣkoṭi shows that he thinks that ultimate reality is ineffable: there are no ultimate truths. A fortiori, what one can say about the ultimate is not contradictory. We have argued that, for Nāgārjuna, there are, indeed, no ultimate truths.[5] But the ultimate is contradictory: there are ultimate truths; indeed, that there are no ultimate truths is one of them. Another is that, from an ultimate perspective (though not a conventional one), there is no distinction between the two truths. It follows that, from the ultimate perspective, the conventional is contradictory as well.

Moreover, the two catuṣkoṭis, we argue, paradoxically express the same insight. Each indicates that there are two truths, that conventional phenomena exist and can be characterized conventionally, and that nothing exists ultimately nor satisfies any description ultimately. Hence, they each indicate the compatibility of the conventional reality of ordinary phenomena with their ultimate emptiness. Moreover, taken together, given the insistence in the negative catuṣkoṭi on the conventional character, and hence the emptiness, of emptiness, they also indicate that the ultimate truth is only conventionally real.

The Catuṣkoṭi and de Morgan Lattices

Catuṣkoṭi means literally "four corners" (in Greek, this is referred to as the *tetralemma*). There are, then, four corners to the space of alethic possibilities. The very name suggests representing the truth values as shown in figure 6.1.

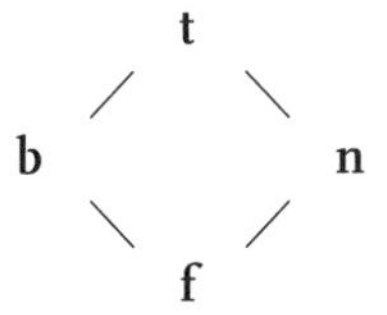

FIGURE 6.1.

Anyone familiar with the semantics of relevant logics, and in particular the Dunn four-valued semantics for first degree entailment, will immediately recognize this as a representation (Hasse diagram) for the four semantic values of that logic.[6] An interpretation of the language, ν, maps every sentence, A, to one of these values, $\nu(A)$. The usual connectives work in natural ways. The value of a conjunction, $\nu(A \wedge B)$, is the *meet* of $\nu(A)$ and $\nu(B)$ (that is, the greatest value less than or equal to both). The value of a disjunction, $\nu(A \vee B)$, is the *join* of $\nu(A)$ and $\nu(B)$ (that is, the least value greater than or equal to both). The value of a negation, $\nu(\neg A)$, is characterized by the following table as shown in figure 6.2.

$\nu(A)$	$\nu(\neg A)$
t	f
f	t
b	b
n	n

FIGURE 6.2.

The striking similarity between the ancient Buddhist view and the contemporary semantics of relevant logic is noted by Priest and Routley.[7] Taking his cue from Nāgārjuna's negative catuṣkoṭi, Sylvan (né Routley) suggested that Nāgārjuna might be thought of as adding a fifth truth value ("none of the above"), meant to apply to statements about ultimate truth.[8] We think that there is something to Sylvan's insight, and we intend to explore it as a way of understanding the notion of awakening.

On the other hand, Nāgārjuna's principal commentators insist that the four koṭis (corners) of the catuṣkoṭi are exhaustive—that there is no fifth option[9]—and Buddhist commentators standardly follow them in this assessment. Our exegesis, if it is to remain faithful to the tradition, must also therefore show that, even if Sylvan is right, the fifth value really is a value that is no value. We will show this as well.

The Great Death, Mountains, and Ox Herding

Though Jōshū, Dōgen, and Hakuin wrote long after Nāgārjuna, and though the influences on this internally heterogeneous Chan/Zen tradition include both Buddhist and Daoist elements, it is illuminating to read Nāgārjuna through the lens of Zen insight. Themes that lie dormant or that are not often brought to the fore in the Indian and Tibetan commentarial literature are sometimes highlighted by Chinese and Japanese Buddhist scholars and practitioners in illuminating ways. Here, we consider the account of awakening, a subject to which these East Asian scholars devoted more explicit attention than did Nāgārjuna.

Jōshū introduced the term the "Great Death" to describe the initial stage of awakening. Dōgen adopted this term,[10] and it gained centrality for Hakuin, who linked it to Dōgen's phrase "the casting off of body and mind."[11] Dying in this way was compared by Hakuin to leaping from a high cliff into a void. One abandons the safe ground of substantialism or reification for the abyss of emptiness, something one can do only if one has confidence that there is, in fact, no bottom. Awakening—resurrection from the Great Death—is the recognition that existence makes sense only in endless free fall. In this free fall, one abandons the need for foundations: for substance as a foundation for attributes; for certain, given, axioms as the foundation for knowledge; for the self as a foundation for experience; for the permanent as the foundation for change; and even for emptiness as the foundation of the conventional. One awakens to the emptiness of emptiness and to the pervasiveness of impermanence and interdependence.

The well-known series of ox-herding pictures provides a nice graphic illustration of this structure (figure 6.3). The first seven pictures record the gradual mastery of the ox, representing the taming of the mind and the gradual analytic understanding of reality. The eighth image is blank, denoting the realization of emptiness. But neither the pictures nor the soteriology can end here. The goal of practice is not the extinction of consciousness, or oblivion to the world, but rather the achievement of enlightened consciousness and of a complete understanding of, and appropriate engagement with, the world. And so the final two pictures return to the beginning, but a beginning informed now

1: Seeking the Ox

2: Seeing the Tracks

3: Seeing the Ox

4: Capturing the Ox

5: Taming the Ox

6: Riding the Ox Home

7: The Ox Forgotten

8: Ox and Man Both Gone

9: Returning Home

10: Entering the City

FIGURE 6.3.

by the realization of emptiness. Awakening does not free one *from* the world; it frees one *for* the world. (This is why Dōgen can insist that practice is awakening. More of this anon.)

All of this is summed up most helpfully in the aphorism that inspired this chapter. Prior to Buddhist reflection, mountains and water—phenomena and change—are perceived as substantially existent, independent things and properties that qualify those things. Some are permanent, some impermanent. Particulars and universals are ontologically independent and are real independently of convention. Buddhist analysis, however, shows these phenomena to be empty of inherent existence, to be insubstantial, and to fail to exist ultimately. Were one to stop here, while the error of taking things to be inherently existent—primal ignorance, as it is called in the trade—would have been expurgated, awakening would not have been achieved. For to stop at this point would be to be stuck with an incomplete understanding both of emptiness and of the kind of reality that mountains and water—phenomena and change—in fact have. This would be to take conventional reality and emptiness to stand to one another as appearance and reality, and so would simultaneously be to deprecate conventional reality and to reify emptiness. Hence, the final moment of the dialectic—the realization that mountains are *just* mountains and that water is *just* water—is essential if practice is to be completed. At this moment, one realizes that for mountains and water to be empty just is for them to exist interdependently and conventionally; for them to exist at all just is for them to be empty of inherent existence. The realization of their emptiness is therefore the realization of their existence, and this is the realization that emptiness and existence are the same thing: the identity of the two truths. The third moment differs from the first just in that the realization of emptiness that mediates them strips away the imputation of inherent existence from the apprehension of the conventional, leaving the conventional just as conventional and transforming the world as seen through primal ignorance into the world as seen through awakened awareness.

The Lattices

We can now connect this dialectic directly to the catuṣkoṭis and to the semantic lattices that represent them. The first lattice (figure 6.4) represents the positive catuṣkoṭi and the first moment of the Zen dialectic. In this lattice, we see that the evaluation function for our language, ν (represented by the squiggly arrows), maps each sentence (such as *A*, *B*,...) into the set of truth values represented by the corners of the lattice. From the standpoint of conventional

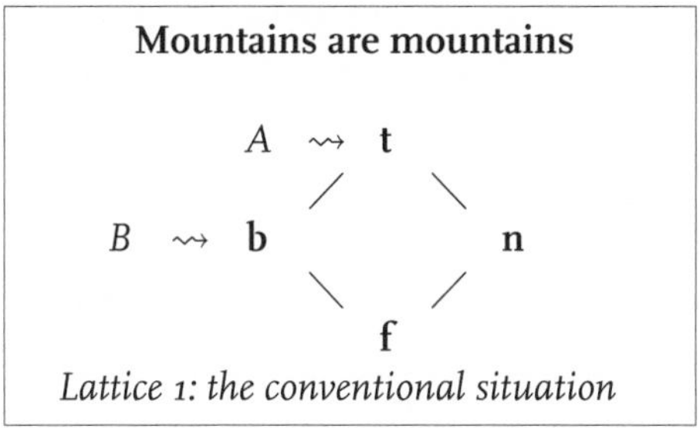

FIGURE 6.4.

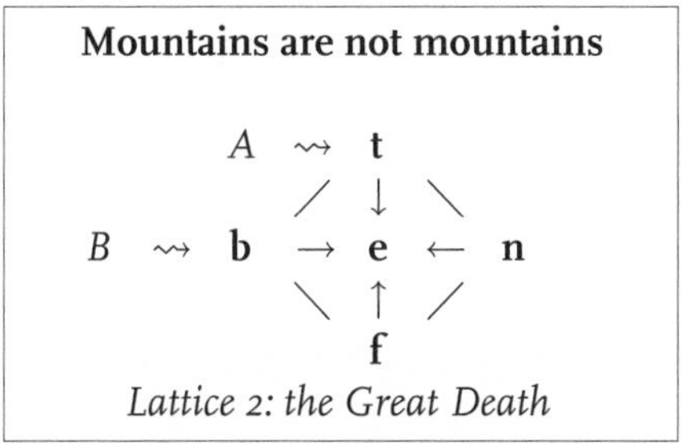

FIGURE 6.5.

truth, some sentences are true; some are false; some are true and false (perhaps in different senses); and some are neither true nor false (perhaps in different senses). But truth values can be assigned. Mountains are, from this perspective, mountains.

The second lattice (figure 6.5) takes us to the second moment of Zen awakening. Here, a second mapping is also represented. A fifth value, *e* (emptiness), is added to the lattice. Though we write it at the heart of the picture, it is an isolated point. That is, according to the ordering, it is incomparable with the other four values. (Strictly, then, this is not a lattice in the mathematical sense; it is just a partial ordering. However, we will continue to describe the structures we are talking about as lattices, since this is an apt description of their appearance.) The value *e* is also a *sink*. That is, if $\nu(A) = e$, then $\nu(A \wedge B) = \nu(A \vee B) = \nu(\neg A) = e$. We now introduce an operator, μ (indicated by the straight arrows), on the semantic values. For any lattice value, V, $\mu(V) = e$. The symbol 'μ' is happily appropriate; for in Japanese Buddhist thought, 'mu' 無 is the ultimate negation. (More of this anon, too.) Given the new structure, the truth values of all sentences are obtained by composing ν and μ. Thus, the truth value of A, e.g., "Mountains are mountains," is $\mu(\nu(A)) = $ e. It is not true that mountains are mountains.

Hakuin and Dōgen, as we have observed, refer to the realization of the emptiness of all things as the Great Death, the casting off of body-mind. They urge that a precondition for awakening is the courage to endure the Great Death, to give up one's commitment to the substantiality, permanence, and ultimate importance of the external and internal worlds, to recognize their emptiness. At that point, mountains are no longer mountains, water is no longer water. All there is, is emptiness.

It is tempting to think that the Great Death and the apprehension of nothing but emptiness is awakening. But again, as we have observed, it is not. To awaken is not to lose the conventional truth; it is to awaken to its conventional nature. The apprehension of emptiness and the dissolution of the conventional are only preconditions. The second lattice collapses all four corners into emptiness and so cannot be a stopping point.

To leap from the high cliff of ignorance requires courage precisely because one is convinced that one will inevitably hit bottom—that there is a ground. Awakening occurs with resurrection from the Great Death and the realization that there are no foundations, whether ontological, epistemological, or logical. Conventional truth is not undermined by this discovery, for conventional truth never presupposed such foundations anyway. Its reality is the reality of changing, interdependent, essenceless phenomena, the ontological status of which is determined by the conventions and concerns with which we approach them, and access to which is mediated by conventional epistemic practices whose warrant is determined in turn by their efficacy in mediating our relations to these variable, essenceless phenomena. Awakening is awakening to the fact that the only reality possible for conventional phenomena is their emptiness and that emptiness just is their conventional reality. Mountains are just mountains, water is just water—neither anything more nor anything less.

Diagrammatically, this last stage is difficult to draw. It is helpful, for a start, to split it into two (see figures 6.6 and 6.7). Recall that μ maps every value to e. Hence, $\mu(e) = e$. The value e is itself "muified"; and since it is empty, there is ultimately nothing for the arrows inside the diamond to map to. This is really a transition state, and the diagram might be better represented dynamically, with the interior of the diamond gradually fading out, giving rise to lattice 4.

The arrows from the sentences now stop at the original truth values. All sentences therefore receive their conventional truth values. The value e is still there, but has canceled itself, and so too the arrows that target it, allowing the original truth values to manifest—to emerge from emptiness.[12] (The four conventional truth values, though they map to e in lattice 3, may still be the targets of the squiggly arrows, since these represent conventional practice and so remain undisturbed by the ultimate analysis represented by the straight arrows.)

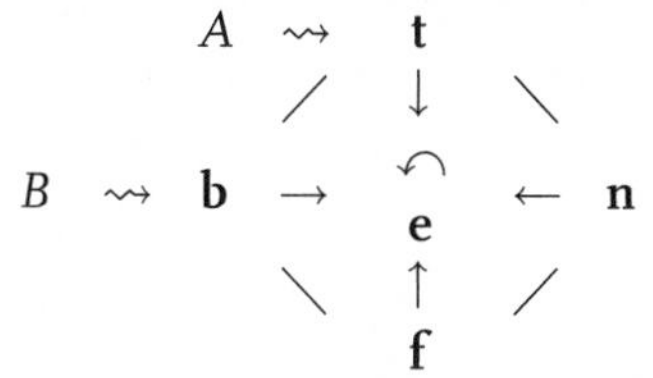

Lattice 3: the emptiness of emptiness

FIGURE 6.6.

Mountains are mountains

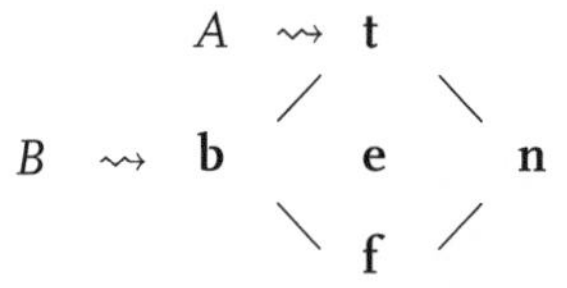

Lattice 4: awakening

FIGURE 6.7.

As figure 6.7 makes clear, we have effectively returned to where we started. True, from the standpoint of conventional reality, the first and last representations may look different. The first does not encode emptiness; the last does. But from the standpoint of ultimate reality, there is no real difference; they are the same. The first lattice had an empty center from the beginning. The final picture only makes that fact explicit. In each, conventional practice proceeds in the context of this empty center and is undisturbed by it.

Internal and External Negation

It is interesting to turn here, for a moment, to traditional Indian logic (Hindu and Buddhist). In Indian logic, it is common to distinguish between two kinds of negation, which we will call *internal* (*paryudāsa*, Tib. *ma yin dgag*) and *external* (*prasajya*, Tib. *med dgag*). The difference between them is that the internal negation of a proposition, or the state of affairs that it describes, implicates the existence of a different state of affairs. Thus, when we say that a certain pot is not blue (internal), we implicate that it is some other color (e.g., red). An external negation—such as that there is no blue pot—has no such implicatures.

An important theme in Madhyamaka commentarial literature is that emptiness is an external negation.[13] When we say that the pot's being blue is empty, we do not implicate that it is some other color, or even that there is a pot there at all. The state of affairs of a blue pot just does not arise. Most important, to say that something is empty is not to implicate the positive state of affairs that it has a certain essence, namely, emptiness.[14]

The transformation from the perspective of the positive catuṣkoṭi (first lattice) to the negative (second lattice) is the transition from the conventional to the ultimate perspective, and hence to the perspective of the apprehension of emptiness. That transition should therefore be marked by some kind of external negation. This is exactly the function of μ. In the context of the second lattice, it is not the case that A is true: A is not ultimately true, in virtue of the emptiness of its subject and predicate. Thus, it takes the value e, which is distinct from t and b. This is not to say that $\neg A$ is true, though. Indeed, it has the same status: all of the four standard possibilities are rejected. Nor is it true to say that the state of affairs that A describes is empty. No positive statement—in fact, no statement at all—is true at this stage of the game. All take the value e.

This is the sense in which emptiness is an external negation. And the fact that it is an external negation is what makes it possible for the recovery of the conventional, represented in the final moment of the dialectic. For if any alternative, even emptiness, were implicated by the negation of the conventional koṭis, it would be hard to see how they could each be recovered and how the conventional world could be preserved. It is precisely the fact that emptiness is such a complete negation that prevents it ultimately from erasing the conventional truth values which it negates. The fact that this falls out so nicely from our account indicates that our use of modern logical apparatus does not take us so far from the canonical Indo-Tibetan tradition after all.

Cogent Inconsistency

The series of lattices also gives us insight into Dōgen's puzzling assertion that practice is awakening. It might seem much more natural to think that practice is a *means to* awakening, and so is precisely what one does when one is *not yet* awakened. If that does seem more natural, then one is indeed not yet awakened, and practice may be necessary. But suppose that one is already awakened. One has realized emptiness and reaffirmed the conventional truth. That conventional truth is not altered by one's realization. It must hence be recognized to be empty once again, and that is practice, and that practice is awakened. But that practice is no different from the practice one initially undertook. And so, that was awakened practice as well. One just didn't realize this.

This, of course, leads us to one of the most puzzling doctrines of East Asian Buddhist philosophy, one disparaged by some Tibetan Madhyamaka philosophers: the doctrine of primordial awakening and of an innate buddha-nature in every sentient being. From the standpoint of one focused on the graduated path to enlightenment, with countless eons of practice before one attains even the second bodhisattva stage, and many more countless eons of practice before awakening, the very idea that one is already awakened seems preposterous. Why put in all that effort to achieve what is already achieved? The claim that, despite being already awakened, one simply doesn't realize it, appears as well to be an incoherent reply. How could buddhas not know that they are buddhas?

Here, though, the Chan/Zen tradition is merely following Nāgārjuna closely—and this is why, in this tradition, sudden awakening is rated as possible. If the two truths really are nondifferent, and if to apprehend the ultimate really just is to apprehend the conventional, what a buddha apprehends is precisely what anyone else apprehends. This does not mean that it is *easy* to see things as a buddha does. Ignorance remains the superimposition of inherent existence on that which is empty. But it does mean that ignorance is not the *absence* of awakened perception, but an *addition* to it. Awakening is simply the realization of the fact that nothing needs to be added to experience. Sudden awakening is possible because of the presence of that primordial awareness.

So, all things have a single nature, and that is emptiness, and that is no nature at all. And that is why each thing can manifest exactly the conventional nature that it has. All of this might seem at first glance to be hopelessly incoherent. We grant its inconsistency: Nāgārjuna and Dōgen are indeed committed to the identity of distinct truths and to the assertion that the essence of all things is their essencelessness. They are also committed to the claim that the objects of awakening and ignorance are both distinct and identical. The fifth value, *e*, with its paradoxical status, is a way of representing this. Nāgārjuna and Dōgen agree that ultimate reality escapes the standard four possibilities, and so acknowledge a fifth; and the fifth is self-dismantling. It is both crucial and idle.

So, inconsistent, yes; incoherent, no. We hope to have made sense of this inconsistent picture of reality. To the extent that we have, we have vindicated Nāgārjuna's use of the positive and negative catuṣkoṭis, his identification of the two truths, and the claim of his most important exegetes that emptiness in Nāgārjuna's system is an external, not an internal, negation. We have also, to this extent, vindicated Hakuin's and Dōgen's account of the Great Death, illuminated the identity of practice and attainment, and explained the ox-herding sequence. And we have shown that mountains are just mountains and water is just water. What more could they be?

NOTES

1. The aphorism occurs in many variants in Chan and Zen literature, but was first attributed to Master Qingyuan in the *Compendium of the Five Lamps* (*Wudeng Huiyuan*, 1252):

> Thirty years ago, before I practiced Chan, I saw that mountains are mountains and rivers are rivers. However, after having achieved intimate knowledge and having gotten a way in, I saw that mountains are not mountains and rivers are not rivers. But now that I have found rest, as before I see mountains are mountains and rivers are rivers. (App 1994: 111–112n2).

2. MMK XVIII.8. Translations are from Tsong kha pa 2006.
3. MMK XXII.11.
4. Garfield and Priest 2003.
5. Ibid.
6. See, e.g., Priest 2001: 8.4.
7. Priest and Routley 1989: 16ff.
8. Ibid.
9. Candrakīrti 2003: 11a–b; Tsong kha pa 2006: 50–54.
10. See Nishijima and Cross 1996.
11. Peter Gregory (personal communication) has speculated that this may have been a misunderstanding of his Chinese teacher Rujing's phrase "casting off the dust of the mind," indicating the elimination of the *kleśa*s.
12. Lattice 4 might therefore also be represented as lattice 3 with its whole interior written *under erasure*.
13. Candrakīrti 2003: 11–12; Tsong kha pa 2006: 50–54.
14. See Candrakīrti's commentary on MMK XV.8 (2003: 92b), in which he compares one who takes emptiness to be an essence with a customer who, when the shopkeeper tells him that he has nothing to sell, asks to purchase some of that nothing.

7

How Do Mādhyamikas Think?: Notes on Jay Garfield, Graham Priest, and Paraconsistency

Tom J. F. Tillemans

Several philosophers and Buddhist studies specialists have taken up the question of whether the philosophers of the Middle Way school, i.e., the Mādhyamikas, use some form of deviant logic, or a logic which would not recognize fundamental theorems, such as the law of double negation elimination, the law of excluded middle, and even the law of non-contradiction. Often this investigation has focused on the tetralemma (*catuṣkoṭi*), with very varied results. In some writings problems about excluded middle or the interpretation of negation in the tetralemma have tended to take precedence over earlier interests about Mādhyamika respect or non-respect for the law of non-contradiction. Indeed it's probably fair to say that, in Buddhist studies at least, attributing contradictions to Nāgārjuna has increasingly fallen out of vogue, such an attribution or tolerance of this view often being considered, by those of a philosophical bent, as tantamount to a trivialization of the Mādhyamika's approach as exclusively mystical or even irrational. Some argue, more or less intuitively, that contradictions are rationally unthinkable. Others invoke a more sophisticated formal problem that anything and everything would follow from a contradiction, so that all reasoning would become indiscriminate; contradictions thus could supposedly never be tolerated by rational individuals on pain of "logical anarchy." In any case, the underlying idea is that, if the Mādhyamika's thinking is not to be trivialized as irrational—and indeed I agree it should not be so trivialized—it would have to rigorously respect the law of non-contradiction.

In what follows, we'll need to be clear on two terms: (1) a logic will be said to be *paraconsistent* if it does not allow every statement to be derived indiscriminately from premises that are contradictory. In short, paraconsistent logics are those in which, contrary to classical logic, a contradiction does not lead to "logical anarchy" or "explosion"; (2) a philosophy is *dialetheist* (i.e., accepts a double truth, *aletheia*) if it accepts that there are at least some statements of contradictions that are true. Paraconsistency and dialetheism clearly are separable for logicians who are interested primarily in the formal handling of inconsistency, all the while maintaining skepticism about there actually being any true contradictions. The two do, however, tend to be taken as a package by logicians and philosophers whose thought is inclined toward acceptance/tolerance of contradiction. For our purposes, as we are dealing with the latter type of thinkers, we will not treat paraconsistency independently from dialetheism.

Now, recently the Australian logician Graham Priest has teamed up with the American philosopher Jay Garfield to significantly elaborate upon certain ideas that they attribute to the second-century C.E. author Nāgārjuna. Priest and Garfield reconstruct this philosophy in terms of a radical type of paraconsistent logic and dialetheism, maintaining that there are some Nāgārjunian arguments that can best be interpreted as evidence of a *rational* acceptance of some true contradictions. In other words, Nāgārjuna (at least implicitly or in a reconstruction of his philosophy) was an advocate of a robust and full-fledged form of dialetheism and thus accepted that, for some statement φ, φ and not-φ was true, but he did not accept that this implied a logical anarchy where any and all statements were derivable. Accordingly, Priest and Garfield's joint paper "Nāgārjuna and the Limits of Thought" does not endorse a laissez-faire acquiescence in any and all contradictions; they do, however, seek to argue that *some* statements of contradictions can be best taken as true given the basic principles of Mādhyamika thought, notably those along the lines of "the ultimate truth is that there is no ultimate truth" or "all things have one nature, i.e., no nature." These Buddhist positions, and others of a logically similar structure and supposedly to be found in Western thinkers like Kant, Wittgenstein, and Hegel, have the common characteristic that Graham Priest has diagnosed as being at the "limits of thought," in that they involve totality paradoxes. The dialetheism comes in when we say that specific sorts of totalities, or "inclosures," exist and that there are at least some things which both are and are not in them.[1]

My Own Take: I Can Readily Accept a Limited Type of Paraconsistency/ Dialetheism in the Prajñāpāramitā and Nāgārjuna, But Priest and Garfield's Robust Form of Dialetheism Seems to Me Unlikely

Graham Priest and Jay Garfield seem to have read my introduction to *Scripture, Logic, Language* as showing that I, like them, accepted Nāgārjuna's "sincere endorsement of contradictions" (Priest 2002: 250 n 2). Well, no doubt, finding out what that book's *svamata* (Tib. *rang lugs*, own take) on paraconsistency and dialetheism might actually be is a difficult task, especially as my views had evolved considerably since an earlier article (reprinted as chapter 9 in Tillemans 1999). It's probably by now high time to set out as clearly as I can what I do accept.

In my introduction to *Scripture, Logic, Language*, I had wanted to indicate that my previous views about Buddhist works not exhibiting any logical deviance still applied to later (i.e., post-fifth-century C.E.) writers, but that things were not so neatly classical originally. I said:

> I don't now know how to exclude that the *Prajñāpāramitāsūtras* are most simply and naturally read as having more or less the contradictions they appear to have. Indeed, that [Edward] Conze–[Jacques] May scenario fascinates me more and more.[2]

I was essentially imagining an attempt at a more or less literal and unhedged interpretation of certain passages in the *Prajñāpāramitāsūtras* and in early Mādhyamika writers like Nāgārjuna, an interpretation which would be independent of and even opposed to that of the later commentators. I found myself in a position where I could no longer rule out an interpretation of this sort on formal grounds or because all contradiction supposedly would be irrational or lead to unlimited anarchical implication. Indeed, the prospect of trying to tread this paraconsistent path seemed to me worthwhile, even heady, in that it seemed to be an attempt to take the provocative and disturbing aspects of the Mādhyamikas' writings seriously, straight-no-chaser, and not explain them away with sophisticated ad hoc solutions or additions to the texts designed to accommodate a type of prescriptive common sense about what was needed so that an author like Nāgārjuna would supposedly be minimally rational.

In *Scripture, Logic, Language* I had spoken about a natural and simple, literal reading of passages in the *Prajñāpāramitāsūtras* that suggested acceptance of contradiction. I was thinking primarily of the "signature formulae" of the *Vajracchedikāprajñāpāramitāsūtra*.[3] These are the oft-repeated statements throughout the sūtra that say that X does not exist or is not the case and that we therefore say that X does exist or is the case. E.g., the Buddha does not have any distinctive marks and that is why one says that he does. Here is a passage from the *Vajracchedikā*:

> buddhadharmā buddhadharmā iti subhūte 'buddhadharmāś caiva te tathāgatena bhāṣitāḥ / tenocyate buddhadharmā iti //
>
> The dharmas special to a buddha, the dharmas special to a buddha, these, Subhūti, the Tathāgata has taught to not in fact be/have dharmas special to a buddha. Thus they are said to be dharmas special to a buddha.

Let's leave aside the somewhat tricky question as to how we should take the Sanskrit compound *abuddhadharmāś ca* (as a *bahuvrīhi* or as a *tatpuruṣa*; I tend to opt for the latter, as do most translations in Buddhist canons). In any case, the simple and natural understanding of the passage, for the moment at least deliberately neglecting commentaries, is that this signature formula is denying something and then later affirming it. We'll delve more into the mysteries of such statements, as well as the commentaries, below.

As for Nāgārjuna, I was only secondarily thinking of his use of the tetralemma: what impressed me was the possibility of a more or less literal interpretation of his system in the sixfold logical corpus (*rigs tshogs drug*). At some points (e.g., in his *Ratnāvalī*) he endorses various Buddhist doctrinal positions (e.g., karmic retribution, etc.), and at other points (i.e., in the *Mūlamadhyamakakārikās*) he clearly denies that there are any such things at all. The fabric of his system, again neglecting commentaries, seems to suggest contradictoriness not unlike that to be found in the signature formulae of the *Vajracchedikā*: such and such is said to be so in certain texts, chapters, etc., and elsewhere, or even in the same paragraph, is said not to be so. My own mentor, Jacques May, many years ago interpreted Nāgārjuna using Hegelian ideas of the contradictoriness of all things; Edward Conze also held a view on the *Prajñāpāramitā* as accepting contradictions; Gadjin Nagao too, I think, was not far from this. I often thought that the debate about Buddhist acceptance (in some sense) of contradictions, a debate that had gone largely out of fashion in professional Buddhist studies, could be profitably revisited once the full resources and rigor of the interpretive tools of non-classical logics were skillfully brought to bear upon informed textual readings. That is now happening thanks to the considerable impetus of Graham Priest and Jay Garfield, and it is, I think, something of a liberating experience to be able to talk seriously about Mādhyamika and *Prajñāpāramitā* thought in these terms without getting bogged down in mind-numbing vagueness or excessive philological data too short on theoretical insight.

My own objections to Priest and Garfield's interpretations concern essentially two points: the role they attribute to totality paradoxes in Nāgārjuna's thought and, especially, the type of dialetheism they attribute to him. While we may well be able to find weak contradictions/dialetheism in early texts, it seems unlikely that early authors endorse, or in any way tolerate, the robust or full-fledged form of dialetheism of which Priest and Garfield speak. Here's what being weak and being strong/robust means in this chapter: we'll speak of an endorsement of a weak contradiction as an acceptance of the truth of a statement φ at some point and an acceptance of the truth of not-φ at another; an endorsement of a strong contradiction, by contrast, means accepting the truth of a conjoined statement, φ and not-φ, i.e., $\varphi \& \neg\varphi$. The move from the weak to the strong variety is not inevitable, and thus a wedge can be driven between a weaker dialetheism (in which weak contradictions are accepted) and the robust dialetheism accepting strong contradictions.

Now, there are, I think, reasons for taking Nāgārjuna and the *Prajñāpāramitā* as accepting weak dialetheism. These reasons will be spelled out below. But in any case, these early authors, if they were dialetheist, could not be dismissed a priori because of looming anarchical implications or some other specter of irrationality. Formally speaking, their logic would involve a recognizable type of paraconsistency and dialetheism; indeed, arguably, it would be significantly similar to what Nicholas Rescher and Robert Brandom developed in their joint book *The Logic of Inconsistency*.[4] In 1992, in a *note liminaire* to a felicitation volume for Jacques May, I had mentioned that Rescher and Brandom's (weak) inconsistency might allow us to rationally reconstruct aspects of a Mādhyamika philosophy in the style of Conze and May. I later discovered that the approach was not unique to Rescher and Brandom: it was, as Koji Tanaka pointed out in his taxonomy of contemporary theories of paraconsistency, initially developed by the Polish logician Jaśkowski and certain other writers, including some of my Canadian compatriots. Tanaka classified these theories as "non-adjunctive" approaches to paraconsistency, i.e., they prohibit the move from individual premises, φ, $\neg\varphi$, to their adjunction $\varphi \& \neg\varphi$.[5] In other words, non-adjunctive paraconsistency enables one to affirm that φ is true and to affirm that $\neg\varphi$ is true—a weak inconsistency—without, however, ever admitting the truth of the statement $\varphi \& \neg\varphi$. This latter statement is a strong contradiction that cannot be accepted as true in the Rescher-Brandom system if dastardly consequences like explosion are to be avoided. The paraconsistency may certainly be disturbing, but it is not irrational.

Priest and Garfield on Nāgārjuna

Although a natural account of the signature formulae of the *Vajracchedikā* and the fabric of Nāgārjuna's six works seems to have their authors granting/ endorsing the truth of φ at some point and endorsing the truth of not-φ at another, we never, to my knowledge, find them giving a clear endorsement of the truth of the conjunction, φ and not-φ.[6] My skepticism about finding full-fledged, or robust, dialetheism in Nāgārjuna is thus obviously going to be out of step here with Priest and Garfield's interpretation. We thus need to look in more detail at why Priest and Garfield thought that there were indeed true adjunctions of φ and not-φ in the Mādhyamika literature and what exactly would be problematic in such a reading of Nāgārjuna.

I have no problems with Priest and Garfield's characterization that what they are doing with Nāgārjuna "is...not textual history but rational reconstruction,"[7] providing of course that history and textual evidence do not seriously clash with, or rule out, that reconstruction. Indeed, the first candidate for paradox that they give, i.e., "The ultimate truth is that there is no ultimate truth," is arguably a consequence or paraphrase of several passages in the *Mūlamadhyamakakārikā*s and in that way can perhaps be claimed to be the thrust of Nāgārjuna's philosophy, if not actually his words.[8] The second, i.e., "all things have one nature, i.e., no nature," is close to a historically attested interpretation of some passages in *Mūlamadhyamakakārikā*s XV about the three characteristics of any intrinsic nature (*svabhāva*): non-fabricated, independent of other things (*nirapekṣa paratra*), and always fixed. It is especially Candrakīrti's interpretation of these passages—notably, his *Prasannapadā* on XV.2—that brings in the idea that Nāgārjuna does not just refute intrinsic natures, but accepts that there is at least one such non-fabricated, independent, and unchanging fixed nature of things, viz., their emptiness (*śūnyatā*).[9]

I shouldn't go into many technical details here about how Priest and Garfield formally present the paradoxes that they see in Nāgārjuna; I'll confine the presentation of inclosure schemata to a long endnote.[10] In any case, Priest and Garfield claim that the Nāgārjunian paradox is like set theoretical paradoxes, where in the case of some totality, or "limit of thought," defined in a certain way, there will be objects that are both included within it and are outside it. They argue that, if we suppose with Nāgārjuna that all things are empty, then the totality of empty, i.e., natureless, things will itself have a nature (i.e., being empty) and that this nature will be both in and not in the totality of empty things. Formulated as an inclosure paradox, it looks potentially interestingly similar to other totality paradoxes, like those of Cantor and Russell.

The connection with other logical paradoxes, if it could be established, would itself be quite important as it would serve in part to answer a charge that these Nāgārjunian paradoxes are simply "rhetorical paradoxes" along the lines of "The Golden Rule is that there is no Golden Rule," "I can resist everything except temptation," and other such cute duplicitous sayings, which are no more than attention grabbers.[11] Undeniably, there is a penchant for such enigmatic, provocative styles of expression in Indian philosophy, so that it would be rather silly to say that *every* use of words in an apparently contradictory fashion in a Sanskrit text is a case of an author embracing dialetheism or saying something exotic of logical interest. The saving grace of Priest and Garfield's Nāgārjunian paradoxes, if they are right, would be that these paradoxes would be cases of a wider East-West phenomenon, i.e., inclosure paradoxes, and would thus not be simply a matter of provocative style. They would supposedly be logical paradoxes in the same way that Russell's and Cantor's paradoxes are.

Although the Nāgārjunian paradoxes would be interesting for comparative philosophers in that they would be East-West discoveries of consistency problems with totalities, there are, it seems to me, some serious problems if we wish to abide by the spirit and letter of Indian texts and also say that Nāgārjuna would advocate true strong contradictions stemming from totality paradoxes. Consider what we do know about the spirit of Indian discussions of totalities. Indeed, inconsistencies in the notion of a totality *do* explicitly and repeatedly figure in Indian philosophy's arguments about the coherence of the notion of *sarva* (all, the totality, the universe), but these derivations of inconsistencies are certainly not *endorsed* by Buddhists as cases of dialetheism or genuine true contradictions, strong or weak. They are instead used by Naiyāyikas, like Uddyotakara in his *Nyāyavārttika* to *Nyāyasūtra* 2.2.66,[12] to *refute* Buddhist doctrines, like the semantic theory of *apoha*, by reductio ad absurdum. The non-Buddhist Naiyāyika argues, for example, that the Buddhist theory of *apoha*, where the term X signifies non-non-X, is impossible in the case of a term like "the totality" or "all" (*sarva*). The reason is that the Buddhist would (absurdly) have to admit that there was something, be it a set or a property or an individual, that was outside the totality of things, because given the principle that any word X signifies non-non-X, "the totality" would express the negation of non-totality (*asarvanivṛtti*); the hidden premise is that there always must be something to negate, a real, existing negandum. Of course, the problem then is that this "something outside the totality" would have to be both outside and not outside the totality of things.

Whatever the value of Uddyotakara's attack, the Buddhists, including Mādhyamikas like Kamalaśīla in his *Madhyamakāloka* and Śāntarakṣita in the *apoha* chapter of his *Tattvasaṃgraha*, repeatedly take great pains to show that these supposed contradictions in the notion of a totality are *not* contradictions at all and that there is a way to preserve consistency in the *apoha* theory by saying that "something outside the totality" (*asarva*) is just a conceptual invention: it is not necessary that an *asarva* actually be real to be the negandum in non-non-totality. In short, the most explicit and frequent discussions about contradictions stemming from totalities are those between non-Buddhists and Buddhists; the Buddhists defend themselves by arguing that acceptance of totalities does *not* lead to any inconsistencies at all. The Buddhists never, as far as I know, *accept* any explicitly formulated argument, non-Buddhist or otherwise, to the effect that *sarva*, the universe, the totality, would indeed be contradictory in the strong or weak senses of contradiction. It would thus be odd that, for them, totality arguments should nonetheless be the major vehicle they use to show true strong contradictions concerning emptiness and other cardinal principles of their philosophy. Earlier, I spoke about the Nāgārjunian paradoxes being supposedly distinguishable from insignificant rhetorical paradoxes because they would turn on major East-West problems about totalities. If I am right in arguing that Buddhists generally do not seem to view totalities as involving contradictions, then the paradoxical passages that Priest and Garfield cite could well also diminish in significance: they would become more like anomalies or enigmatic expressions than evidence of common East-West fellowship in discerning contradictions at the limits of thought.

Turning to the letter of the texts, I would argue that not just are totality arguments used differently in Indian philosophy from the way Priest and Garfield would have them used, but that it seems rather implausible to say that Nāgārjuna himself accepted any true strong contradictions at all: indeed, he seems to give pretty good textual evidence that he does not. For example, in *Mūlamadhyamakakārikā* XXV.14 he gives what looks like a clear prohibition against strong contradiction:

> bhaved abhāvo bhāvaś ca nirvāṇa ubhayaṃ katham / na tayor ekatrāstitvam ālokatamasor yathā /
>
> How could both non-being and being pertain to nirvāṇa? Both are not present in one place, just as light and darkness [are not present in one place].

Even more explicit in banning true strong contradiction is Candrakīrti's comment:

> bhāvābhāvayor api parasparaviruddhayor ekatra nirvāṇe nāsti saṃbhava iti // bhaved abhāvo bhāvaś ca nirvāṇa ubhayaṃ katham / naiva bhaved ity abhiprāyaḥ /

For being and non-being too, there is no possibility for the two mutually contradictory things (*parasparaviruddha*) to be present in one place, i.e., nirvāṇa. Thus, how could both non-being and being pertain to nirvāṇa? The point is they could not at all.

The argument is situated in the context of the fourfold negation of the tetralemma (*catuṣkoṭi*), where an opponent suggests that nirvāṇa both is and is not; in short, the opponent is advocating that a true strong contradiction would apply. Nāgārjuna and Candrakīrti reply that such a true contradiction is not possible. Now, there is no indication whatsoever that their reasoning is restricted to some isolated specific case, i.e., nirvāṇa. It looks pretty clearly generalizable: no true strong contradiction in this case, because no true strong contradictions at all. To suggest otherwise and say that there are some true strong contradictions in certain specific cases makes for a circumscribed rejection of the third lemma of the tetralemma that is hard to reconcile with fundamental texts of the Mādhyamikas. Indeed, there is solid evidence (e.g., in the work of Nāgārjuna's disciple Āryadeva, in Candrakīrti, and in others) that the essence of the Mādhyamika method is that the rejection of the four lemmas in the tetralemma is and must be generalizable, and that is the way a Mādhyamika should *always* proceed in criticizing philosophical positions. This is the point of the famous verse 22 in Āryadeva's *Catuḥśataka* XIV, which advocates negating all four positions:

> sad asat sadasac ceti sadasan neti ca kramaḥ / eṣa prayojyo vidvadbhir ekatvādiṣu nityaśaḥ //
>
> Being, non-being, [both] being and non-being, neither being nor non-being: such is the method that the wise should always use with regard to identity and the like [i.e., all other theses].

Again, it would be quite odd if a Buddhist were to allow that, in spite of verses like this, Nāgārjunian totality paradoxes nonetheless yielded true strong contradictions that were exceptions to the rejection of the third lemma.

Nāgārjuna and the Prajñāpāramitā Unhedged

Let me try to make the best case I can for a paraconsistent, dialetheic interpretation of Nāgārjuna and the *Prajñāpāramitāsūtras*. Instead of totality arguments suggesting some form of paraconsistency and dialetheism, as Priest and Garfield have it, I think that it is the whole system that suggests a type of paraconsistency/dialetheism on a natural reading, and in particular it is the use of the two truths, conventional (*saṃvṛtisatya*) and ultimate (*paramārthasatya*).

Here's what I take to be a key problem in early Mādhyamika and *Prajñāpāramitā* texts. Suppose the Buddhist author says (more or less explicitly) that φ is true and also says that not-φ is true, as the Mādhyamikas and the author(s) of the *Prajñāpāramitāsūtras* are wont to do when they say that dharmas, aggregates, buddha-marks, karma, suffering, etc., exist and also say that they do not exist, i.e., are empty. Are hedges and parameters, like the qualifiers "conventionally" and "ultimately," implicit or somehow built into φ and not-φ, respectively, so that there is only a pseudo-appearance of contradiction?[13] Or is it the same statement without any implicit parameters whose truth is being endorsed (for one set of reasons, say, conventional) at some point in the text and rejected (for another set of reasons, say, ultimate) at other points in the text?

By way of illustration of the two approaches, let us go back to the signature formulae of the *Vajracchedikāprajñāpāramitāsūtra*: X does not exist/is not the case, and thus we say that X does exist/is the case. For example, the Buddha doesn't have any distinctive marks and that is why one says he does. Now, these types of statements can be and have been approached in both above-mentioned ways. We could do what the eighth-century Indian Mādhyamika Kamalaśīla did in his *Vajracchedikāṭīkā*, which was a kind of common later Buddhist interpretive stratagem, namely, clearly differentiate the perspectives involved: the buddha-dharmas, etc., are not buddha-dharmas, etc., looked at ultimately, and they are buddha-dharmas and so forth, looked at from the point of view of conventional truth.[14] We either could add explicit qualifiers right into the wording of the respective affirmative and negative statements (as did, for example, the Tibetan writer Tsong kha pa [1357–1419]), or we could leave the actual wording in the sūtra unchanged but say, as did Kamalaśīla, that qualifications of perspective have to be understood as implicitly present. In any case, for our purposes, the result is more or less the same: the appearance of any contradiction (strong or weak) vanishes. There would be nothing more logically provocative here in endorsing both statements than there would be in endorsing the statements "It is ten o'clock" and "It is not ten o'clock," when we also know that the first statement concerns Eastern standard time and the second concerns Pacific standard time.

The alternative approach leaves the provocation of the signature formulae intact à la Conze et al., i.e., we would say that the same completely unparameterized statement is being affirmed and negated. In short, we would use no explicit parameters nor implicit time-zone-like switches of perspective along the lines of Tsong kha pa or Kamalaśīla, but only, at most, different kinds of supportive reasoning as to why the one statement is true and why its denial is true. Thus, the sūtra author(s) would have good reasons to say that dharmas or buddha-marks do exist (e.g., to account for truths that must be accepted in the world, or at least among Buddhist worldlings) and other good reasons to say that they don't (e.g., to give an account of their ultimate status, emptiness). Indeed, this move might well bring out just how close and inseparable conventional and ultimate truths are for early Mahāyāna Buddhist authors: as Nāgārjuna had himself often repeated, the conventional truth, i.e., saṃsāra, is nothing but (*eva*) the ultimate truth, i.e., nirvāṇa, and vice versa. Put in our terms, the two truths are so close that the very same unparameterized statements about dharmas, aggregates, suffering, etc., are both asserted and denied.

There is, I think, a good reason to prefer the second style of interpretation and be suspicious about the imposition of hedges and parameters and other attempts at nonliteral nuancing of early Mādhyamika writings. Simply put, if we can read Nāgārjuna and the *Prajñāpāramitā* without qualifiers and pretty much literally in their acceptance and rejection of the world and Buddhist schemata, let's go ahead and do it: they are interesting, rational, and intelligent as is, and charity may not require anything more; there is no need for our prescriptive common sense. This is about the most straightforward and persuasive exegetical argument I can muster for interpreting these writers as embracing paraconsistency and dialetheism.

A not infrequent, but in my view less persuasive, argument is that a nuanced and finessed approach would invariably be wrong, or even be a travesty of the Mādhyamika approach, because it would bring in philosophical theses by the back door and thus fatally weaken the whole quietist project that Nāgārjuna sought to promote. Indeed, there is a traditional Sa skya pa interpretation of Mādhyamika thinking that goes a considerable distance in fleshing out this argument. I'm thinking of the *lTa ba'i shan 'byed* of the fifteenth-century Tibetan writer Go rams pa bSod nams seng ge (1429–1489), probably the most explicit traditional source I know for a potentially coherent, unparameterized interpretation of Nāgārjuna and the *Prajñāpāramitā*. Go rams pa's target was, of course, Tsong kha pa, who advocated adding qualifiers like "ultimately" (*don dam par*) or "truly" (*bden par*) to all of the negative statements made by Mādhyamikas: things are not ultimately/truly produced, are not ultimately/truly existent, and so on and so forth for all properties a person might wish to attribute.

Go rams pa's main point, in his refutation of Tsong kha pa, was that, if a Mādhyamika commentator adds that kind of ultimate parameter and thus gives a nonliteral interpretation of Nāgārjuna's negative statements, he has in effect denatured the whole Nāgārjunian dialectic to the degree that it will no longer be able to accomplish its (religious) purpose of quieting philosophical speculation and attachment—and irenic quietism, or complete "freedom from proliferations" (*spros bral*, Skt. *niṣprapañca*), is, for Go rams pa, the main point of the Mādhyamika's negative dialectic. His alternative is thus to take literally the idea of *yod min med min*, "not existent, not nonexistent," and not add any qualifiers like "ultimately"/"truly," the danger being that, by negating "ultimately φ" instead of φ itself for any statement, the Mādhyamika thinker will arrive at smugness about being free of positions, but will in fact remain as attached to the truth of φ as any other realist philosopher. Qualifiers and hedges, so the argument can be paraphrased, make everything a little too neat and refute straw men.

This argument, however, doesn't look to me to be as telling against *all* Mādhyamika uses of parameterization as Go rams pa would want it to be. Go rams pa (and critics like him) would surely be right in opposing the tendency of many followers of Tsong kha pa to rather glibly trot out the provisos "truly" or "ultimately" whenever the philosophical going got tough. However, differentiating between "truly X" and "X" can be more than that and can reflect a repeated self-examination—i.e., a type of phenomenological analysis of our *Lebenswelt*—to discern nonobvious recurring features of how we superimpose true/ultimate status upon otherwise innocent conventional things. In fact, Tibetans have argued that recognizing what is to be refuted (*dgag bya*) and what is to be conserved (i.e., true existence and conventional existence, respectively) is one of the most difficult, and most necessary, points in a sophisticated Mādhyamika philosophy. As I have argued elsewhere, this approach is more in step with later Indian Mādhyamika thought than is generally conceded.[15] The upshot would be that Go rams pa's traps of parameterization would tell against an overly facile or dogmatic resort to the tactic. No doubt, much use of qualifiers was often little more than rote repetition of doxa, but I suspect that it was not always and need not be.

In any case, let's suppose we adopted an unqualified reading either because simplicity and naturalness are (all other things being equal) better than complex additions and hedges, or perhaps because of Go rams pa–style quasi-religious arguments. Where does this unhedged interpretation of Nāgārjuna and the *Prajñāpāramitā* take us in terms of logic? I would say the following: it leads to a type of paraconsistent logic according to which Nāgārjuna will in certain discussions admit that φ is true (for worldly, doctrinal, or even Abhidharmic reasons) and in other contexts that $\neg\varphi$ is true (for reasons involving the emptiness of intrinsic nature); however, Nāgārjuna will recognize no good reasons at all to ever admit the truth of the conjunction $\varphi \ \& \ \neg\varphi$. There will be no such reasons, because Nāgārjuna, as I argued earlier, is deeply respectful of the third negation in the tetralemma, a negation which he generalizes to apply to every statement. In short, we end up with Nāgārjuna accepting non-adjunctive paraconsistency and weak dialetheism. He could not, however, hold strong dialetheism if the Mādhyamika is not to run afoul of his own prohibitions. For Nāgārjuna, there is no φ, such that $\varphi \,\&\, \neg\varphi$ is true.

Up until now my argument has been essentially that, whatever the philosophical merits of blocking the move from weak to strong dialetheism, Nāgārjuna and the *Prajñāpāramitā*, interpreted quite literally, *do* seem to have blocked precisely that move. But, given that adjunction generally seems an obvious and inevitable logical operation to most people, why might a Mādhyamika nonetheless embrace a non-adjunctive approach, apparently tolerating weak contradiction but eschewing the strong? If we stay in the spirit of Go rams pa, the beginnings of an answer might be found in the Mādhyamika thinker's quietism, his refusal to engage himself on how things really are. Asserting a strong contradiction of the form $\varphi \,\&\, \neg\varphi$ could quite easily be taken (and was supposedly so taken by certain non-Buddhists) as a definite position with a commitment to there actually being a contradictory state of affairs, while stating φ at some point (for worldly reasons) and then its negation at another (because of emptiness) would have the effect of annulling the commitment to what was previously stated, and thus would be considerably less likely to engage one in a position or thesis. Indeed, the same process of annulment would apply to stating $\neg\varphi$ and then denying it too, resulting in a return to a perspective where φ can be once again endorsed but without hypostasis or grasping at how things really are. A non-adjunctive use of the two truths may thus be a systematic use of inconsistency in the service of quietism: no position would escape annulment.

The logic of Nāgārjuna would be paraconsistent/dialetheic, but with nonetheless well-defined areas in which classical logic would function. Non-adjunctive paraconsistency and weak dialetheism would, as I have been arguing, apply in a general manner to the so-called six logical works (*rigs tshogs drug*) of Nāgārjuna, which sometimes treat of things worldly and then deny those same things elsewhere in discussions of emptiness, i.e., *śūnyavāda*. They would also apply when Nāgārjuna discusses the ultimate status of things in systematically negative terms: they would thus apply to discussions of emptiness, like in the tetralemma, where Buddhists endorse $\neg\varphi$, $\neg\neg\varphi$, but do not endorse the adjunction $\neg\varphi \,\&\, \neg\neg\varphi$, nor a fortiori $\varphi \,\&\, \neg\varphi$.[16] Also, if we wish, the passages that Priest and Garfield took as evidence for Nāgārjunian dialetheism could still be taken as showing paradoxes: the relevant inclosure schemata would just have to be reinterpreted in terms of weak contradictions, rather than the strong variety. Paraconsistency and dialetheism (of any sort) would not, however, figure in ordinary discussions about purely conventional matters, like the usual and banal reasonings about fires on smoky hills, sound being impermanent, fire being hot, and other such discussions about non-ultimate states of affairs acknowledged in common by Mādhyamikas and realists. Nor would they be applicable in the numerous reductio ad absurdum (*prasaṅga*) arguments where Nāgārjuna seeks to show inconsistencies in his opponents' positions. These reductio usually proceed by deriving φ at some point and $\neg\varphi$ at another; the adjunction of the two gives the needed contradiction. Clearly, a Mādhyamika debater could not allow even weak contradictions, if he were to hope to vanquish his realist opponent by playing according to the rules of the latter's own game.

Caveats and Conclusions

I think this is about as far as I can go in making the case for paraconsistency and dialetheism in early Mādhyamika and the *Prajñāpāramitā* texts. In any case, later Mādhyamika philosophy in India or Tibet—or, in other words, Nāgārjuna's philosophy as viewed by commentators from about the sixth century C.E. on—is another story and *is* much more inclined to parameterization. It is also much more conservative about consistency. There are more explicit prohibitions against *virodha/viruddha* (contradiction), a fact which makes it more difficult to read the later Mādhyamika scholastics as tolerating or advocating any weak or strong contradictions. Significant too is that the later Mādhyamika writers were, with one or two exceptions, under the spell of Dignāga's and Dharmakīrti's logic, so that there was an attempt to harmonize Mādhyamika thought with a logic for realists. Numerous examples of disambiguation, parameterization, and other relatively predictable moves of paradox resolution can be given. Suffice it to stress for our purposes that true (strong or weak) contradictions were anathema for the logicians of the Dignāga-Dharmakīrti school and that there is every reason to think they were too for later Mādhyamikas, like Kamalaśīla, Śāntarakṣita, and many others, who saw themselves as under the same constraints as their logician co-religionists. There was a significant change in orientation between Nāgārjuna and later commentators (especially those of the majority *Svātantrika/Rang rgyud pa persuasion), and that change was largely due to the overwhelming influence of the Dignāga-Dharmakīrti school on Indian Buddhist thought.[17]

Does this evolution mean that later Indian or Tibetan Mādhyamika thought, with its parameterization and classical logic, is inauthentic or without philosophical value as a development of Nāgārjuna's stance? Of course not, unless authenticity and value demand no evolution, a kind of pure doctrinal deep freeze. Indeed, many of the more significant philosophical analyses in Nāgārjuna as viewed via later Mādhyamikas—e.g., the identification of what is to be refuted (*dgag bya*) and its distinction from what is conventionally so, the part-whole arguments, causality, dependence and intrinsic natures, the critique of epistemology—do not seem to depend necessarily upon an acceptance of paradox. These subtle analyses and others can be and were pursued by later Indo-Tibetan thinkers using a classical logic; there is no reason at all to think that these people badly missed the boat. While I have been arguing that the early Mādhyamika and *Prajñāpāramitā* literature may well be best read as dialetheist, it would be a somewhat stultifying mistake to see the whole, or even the essentials, of this philosophy, or of Buddhism for that matter, as turning irrevocably on a use of non-classical logic and acceptance of contradiction.

In conclusion, I would maintain the historical hypothesis first advanced in *Scripture, Logic, Language*: not only did the philosophical debates and doctrines evolve over time with Buddhist scholastic thinkers, but the logic seems to have evolved away from a rather complex architecture to one of increasing homogeneity, simplicity, and classicalness.[18] Logical simplification also happened elsewhere in Indian thought. A number of researchers[19] have looked at Indian and Tibetan logicians' problems in explaining their theories of valid reasons: with time, the formal aspects became ever simpler even though the philosophical analyses often became increasingly subtle. Something similar seems to have happened in the case of the Mādhyamikas.

NOTES

The present chapter, in true Buddhist fashion, went through several incarnations in quite different realms. Initially, a much longer version was read to Buddhist studies colleagues in Calgary and, a year later, to argumentation theorists in Tokyo. The present version was presented in Cambridge in November 2005 at the colloquium on Buddhism in Logic and Analytic Philosophy. I'm indebted to several participants for helpful criticism, including Graham Priest, Jay Garfield, and Koji Tanaka.

1. For the technical details on what an inclosure is, see note 10 below. The joint article by Priest and Garfield, "Nāgārjuna and the Limits of Thought," appears in Priest 2002 as well as in Garfield 2002c. My page references are to Priest 2002.

2. Tillemans 1999: 18.

3. I owe the phrase "signature formula" to Paul Harrison, who discusses these passages in the introduction to his forthcoming new translation of the *Vajracchedikā*.

4. Rescher and Brandom 1980. See Tillemans 1992: 11–12.

5. See Tanaka 2003: 29–30.

6. The only potential counterevidence here might be the "positively formulated" tetralemma found in *Mūlamadhyamakakārikā* XVII.8, which states

that everything is real (*tathya*), everything is not real, everything is both real and not real, and everything is neither, and that this is what the Buddha taught. However, as Candrakīrti and other commentators make clear—and as the overwhelming use of the negative tetralemma in Nāgārjuna seems to bear out—this series of positive statements is an exceptional case and is best seen as a graded hierarchy of provisional stages aiding specific disciples (with diminishing degrees of obscuration) on their way to understanding emptiness. It seems that the verse essentially provides a hermeneutics to resolve the seeming conflicts among the extremely diverse views preached in the scriptures: the lowest view is realism's affirmation of things, then its denial, an acceptance of both, and then the rarefied "neither-nor" position for the "scarcely obscured" student. The contradiction in the third lemma is thus best seen as at most a pedagogically useful transitional stage for certain individuals, as is the affirmation in the first; it does not represent the dominant Nāgārjunian standpoint, in which a fourfold denial of all such positions clearly is key. See Ruegg 1977: 5–7, 63–64n71.

7. Priest 2002: 251.

8. It's worth mentioning, however, that later Tibetan commentators would hedge this statement to make a distinction between ultimate truth and what is ultimately established (*don dam par grub pa*) so that we end up with the tamer principle that the ultimate truth is the ultimate truth but, like any other dharma, is not ultimately established. The ultimate truth would not be that there is no ultimate truth, but rather that nothing is ultimately established.

9. See *Prasannapadā* (La Vallée Poussin 1903–1913: 264.12–265.2):

> atha keyaṃ dharmāṇāṃ dharmatā? dharmāṇāṃ svabhāvaḥ. ko 'yaṃ svabhāvaḥ? prakṛtiḥ. kā ceyaṃ prakṛtiḥ? yeyaṃ śūnyatā. keyaṃ śūnyatā? naiḥsvābhāvyam. kim idaṃ naiḥsvabhāvyam? tathatā. keyaṃ tathatā? tathābhāvo 'vikāritvaṃ sadāiva sthāpitā. sarvadānutpāda eva hy agnyādīnāṃ paranirapekṣatvād akṛtrimatvāt svabhāva ity ucyate.

Note that, in this vein, there is also an important passage from the *Aṣṭasāhasrikāprajñāpāramitāsūtra* quoted in the autocommentary to Nāgārjuna's *Vigrahavyāvartanī*. See Priest 2002: 266. On the senses of *svabhāva*, see also de Jong 1972. For Tsong kha pa's non-paradoxical reading of these and related passages, see Magee 1999.

10. Here, briefly, is how it goes. The key formal notion that they introduce is that of an "inclosure": a totality set Ω is an inclosure if (1) its members have a property φ and have a certain property ψ; and (2) there is a "diagonalizing" function δ that assigns to each subset x of Ω whose members have ψ a new object that is not in the subset x but is still in Ω. Applying that function δ to Ω itself, we get an object that both is and is not a member of Ω. Symbolically, here are Priest's conditions for an inclosure:

> $\Omega = \{y{:}\varphi(y)\}$ exists, and $\psi(\Omega)$.
> For all x such that x is a subset of Ω and $\psi(x)$, $\delta(x)$ is not a member of x.
> $\delta(x)$ is a member of Ω.

See Priest 2002: 134 for the inclosure schema. In the Nāgārjunian inclosure paradox, Ω is the set of all empty things, i.e., things without intrinsic nature; these things have the property ψ, i.e., having a common intrinsic nature. The diagonalizing function δ assigns to the subset x the nature of the things in x. Since $\delta(x)$ is a member of X, it does not have an intrinsic nature. The subset x, however, has the property ψ and thus consists of things which do have a common intrinsic nature. Therefore, $\delta(x)$ is not a member of x. Applying δ to Ω itself, we have the result that $\delta(\Omega)$ is a member of Ω and $\delta(\Omega)$ is not a member of Ω. The nature that δ assigns to Ω is emptiness. Thus, emptiness is empty of intrinsic nature and is not empty of intrinsic nature.

11. On the distinction between logical and rhetorical paradoxes, see Rescher 2001: 4. See Tillemans 1999: 195–196 on some examples of the stylistic tendency in Indian philosophy to use seemingly paradoxical modes of expression. Often it is quite clear (e.g., by looking at auto-commentaries) that these are only rhetorical paradoxes.

12. See Uddyotakara's *Nyāyavārttika* (1936: 687): na punaḥ sarvapada etad asti, na hy asarvaṃ nāma kiṃcid asti yat sarvapadena nivartyeta (For the word *sarva*, though, this [exclusion] is not to be. Indeed, there is nothing at all called *asarva* (what is outside the totality) that would be negated by the word *sarva*).

For further references to the debates concerning *sarva*, see also Keira 2004: 92n139. The same objection of potential contradiction figures in discussions of totalities in other contexts, e.g., Buddhist accounts of "knowledge of all," viz., omniscience (*sarvajñā*) and the Buddhist doctrine of all being momentary. The Buddhist reply is again the same attempt to dissipate the apparent contradiction.

13. Cf. Priest 2002: 151 on parameterization:

> "The stratagem is to the effect that when one meets an (at least prima facie) contradiction of the form P(a)!, one tries to find some ambiguity in P, or some different respects, r1 and r2, in which something may be P, and then to argue that a is P in one respect, P(r1,a), but not in the other, ¬P(r2,a). For example, when faced with the apparent contradiction that it is both 2 p.m. and 10 p.m., I disambiguate with respect to place, and resolve the contradiction by noting that it is 2 p.m. in Cambridge and 10 p.m. in Brisbane."

14. See, for example, Kamalaśīla's discussion on the sūtra's formula concerning "heaps of merit," i.e., *bsod nams kyi phung po*, in *Āryaprajñāpāramitāvajracchedikāṭīkā* (1994: 296–297).

15. See Tillemans 2001: 20–29 and Tillemans 2004.

16. An interesting question, which can only be very briefly taken up here, is how the Mādhyamika blocks the move from $\neg\varphi$, $\neg\neg\varphi$ to φ & $\neg\varphi$. Is it because he does not accept adjunction or because he (also) does not accept a law of double negation elimination? The status of the latter law is unclear among Indian and Tibetan Mādhyamikas. Many contemporary scholars have thought that *paryudāsa* (implicative) negation is subject to the law of double negation elimination, but that the *prasajya* (non-implicative) negation in the tetralemma must not be subject to such a law. Unfortunately, all this is nonobvious and cannot be taken for granted, varying

rather with the philosophical stances of the schools. Some Tibetan Mādhyamikas do go in that direction, but using other terms. Go rams pa uses the term *dgag pa gnyis kyis rnal ma go ba* (understanding the positive via two negations), which clearly corresponds to a law of double negation elimination. He argues that the Mādhyamika does *not* accept such a law; see, e.g., the argument against Tsong kha pa in Go rams pa 1988: 51–52. Tsong kha pa, by contrast, takes it as virtually self-evident that Mādhyamikas, indeed everyone, must accept double negation elimination; see his use of *dgag pa gnyis kyis rnal ma ston pa* in his *rTsa shes ṭīk chen* (1973: 43–44). In fact, as Pascale Hugon has pointed out to me, the term is Indian in origin and is found in the third chapter of Dharmakīrti's *Pramāṇaviniścaya*. We find there the phrase *pratiṣedhadvayena prakṛtagamanāt* (Tib. *dgag pa gnyis kyi rnal ma go ba'i phyir ro,* sDe dge edition 224b). It seems clear that Dharmakīrti, at least, and possibly the Mādhyamikas who felt strong affinities with his thought recognized double negation elimination. My thanks to Pascale Hugon for references to Dharmakīrti and to José Cabezón for reminding me of the importance of the term in Go rams pa.

17. I have taken up the subject of the Svātantrika-Mādhyamika debt to the logicians in "Metaphysics for Mādhyamikas" (Tillemans 2003).

18. Tillemans 1999: 17:

> "[O]n this scenario Buddhist thought would have a history of going from the very provocative logic of certain Mahāyāna sūtras, and perhaps even Nāgārjuna, to the tamer logic of the scholastic. The later Indo-Tibetan scholastic, not surprisingly perhaps, would turn out to have an increasingly conservative reaction to the original writings of their tradition, arguing that the paradoxical or provocative aspects just cannot be taken at face value, but must be explained away with qualifiers and hedges."

19. See, e.g., Oetke 1996.

8

A Dharmakīrtian Critique of Nāgārjunians

Koji Tanaka

It has been slowly recognized that philosophers in non-Western traditions, such as Buddhist and Chinese philosophers, have developed rigorous philosophical traditions—as rigorous as those of their Western counterparts—and that their concerns and problems are often the same as those of Western philosophers, although their solutions are often different. In their discussion of Nāgārjuna, Jay L. Garfield and Graham Priest (2003) attempt to emphasize and expand upon this recognition. They rationally reconstruct (rather than provide a systematic exegesis of) Nāgārjuna's thought and arguments as an example of an East-West philosophical dialogue. Garfield and Priest show that Nāgārjuna's thought exhibits a structural similarity to the thought of some of the major figures in the Western tradition. They claim that, given the enormous influence that Nāgārjuna has had on the Buddhist philosophical tradition,[1] their rational reconstruction of Nāgārjuna is an important contribution to the East-West dialogue and thus to philosophy as a whole.

More importantly, Garfield and Priest claim that their rational reconstruction of Nāgārjuna provides a new lesson to Western philosophers. According to their reconstruction, Nāgārjuna argues that all things lack a fundamental nature, including emptiness, yet they all have the same fundamental nature, i.e., emptiness; hence, all things both have and lack that very nature. And given that Nāgārjuna is concerned with the fundamental nature of all things, Nāgārjuna's paradox is considered to be an ontological paradox.

In this chapter, I will not focus on the exegetical accuracy of Garfield and Priest's reconstruction of Nāgārjuna. What I will focus on is the implication that Garfield and Priest draw from this reconstruction. They argue that Western philosophers haven't seen an ontological paradox of the sort that Nāgārjuna is interpreted as presenting and, thus, that Western philosophers can learn an important lesson from Nāgārjuna. While I welcome attempts to abstract new lessons from Nāgārjuna and, in general, from non-Western philosophers, their claim that Nāgārjuna can provide us with something new indicates the problematic nature of their overall project.

My concern with Garfield and Priest's project is roughly the following. For Nāgārjuna's paradox to provide a new insight, Nāgārjuna and Western philosophers must share a common ground. As Davidson has famously argued, it is only on the basis of a common ground that a genuinely meaningful dialogue is possible. Without such a common ground, we cannot discern that others' utterances are even utterances, let alone meaningful ones.[2] Garfield and Priest do not establish such a common ground; such a supposed common ground is simply a working assumption of their thesis. However, given that Nāgārjuna's paradox is the sort of paradox that Western philosophers have never seen before, one might suppose that this would indicate an absence of the relevant common ground necessary for genuine dialogue. In this chapter, I shall pursue this supposition and argue that Garfield and Priest have failed to show that Nāgārjuna's ontological paradox relevantly intersects with the philosophical interests of Western philosophers. In particular, I will try to show that the focus on Nāgārjuna in an attempt to forge an East-West dialogue is problematic.

The crux of my argument will turn on showing that Nāgārjuna *does not* and *cannot* make an important conceptual distinction that seems to have made the development of twentieth-century analytic philosophy possible. Significantly, while the possibility of the analytic tradition depends on this conceptual distinction, this distinction is not itself made explicit in this tradition. However, it seems that we can make this distinction explicit by examining the thought of Dharmakīrti, which is the strategy I shall pursue in this chapter. My argument shall proceed as follows. First, I shall explicate this conceptual distinction in the context of Dharmakīrti's philosophy. Second, I shall show how twentieth-century analytic philosophy presupposed and developed one aspect of this distinction. Third, I shall show that Nāgārjunians[3] do not have the resources to make this distinction and, hence, do not have a relevant common ground for dialogue with Western philosophers. Finally, I shall conclude with some reflections on the usefulness (or lack thereof) of appealing to Nāgārjuna as the basis for East-West dialogue and the contrasting promise of pursuing dialogue with the logical tradition developed by Dharmakīrti. In order to see my Dharmakīrtian critique of Nāgārjunians (i.e., Garfield and Priest), let us turn to a Dharmakīrtian perspective, which will be used to analyze twentieth-century analytic philosophy.

A Dharmakīrtian Perspective

It must be stated at the outset that Dharmakīrti was an epistemologist and logician. He wasn't an original thinker with respect to metaphysics and ontology. Dharmakīrti's ontology is a variant of that of the Abhidharma (as depicted in texts such as Vasubandhu's *Abhidharmakośa*). His innovations can be found in the fields of epistemology and logic. The primary aim of Dharmakīrti's philosophy was to explain the possibility of knowledge (to use Kant's phraseology) based on Abhidharma ontology, which is an ontology of particulars. The project of Dharmakīrti was to illuminate what makes knowledge and logic possible.

Dharmakīrti's epistemology is based on two distinct faculties of cognition: perception and conception. He holds that our cognitions obtain data through perception. It is through perception that we can interact with the world. Perception, however, simply "holds" the data as undetermined manifolds and doesn't "organize" the data in any way. It is conception that organizes the data delivered to cognition through perception and provides a determinate content to it. Hence, for Dharmakīrti, it is conception that makes our interaction with and our experience of the world meaningful.[4] Consider, for example, the statement "This jar is impermanent." Perception simply holds a thing insofar as it delivers some sensible impression to cognition. Upon perceiving a certain figured thing, it doesn't make sense to say that it is a chair or a table or a range of other possibilities, since perception does not organize the data. Thus, saying that it is a jar presupposes a judgment that eliminates other possibilities. Judgments that eliminate other possibilities in this way constitute the concept *jar.* In the same way, a judgment is made that the jar is impermanent based on the fact that the thing which is perceived is judged to be not permanent. Thus, this judgment eliminates the possibility that the thing which is perceived be judged to be permanent. But it also eliminates the possibility that the thing which is perceived be judged to be unconditioned, etc., even if the same (perceived) thing may be judged as impermanent. Asserting the statement "This jar is impermanent" presupposes the judgments just described. That is, in asserting the statement, one *says* that the thing which is judged to be not a chair, not a table, etc., is subsumed by that which is judged to be not permanent, not unconditioned, etc. This is essentially Dharmakīrti's *apoha* theory.[5]

An important point to note in the above discussion of the *apoha* theory is that Dharmakīrti focuses on language and linguistic acts. That is, *apoha* is a theory of language. Dharmakīrti is concerned with the content of what we say. For Dharmakīrti, when certain sensible impressions are delivered to our cognition, perception doesn't hold a jar as such. The perceived sense data are undetermined with respect to whether that which is perceived is a jar or anything else. It is conception that makes the determination possible. For Dharmakīrti, the statement "This jar is impermanent" isn't about the thing *jar* (the referent of the statement's subject). Instead, the statement is expressing that the thing which is judged to be not a chair, not a table, etc., be subsumed by that which is judged to be not permanent, etc. That is, in asserting a statement, one is to express *apoha* (i.e., elimination) and not assert an object.[6]

Now, as one might have noticed, the dichotomy between perception and conception creates a problem for Dharmakīrti. Without getting into too many details, it is easy to see that there is a difficulty in explaining how conception could latch on to the world. *Jar*, for Dharmakīrti, is essentially a concept. As such, it's not what is or can be perceived. *Jar*, for Dharmakīrti, seems to be a fictional construction that we superimpose onto the world. Since inferences (*anumāna*) operate at the level of conception, Dharmakīrti doesn't seem to be able to "ground" inferences (and concepts) in the world.

While this may simply illuminate Dharmakīrti's Yogācāra background, Dharmakīrti in fact tries to account for this difficulty and spends a substantial amount of time and effort in so doing. He develops a sophisticated causal account to meet the challenge.[7] What I am interested in here, however, is not whether Dharmakīrti has succeeded or failed to ground concepts and inferences in the world. Rather, I am interested in the thought that, in asserting a statement, one expresses the elimination of some possible judgments instead of asserting an object. This thought seems to presuppose a distinction between the question of *grounding* and the question of *what is said* in a statement, utterance, etc. That is, we can derive from Dharmakīrti's thought the distinction between the following two questions:

(1) What is a statement about?
(2) What does a statement say?

The first question is to focus on "the things in the world" that account for the objectivity of a statement. Dharmakīrti's answer to the first question is that a statement is about the particular things in the world that cause similarities and dissimilarities in judgment. Because of the sharp dichotomy between perception and conception, Dharmakīrti has a hard time grounding conception in a world which can only be perceived, i.e., there is nothing in the world to which a concept refers or corresponds.

Whether or not his causal account provides a satisfactory answer to the first question that can account for the objectivity of a statement, Dharmakīrti seems more successful in answering the second question. Dharmakīrti argues that what a claim, such as "This jar is impermanent," does is say that the thing which is judged to be not a chair, not a table, etc., is subsumed by that which is judged to be not permanent, etc. That is, a statement expresses cognition's elimination of other possibilities. Since it is "true" that, for example, there is a jar instead of a chair in reality, the statement "truly" says that a jar is impermanent. Thus, by focusing on the second question, Dharmakīrti is able to account for the objectivity that conception and inferences have.

What many commentators and adversaries of Dharmakīrti, whether traditional or modern, overlook is that Dharmakīrti can separate the two questions as distinct. The first question forces us to focus on the furniture of the world that may ground our claims. It thus leads us to investigate what there is, i.e., ontology. The second question is essentially a semantic one. It focuses on what a statement, utterance, sentence, or claim says or expresses. As we will see below, it is this second question, as distinct from the first question, that led to the development of twentieth-century analytic philosophy.

Twentieth-Century Analytic Philosophy from a Dharmakīrtian Perspective

Philosophy in the West is said to have taken a linguistic turn in the twentieth century. Twentieth- (and twenty-first-) century analytic philosophy is often characterized in terms of its focus on language. It is often thought that, during the twentieth century, it became increasingly important to reflect on what we are saying in making an assertion. Moreover, it is also often thought that it was Frege who, in the late nineteenth century, put this linguistic focus at the center of Western philosophical activity. Indeed, it was this focus that led him to develop his logical theories, particularly his quantification theories, which form the backbone of twentieth-century analytic philosophy.

Frege took sentences such as "Venus has zero moons" to be primarily expressing not the given object *Venus* but the concept *the moon of Venus*. For Frege, a *concept* is a function from the objects that are named in a sentence to a truth value. It subsumes named objects in terms of truth values. Only under the subsumption of a concept can objects be recognized as those suggested by the names in sentences. A concept, by subsuming objects, provides us with a way of signifying the objects.[8] In this way, Frege takes the content expressed by the sentence to be concepts that subsume named objects. Thus, in the sentence "Venus has zero moons," given that there is in fact nothing that can be subsumed by the concept *the moon of Venus*, the concept and thus the sentence give rise to truth. What the sentence expresses is the concept *the moon of Venus*. Since the truth of the sentence reflects an objective fact, Frege can secure objectivity. It is through this focus on the question of "What does a sentence say about the named object?" that Frege can accommodate objectivity.

Frege's celebrated quantification theories are based on the same idea. Since it is a function, a concept itself can be an argument of another function. Frege viewed quantifiers as higher-order functions that treat first-order functions as arguments and a truth value as the value. Thus, in a sentence such as "There is a moon of Venus" (or "Something is a moon of Venus" to make the quantifier more explicit), the function which takes *the moon of Venus* as an argument yields falsity—for there is nothing that can be subsumed by the concept *the moon of Venus*. In this way, the existential quantifier is concerned with the concept *the moon of Venus*: the quantified sentence *expresses* the fact about the concept *the moon of Venus* that there is nothing that can be subsumed by the concept. Frege's quantified logic, which became essential for the development of twentieth-century analytic philosophy, developed on the basis of this idea. The linguistic turn of twentieth-century analytic philosophy was made possible by Frege's focus on the second question: "What does a sentence say?"[9]

The same perspective can be used to view the twentieth-century development of logic, which played an important role in the twentieth-century development of analytic philosophy. While the twentieth-century development of logic is as diverse as that of analytic philosophy, the key logical notions were provided by Tarski.[10] Tarski's account is metamathematical (as he called it). His approach is to *define* (or *stipulate*) a notion of truth at a metalevel (i.e., a metamathematical level). It is from this level that an inference can be formalized with respect to logical constants in the object language. By applying the notion of truth as defined at the metalevel, an inference in the object language can be evaluated with regard to its validity. Thus, Tarski's metamathematical approach to logic focuses not on the things in the world but on language. The question of the things in the world (i.e., what is there?) is essentially defused at the metamathematical level where a definition of truth is defined (stipulated). While Tarski's account may have consequences for ontology, as was shown by Quine (1969), it focuses on the (syntactic) forms that statements express. It is this focus that is characteristic of the twentieth-century development of logic.

A Dharmakīrtian Critique of Nāgārjunians

We are now in a position to put forth a Dharmakīrtian critique of Nāgārjuna and Nāgārjunians (i.e., Garfield and Priest). As one might expect, the critique is based on the distinction that Dharmakīrti makes (or could have made) between the following questions:

(1) What is a statement about?
(2) What does a statement say?

This distinction is also important in understanding the main characteristic of twentieth-century analytic philosophy. I will show in this section that Nāgārjuna *does not* and *cannot* make this distinction. This will show that an exclusive focus on Nāgārjuna doesn't provide us with a genuine basis from which an East-West dialogue can be meaningfully carried out in a contemporary philosophical context.

In his *Mūlamadhyamakakārikā*, Nāgārjuna sets out to refute the ontology of essence. He presents numerous arguments to show that things don't exist essentially—that is, that things are empty (of essence or inherent existence). Nāgārjuna's thesis of emptiness can be understood in various ways. One way to understand it is that Nāgārjuna rejects the idea that there is something about an object that makes a certain statement true. For example, in a statement such as "Venus has zero moons," he can be seen as arguing that there is nothing essential about Venus, nor anything else in the world, that makes this statement true. Thus, Nāgārjuna's thesis of emptiness responds negatively to Dharmakīrti's first question for any claim one may assert; i.e., ultimately, there is nothing that a statement is about. As the centrality of his emptiness thesis shows, Nāgārjuna's philosophical interest seems exclusively focused on this question.

While this seems to be true, it also seems true from a Dharmakīrtian perspective that Nāgārjuna implicitly addresses the second question in a way which is distinct from the first question. Having shown that there is nothing that a statement is about, Nāgārjuna can be seen as trying to account for the possibility of asserting such statements. Since it is true that Venus has zero moons, we can assert such a statement even though there is ultimately nothing that the statement is about. One can think of this fact as the reason that Nāgārjuna introduces the notion of the two truths: ultimate truth and conventional truth. *Ultimately*, there is nothing that any statement is about. Nonetheless, we talk as if it were true that Venus has zero moons. For Nāgārjuna, it is *conventionally* true that Venus has zero moons. Thus, when we utter such a statement, we don't say anything about anything in the world. Instead, we express a convention that Venus has zero moons. A convention doesn't have any ontological significance; rather, it is what governs our discourses. This shows that, when Nāgārjuna raises the notion of two truths, he seems to implicitly feel the pull of Dharmakīrti's second question, "What does a statement say?"

However, though a Dharmakīrtian can read Nāgārjuna as addressing this question, Nāgārjuna never thematized the notion of conventional truth as a response to the second question. In fact, his interest is primarily with the first question. Nāgārjuna's identification of the ultimate and conventional truths in *Mūlamadhyamakakārikā* XXIV.18, which is often considered to be the climax of the text, seems to put conventional truth on the same plane as ultimate truth. That is, the issue of conventional truth comes down to the lack of what a conventionally true statement is about. Nāgārjuna thus steers away from the second question, "What does a statement say?" and refocuses on the first question, "What is the statement about?" Hence, Nāgārjuna does not and cannot properly address the second question.[11]

Nāgārjunians such as Garfield and Priest seem to have capitalized on this point. Their argument to demonstrate Nāgārjuna's profound contradiction (ontological paradox) takes a distinctively ontological turn. Details of exegetical accuracy don't concern us here.[12] What concerns us is their acknowledgment of the above discussion. They claim that "Nāgārjuna's enterprise is one of fundamental ontology,"[13] and this is his unique contribution to philosophy, both East and West. They go so far as to suggest that Nāgārjuna's enterprise doesn't actually intersect with that of twentieth-century philosophers:

> One might fairly ask, as have many on both sides of this planet, just *why* paradoxes of expressibility arise. The most obvious explanations might appear to be semantic in character, adverting only to the nature of language. One enamoured of Tarski's treatment of truth in a formal language might, for instance, take such a route.... But Nāgārjuna's system provides an ontological explanation and a very different attitude toward these paradoxes, and, hence, to language.[14]

Priest also acknowledges this fact and justifies taking the ontological turn:

> [Discussions on Nāgārjuna (and Heidegger)], which put *what is* at centre stage, certainly mark an ontological turn in focus. The philosophy of language took pride in twentieth-century philosophy. Certainly there is no going back to how things were before this. But maybe this century will see a return to the mainstreaming of a more traditional philosophical issue, the nature of reality—and if I am right, a nature that is contradictory.[15]

There are three things that need to be said here. First, central to the Nāgārjunians' ontological turn seems to be their realist commitment. Just before justifying the ontological turn, Priest writes, "I am enough of a realist to hold that there must be something about reality that makes [statements true]. . . . When I say that reality is contradictory, I mean that it is such as to render those contradictory statements true."[16] As we saw above, Nāgārjuna can be seen to reject, rather than assert the negation of, the idea that there is something in the world that a statement (whether contradictory or not) is about. But this is exactly the realist principle that Priest endorses in order to take the ontological turn. Nāgārjuna's ontological turn seems to be concerned with a rejection of certain ontological commitments (to give it a Quinean ring), while Priest's seems to put something back into reality, i.e., an ultimate nature of the things that a statement is about. It seems that the Nāgārjunians' (or Priest's, at least) ontological turn has been taken on an inconsistent ground. Nāgārjunians might reply that I am superimposing my Dharmakīrtian perspective onto Nāgārjuna and treating Nāgārjuna's ontological turn not in Nāgārjuna's terms but in my own Dharmakīrtian terms. I do admit that I am reading something into Nāgārjuna's thought. However, Garfield and Priest themselves claim that Nāgārjuna is concerned with the rejection of certain ontological commitment.[17] If Nāgārjuna's rejection of certain ontological commitment must be cashed out differently from the way it is presented in the above discussion, Garfield and Priest owe us an explanation. Moreover, if Garfield and Priest claim that it is the ultimate nature of reality which the rejection of ontological commitment *entails* that is shown to be contradictory, then the contradiction is that Nāgārjuna takes (as the entailment shows) and doesn't take (as the rejection of ontological commitment shows) the ontological turn. If this is correct, then it's not that reality is contradictory for Nāgārjuna, but that the attitude toward ontology is contradictory (both a pro and a con attitude toward ontology are present at the same time). While the point here is a contentious one, it is now shown that it's not clear that Nāgārjunians such as Garfield and Priest can endorse the ontological turn as easily as they do.[18]

Second, by putting this difficulty aside, we could, perhaps, take an ontological turn in the twenty-first century and go back to the ontological issues that seem to have captured the imagination of the Greeks, as Priest suggests. Investigations into ontology may also be important in the overall development of philosophy. However, if we followed the Nāgārjunians' advice on this, we wouldn't have a basis for a genuine East-West dialogue. Hence, an East-West dialogue would be impossible, for such a dialogue requires a common ground, as stated earlier.

Third, it's not only that Nāgārjuna does not and cannot give us a platform on which an East-West dialogue is made possible, but also that he does not provide us with enough philosophical resources to make an important distinction. The two questions with which we have been concerned in this chapter are quite distinct, as I've shown through the thought of Dharmakīrti. Since this distinction does make sense (as I have been showing), there is a reason to respect it. On a Nāgārjunian perspective, however, the second question, "What does a statement say?" cannot properly be raised (it's not merely that it *isn't* raised). From a Dharmakīrtian point of view, Nāgārjunians have too limited resources to even raise this important question.

In Reflection

I often think of Nāgārjuna in parallel with Aquinas. Aquinas was, I believe, a philosophical giant. He was a good philosopher and presented profound arguments. Nonetheless, it is a fair question to ask how influential he is from a twenty-first-century philosopher's point of view. There certainly are philosophers who take Aquinas seriously. For instance, in doing (Christian) philosophy of religion, one simply can't ignore Aquinas. But outside this focused field, Aquinas's influence can hardly be found these days. This seems to be because his philosophical interests are seen as limited from a contemporary point of view.

Nāgārjuna was also a philosophical giant. It is possible that he exerted an enormous influence on the subsequent development of Buddhist philosophy.[19] At least, it seems impossible to ignore Nāgārjuna in a (contemporary) study of Buddhist philosophy. Yet his philosophical interests are very limited. Nāgārjuna's enterprise doesn't seem to be able to offer a common ground with contemporary analytic philosophers and logicians. Contemporary logic seems to have developed as a result of a linguistic turn and a focus on the question "What does a statement say?" as distinct from the question "What is a statement about?"[20]

This point can be generalized. From a contemporary logician's point of view, an account of the history of Western philosophy which doesn't take into consideration the logic tradition can hardly be thought of as a satisfactory account. If a satisfactory account were to be given (not that a complete account can be given in one's lifetime), one would have to consider such figures as Aristotle, Kant, Frege, Russell, and Wittgenstein, to name just a few representatives, as well as the influence that their thought on logic had on the development of Western philosophy. The same is true of Buddhist philosophy.

Without examining the logic tradition (i.e., the Dignāga-Dharmakīrti tradition) and the influence it had on the development of Buddhist philosophy, one couldn't be said to have given a satisfactory account of Buddhist philosophy (not that a complete account can be given in one's lifetime).

The above discussion is significant since the question of the existence of philosophy in the East often turns on the alleged lack of logic in Eastern philosophy. A typical defense often emphasizes that certain forms of argumentation, such as Nāgārjuna's use of the *catuṣkoṭi*, can be formalized using formal logic. But it is one thing to show that one's thought can be formalized in formal logic, and quite another to show that one has developed a logic tradition. Showing that Aquinas's thought can be formalized in terms of classical first-order logic doesn't make him a logician, nor does it make him relevant to the development of logic. There are a very few scholars who have tackled head-on the allegation that Buddhist philosophy lacks the development of logic and have made useful observations from a contemporary logician's perspective.[21] It is hoped that subsequent studies in Buddhist philosophy transcend Nāgārjuna's and the Nāgārjunians' enterprise and start addressing issues that truly concern logicians and analytic philosophers.

NOTES

1. Garfield and Priest state:

> [Nāgārjuna's] influence in the Mahāyāna Buddhist world is not only unparalleled in that tradition, but exceeds in that tradition the influence of any single Western philosopher in the West. The degree to which he is taken seriously by so many eminent Indian, Chinese, Tibetan, Korean, Japanese, and Vietnamese philosophers, and lately by so many Western philosophers, alone justifies attention to his corpus. (Garfield and Priest 2003: 1)

It's certainly true that Nāgārjuna and the Madhyamaka (the school which follows Nāgārjuna) had an enormous impact in Tibet. However, it's not clear that Nāgārjuna's thought and philosophy were as influential in China, Korea, and Japan (i.e., East Asia) as Garfield and Priest contend. This seems true despite the fact that Zen Buddhism lists Nāgārjuna as one of its patriarchs: it is one thing to list Buddhists who are considered to be important, but it is quite another to find their philosophical influence in subsequent developments. For a discussion of the exaggeration of the influence of Nāgārjuna, see Hayes 1994.

2. Davidson 1984; also see Davidson 2001. For a discussion of Davidson's thesis in the context of comparative philosophy, see Tanaka 2006.

3. The term "Nāgārjunians" in this chapter refers primarily to Garfield and Priest, rather than to the historical followers of Nāgārjuna, such as Candrakīrti and Tsong kha pa. The historical account of the issues addressed in this chapter, such as

the Madhyamaka's (attempted) synthesis with Dharmakīrti's philosophy, is a complex one and deserves a treatment of its own.

4. This way of cashing out Dharmakīrti's epistemology gives it a Kantian overtone. Indeed, I have used Kantian terminology to explain the core of Dharmakīrti's epistemology. While I don't claim that Dharmakīrti would explain his project in such Kantian terms, I nonetheless think that it is useful for contemporary philosophers to put Dharmakīrti's epistemological project in these terms. And, given that I am mainly concerned in this chapter with East-West dialogues in the contemporary context, I am not deterred by criticisms raised against my Kantian reading. For parallels between Dharmakīrti and Kant, see also Arnold 2005a, Dreyfus 1997, and Tanaka 2007.

5. For a more complete account of Dharmakīrti's (as well as Dignāga's) *apoha* theory, see, e.g., Dreyfus 1997, pt. 3; and Dunne 2004: 113ff.

6. It must be noted that this account of Dharmakīrti seems to accord more with Sa skya rather than dGe lugs interpretation. My non-neutrality was brought home to me during discussions of Dharmakīrti with Georges Dreyfus and Tom J. F. Tillemans.

7. Dharmakīrti's causal account is roughly as follows. The formation of the concept *jar*, for example, based on the perception of a certain shaped thing, isn't arbitrary. The concept *jar* is constituted by judgments that eliminate dissimilar possibilities. This means that judgments are made based on similarities and dissimilarities. These similarities and dissimilarities in judgments are caused by the (particular) things in the world. Thus, the objectivity of conception is secured by causation (in the world) that brings about the similarities and dissimilarities in judgments.

8. See Frege 1884. A full account of concepts in Frege must take into account sense (*Sinn*) and reference (*Bedeutung*).

9. See Frege 1884 and 1891. Whether or not this is an accurate picture of the history of twentieth-century philosophy, I let the reader judge. Nonetheless, it is commonly accepted that the linguistic turn owes a great debt to Frege.

10. Again, I am open to criticism regarding this picture of the twentieth-century development of logic. Nonetheless, without grasping Tarski's approach, it's not clear that we can be said to be doing logic. As Etchemendy remarks, Tarski's account has become "common knowledge" (1990: 1).

11. I stress once again that I am not concerned here with the long history of Buddhist discussions of the exegetical issues.

12. In this chapter, I don't take any explicit stance toward Garfield and Priest's exegetical accuracy. For a critique of their reading of Nāgārjuna—which gave me some inspiration to write this chapter—see Tillemans' contribution in the present volume (originally delivered as a paper in the conference on Buddhism in Logic and Analytic Philosophy).

13. Garfield and Priest 2003: 15.

14. Ibid.: 15–16.

15. Priest 2002: 295.

16. Ibid. I am not sure whether Garfield would accept this form of realist commitment. If not, my critique here applies only to Priest.

17. For example, Garfield and Priest write: "Much better to read Nāgārjuna as rejecting excluded middle for the kind of assertion the opponent in question is making, packed as it is with what Nāgārjuna regards as illicit ontological presupposition" (2003: 8).

18. I don't categorically deny that Nāgārjuna was a realist. He *might* have accepted the thesis that the states of affairs in reality are independent of what we think of them. (However, Siderits 2003 offers a more antirealist reading of Nāgārjuna.) If this is correct, then this realist thesis comes apart from Priest's realist thesis. In fact, one of the lessons of Nāgārjuna seems to be that the independence thesis of realism comes apart from the truth-making thesis of realism. (No doubt, this point deserves more attention. However, I will leave a discussion on this point for another paper.)

19. But, as indicated earlier, I think that Nāgārjuna's influence has been exaggerated.

20. Of course, there are exceptions in the context of contemporary analytic philosophy. Derek Parfit, for example, would have benefited from Nāgārjuna, as Siderits 2003 demonstrates. However, as Finnigan (2005) shows, one must examine Parfit and Nāgārjuna with respect to the semantic question, not the question about *aboutness*, in order to make such a comparative (or fusion) philosophical examination complete.

21. Most notable are Bimal Krishna Matilal and Tom J. F. Tillemans; see, e.g., Matilal 1985 and Tillemans 1999.

9

Would It Matter All That Much if There Were No Selves?

Raymond Martin

Reductionism about a kind of thing is the view that things of that kind just consist in things of a more basic kind. Buddhism and Western philosophy have each appealed to reductionism to argue that, strictly speaking, there is no such thing as a self, or person. Mark Siderits put this point nicely:

> The Buddhist view of non-self... says that the existence of a person just consists in the occurrence of a complex series of impermanent, impersonal *skandhas*. But Buddhists are not the only ones to hold a reductionist view of person. On some interpretations, both Locke and Hume held such a view. More recently Derek Parfit has given a sophisticated defense of reductionism about persons, which he explains as the denial that the continued existence of a person involves any "further fact" over and above the facts about a causal series of psychophysical elements.[1]

Parfit's view, in a little more detail, is that the existence of a self, or person (in what follows, I shall use *self* and *person* interchangeably), just consists in the existence of a brain and body and the occurrence of a series of interrelated physical and mental events.[2] There is more to Parfit's view. But, in what follows, just this portion is what I shall mean by *reductionism about the self.*

How important would it be *practically* if reductionism about the self were both true and believed to be true? Buddhist and Western philosophers tend to agree that it would be a big deal, but for different reasons. Buddhists have held, and still do hold, first, that belief in the self—at least in the way in which almost everyone believes in it—is a major source of suffering, and, second, that the realization that there is no self is life changing in an extremely positive way: "Buddhists say... that becoming enlightened, coming to know the truth of reductionism, relieves existential suffering. They also say that it makes one more concerned about the welfare of others."[3] In the West, both proponents and critics of the idea that there is a substantial and enduring self have focused on what many have taken to be more pessimistic implications, especially the worry that, if there were no self or even if there were no substantial and enduring self, then there would be no reason for future-oriented self-concern, including prudence. Bishop Butler, for instance, who believed that the self is a simple immaterial substance, tried to counter John Locke's relational theory of personal identity with the criticism that, if selves were to consist only in parts that do not endure, then it would be a mistake "to imagine our present selves interested in anything which befell us yesterday [or] will befall us tomorrow." Under such circumstances, he said, "our present self is not, in reality, the same with the self of yesterday, but another like self or person coming in its room, and mistaken for it; to which another self will succeed tomorrow."[4] Many Western philosophers have echoed Butler's worry.[5]

My main goal, in the present chapter, is to put this worry about future-oriented self-concern to rest. To do this, I shall argue that whatever difficulties there may be in justifying future-oriented self-concern, they are no greater for skeptics about the self than they are for believers. A secondary goal will be to show that some recent Buddhist commentators have exaggerated the extent to which those who deny the existence of a substantial and enduring self need, for practical purposes, to pretend that one actually exists. I shall argue that not much pretense is required.

East Meets West

It is surprising how similar are the concerns of ancient Buddhist philosophers about reduction of the self to those that preoccupy contemporary analytic philosophers. In Buddhist philosophy, concern over whether the self or person is real and, if real, real in what sense, was present from the beginning. The Pudgalavādins, who appeared within a few centuries of the death of the Buddha and included several of the early schools of Buddhism, maintained that persons (*pudgala*) are both distinct from the five aggregates (material form, feeling, ideation, mental forces, and consciousness) and real. Other

Buddhist philosophers who were reductionists, such as Vasubandhu (flourished c. 360 C.E.), argued in opposition to the Pudgalavādins that persons or selves, while real, are nothing but the aggregates.

In the idiom of contemporary analytic personal identity theory, the Pudgalavādins, while not arguing for anything like an immaterial substance, were nevertheless arguing that the self is what Derek Parfit would call "a further fact," while Vasubandhu, like Parfit, was arguing that the self, while real in a sense, is not a further fact. Vasubandhu seems also to have subscribed to two other views for which Parfit is famous: that it is possible to describe reality completely in impersonal terms (the impersonal description thesis); and that it is an *empty question* whether something that is agreed to be constituted out of other, more basic things "really exists."[6]

Mādhyamika Buddhist philosophers, such as Nāgārjuna (c. 150–250 C.E.), Āryadeva (c. 180–250 C.E.), and Candrakīrti (c. 600–650 C.E.), denied both that selves are reducible to the aggregates and that they are distinct from the aggregates. They thus rejected realism about the self altogether. By claiming that what is ordinarily taken to be belief in or reference to the self is actually an act of appropriating (*upādāna*) one's experiences, emotions, and body, they focused instead on the self's seeming ownership of these things. According to Candrakīrti, for instance, the proper explanation of our sense that we "own" our experiences, emotions, and bodies is that our everyday conception of self consists in "an appropriative act of laying claim to the elements of the psychophysical aggregates, an act that does not require there to be any 'entity' or 'object' that is the self."[7]

In the West, one of the earliest indications of interest in the question of whether there is a substantial and enduring self occurs in a scene from a play written in the fifth century B.C.E. by the Greek comic playwright Epicharmus. In this scene, a lender asks a debtor to pay up, and the debtor replies by asking the lender whether he agrees that anything that undergoes change, such as a pile of pebbles to which one pebble has been added or removed, thereby becomes a different thing. The lender says that he agrees with that. "Well, then," says the debtor, "aren't people constantly undergoing changes?" "Yes," replies the lender. "So," says the debtor, "it follows that I'm not the same person as the one who was indebted to you and, so, I owe you nothing." The lender then hits the debtor, knocking him to the ground. When the debtor protests loudly at being thus abused, the lender replies that his complaint is misdirected since he—the lender—is not the same person as the one who struck him a moment before.[8]

In spite of such sophistication about the self, there is not much evidence that Epicharmus or other Greek or Roman philosophers seriously entertained the idea that selves or persons do *not* really exist—that is, that they are fictions. In the West, that idea came onto center stage in the late seventeenth century, via Locke's famous remark that *person* is a forensic term, which Locke made immediately after giving a relational account of personal identity over time. These two proposals—that the self is a fiction and that, whether a fiction or not, the self over time should be understood relationally—tended to be lumped together in the minds of many of Locke's eighteenth-century critics. Butler, for instance, thought that it followed from Locke's relational view that each of us would be a persisting self only in a fictitious sense. He thought that this consequence refuted Locke's view, but not that it *proved* it wrong. Rather, he thought, it enabled people to *rationally intuit* that it is wrong: "the bare unfolding of this notion [that selves are fictitious] and laying it thus naked and open, seems the best confutation."[9]

In Mādhyamika Buddhism, the radical suggestion that the self is a fiction was expressed as the view that it is conventionally, but not ultimately, true that selves or persons exist. Many Western philosophers with reductionistic proclivities would be comfortable with this much of Mādhyamika Buddhism.[10] However, in the view of Mādhyamikas, just as it is merely conventionally true that selves exist, so too it is merely conventionally true that brains, bodies, and interrelated physical and psychological events exist. Few Western reductionists about the self—indeed, few Western philosophers of any sort—are willing to go that far. Instead, most would insist on making sense of something pretty close to normal human values from a point of view according to which brains, bodies, and interrelated physical and psychological events exist not just conventionally, but actually. Hence, some of them are reluctant to say that selves or persons are fictional or, if they do say this, are reluctant to say that selves are fictional *merely because* they strongly supervene on subpersonal parts and relations. In sum, so far as the West is concerned, whereas the original critics of Locke's radical suggestion that selves or persons are fictions tried to defeat his view in order to save the traditional idea that the self is an immaterial soul, in the twenty-first century critics of the view that selves or persons are fictions tend to be nonreductive materialists. As a consequence, in the West, the contemporary philosophical battle is no longer, as it once was, between religion and science, but over how best to understand notions such as *supervenience* and *realization*.[11]

It may seem that the Mādhyamika Buddhist idea that every (composite) thing to which we might reduce the self is at best only conventionally real is more radical than the contemporary Western idea that the self is reducible to subpersonal parts that are real. But, in one respect, the Buddhist view may be less radical. On most contemporary Western reductionistic views, there is something metaphysically special about the self that distinguishes it from the subpersonal parts to which it may be reduced. The self seems to be a thing, but is not a thing; the subpersonal parts are things. On versions of Buddhism according to which *everything* goes into the same hopper, there is nothing metaphysically special about the self. Yet, most Buddhists have wanted to say that there is something special about the self—perhaps not metaphysically special, but special in its being an illusion, or in the way that it is an illusion, or in the role that it plays as an illusion in our relationships to ourselves and the world.

Contemporary Western analytic philosophers—as we shall see, like some of their contemporary Buddhist counterparts—are divided about whether and, if so, to what degree and in what way selves or persons are expendable. Some, including Mark Johnston and John McDowell, argue that selves are not expendable since one needs them in order to make sense either of human values or of epistemology, or both.[12] However, Western philosophers tend to hedge their bets. For instance, in response to Parfit's arguments that there is no "further fact" to the existence of selves or persons, Johnston, in an effort to shore up the reality of the self while simultaneously distancing himself from Cartesians, has called the selves to which he thinks one should be committed *ordinary further facts*, as opposed to *superlative further facts*.[13] Johnston's view, interestingly, seems to be virtually identical to that of the Pudgalavādins.

Reductionism and the Extreme Claim

Reductionism about the self is a metaphysical view that does not commit one to any particular normative theory or to any view about how on relational grounds personal identity over time should be understood. Specifically, it does not imply that personal identity is not what matters primarily in survival, nor that what does matter, à la Parfit, is psychological connectedness and continuity. These latter claims are in addition to reductionism about the self. Even so, in the West today, reductionism about the self, particularly with respect to its implications for the rationality of future-oriented egoistic concern, is a controversial thesis. An important challenge to it is a contemporary version of Butler's claim that, if reductionism about the self were true, then people would have no reason to be especially concerned about their own futures. Parfit calls this challenge the *extreme claim* and contrasts it with what he calls the *moderate claim*, which is the claim that relation R, which Parfit defines as psychological continuity and connectedness with any cause, does allow one reason for special concern.[14]

The intuition on which the extreme claim seems to rely, and what has made it seem plausible to many critics of reductionism about the self, is that future stages of the series of events that on a reductionist view constitute the self are, in effect, *others*. As a consequence, it is said, the current stages of the series would have no *egoistic* reason to be especially concerned about subsequent stages. In a partial concession to this view, Parfit argues that one has moral, rather than self-interested, reasons to be concerned about future stages of oneself.

It is incumbent upon those who claim that reductionism about the self would not be a big deal practically to explain what's wrong with the extreme claim. In my view, the main thing wrong with it is that reductionists about the self can appeal to continuer-interest, instead of self-interest or morality, to justify the rationality of future-oriented surrogates of egoistic concern, including prudence. This is the main thing for which I will argue in the remainder of this section. If this is right, then some of the reasons that have been given to support the view that reductionism about the self motivates revisionist views about what one should or should not value, or about how one should or should not behave—and hence that reductionism would be a big deal practically—do not succeed. Of course, reductionism about the self still might be a big deal practically, for other reasons. I don't think it is, but I shall not argue for that in the present chapter. Instead, in the final section, I shall conclude by explaining why the only practical concession that reductionists about the self need to make to personhood conventions may be to adopt an attitude that I shall call *thin ironic engagement*.[15]

The extreme claim is supposed to be a problem for reductionists about the self that does not arise for nonreductionists about the self (henceforth, *selfists*). My first objective is to show that the same problem arises for at least some selfists, in pretty much the same form that it arises for reductionists. So, if the extreme claim is a problem for reductionists, it is also a problem for these selfists.

If one is a selfist about persons, then one believes that each of us who persists as the same person we are now does so in virtue of some further fact that is over and above what a reductionist would acknowledge to exist. The most extravagant version of such a further fact is a Cartesian ego. Less extravagant versions include the further facts postulated in the views of the Pudgalavādins and of Mark Johnston. In any case, on a selfist view, since future stages of oneself are clearly not others but oneself, it has seemed to many that there is no issue either about what justifies future-oriented egoistic concern or about our entitlement to own, or to anticipate having, the experiences of ourselves in the future.

But this seeming advantage of selfism does not accrue to all versions of selfism. Metaphysical punctualists (or episodics), who believe that the self is real but that it does not last for long, may also be selfists. Galen Strawson, for instance, has argued for the view that selves are real but last only for a few seconds. He claims that there is a series of such selves associated with what we would call an individual person, a claim that he calls the *pearl view*.[16] Strawson is a materialist and may or may not be a selfist. But whatever his view about reductionism, one could subscribe to his pearl view, for pretty much the same reasons that he gave to subscribe to it, and be a selfist. For instance, one could subscribe to his pearl view and hold that selves are like Cartesian egos in being immaterial and indivisible. Since a punctualist (or an episodic) believes that the self does not last for long, a punctualist who is also a selfist has pretty much the same problems as a reductionist in justifying future-oriented egoistic concern. Future pearls on the string, whatever their metaphysical status, are still "others."

But surely, it may seem, among selfists punctualism is a minority view. So even if a selfist who is a punctualist would have a problem justifying future-oriented egoistic concern, what about selfists who are not punctualists? What, for instance, about selfists who hold that the self is real and spans the entire lifetime of the person whose self it is. In my view, even such a selfist has a problem, similar to that faced by a punctualist, in justifying future-oriented egoistic concern. His problem is to explain why *me-now*, that is, the current temporal stage of himself, should be egoistically concerned about *me-later*, a future temporal stage of himself.

What a selfist who is not a punctualist would no doubt reply to this problem is that me-now should care about me-later because both are parts of me (or, alternatively, because both *are* me). I shall call this reply the *me-consideration*. Such selfists claim that the me-consideration adequately justifies future-oriented egoistic concern. However, the me-consideration's being an adequate justification depends at least on one's being justified in believing in the existence of selves, or in the existence of the further fact, and whether anyone is so justified is open to question. But even if the further fact is acknowledged to exist, one still might question whether the me-consideration is an adequate justification of future-oriented egoistic concern.

Suppose, for instance, that one's further fact persists, but one's psychology does not persist. Would the fact that there will be future stages of such a person, even if that person continues to be oneself, justify special concern? It is not obvious that it would. And even if both the further fact and one's psychology were to persist together, it would not follow that me-now *should* care in the special-concern way about me-later. One reason it would not follow is that *is* does not imply *ought*; hence, me-later's *being* a future stage of me-now does not *imply* that me-now *should* care in the special-concern way about me-later. Another reason it would not follow is that me-now may not *identify psychologically* with me-later in a way that supports special concern; for instance, me-now may not anticipate having the experiences that will be had by me-later.

It might be objected that it would be pathological for me-now not to anticipate having the experiences of me-later—for instance, for you not to anticipate having the experiences of yourself in the future. But even if under ordinary circumstances such a failure to anticipate would be pathological, it is question begging to assume that it would necessarily be pathological in extraordinary circumstances. Consider, for instance, teleportation. A man enters a transmitting station on Earth. His body and brain are scanned and simultaneously decomposed, as the information scanned is sent to a receiving station on Mars, where one and only one exact replica of what he was on Earth is produced. Is that Martian replica the same person as he was on Earth? Some psychological continuity theorists would argue that he is the same person. Suppose they are right—that is, right that the best way to extend prevailing criteria of personal identity is to answer that, yes, he is the same person. Even so, someone entering the transmitting station on Earth could sensibly ask why he should care about extensions of the prevailing criteria of personal identity to cover exotic cases, and hence why he should care about the fate of his replica on Mars. The answer, that because on these extended criteria the Martian replica will be himself, does not answer this question.

Something like this worry is ultimately what is the matter with John Perry's suggestion that going out of existence and being continued by a physical and psychological replica of oneself would be as good as being continued by oneself. Perry says it would be as good because what matters so far as one's continued existence is concerned is merely continuing one's projects, and one's replicas could do that as well as oneself.[17] Something similar is also what is the matter with Parfit's suggestion that a person on a "branch-line" on Earth ought not to be too concerned about his own impending death in a few days since his exact replica of a few days earlier will be living safely on Mars. A sticking point with both views is that most of us would care egoistically—and, it would seem, would care rationally—about more than just there being someone in the future whose body and psychology are qualitatively similar to our own; and one would care more even if one were to learn that, by some rational extension of prevailing criteria of personal identity, that person in the future is oneself.

What more might one care about? For one thing, one might also care about there being someone in the future whose experiences one can anticipate having. And while some of us would be capable of anticipating having the experiences of our replicas, some of us would not, even if we thought correctly that we were rationally entitled to anticipate having them.

What, then, of the reply that one's failure to anticipate having the experiences and performing the actions of a replica who—on the basis of a rational extension of prevailing criteria of personal identity—is justifiably regarded as oneself in the future would be pathological? In the case of exotic examples, such as teleportation, it is hard to see how one could defend this claim without begging the question. If, by every normal human standard, one is not dysfunctional in any way, then one's failure to anticipate having the experiences of a Martian replica might just be a feature of the way in which some psychologically healthy people anticipate the future. In normal circumstances, what would be rational and what would be psychologically healthy may go hand in hand, but in exotic circumstances they may not.

But, just as one might in exotic circumstances fail to go along with what in conventional circumstances would be rational and still be psychologically healthy, so also one might even in normal circumstances fail to go along and still be psychologically healthy. Parfit's young Russian nobleman example, in which a person tries to identify with a future stage of himself whose values he finds abhorrent, is a case in point.[18] In addition, one could argue, as many Buddhists have argued, that our normal pattern of egoistic expectations is not healthy. In the context of discussion of the philosophy of the self, the import of these reflections is that appealing to the psychopathology accusation as a way of defending the rationally coercive power of the me-consideration is problematic. Perhaps one could solve all of the problems mentioned without sullying the rationally coercive power of the me-consideration, but this seems doubtful.

In sum, the me-consideration by itself is not an adequate justification of future-oriented egoistic concern because one can sensibly ask why me-now should have special concern for me-later. The reply "because me-later is me" is not an adequate answer to this question. Nor is the reply "because me-now and me-later are both parts of me." In both cases, one can still ask sensibly for a further justification of future-oriented egoistic concern. This is especially apparent if the issue of which view, if any, of the same person over time is most plausible hinges on considerations of utility. But if the me-consideration is not a fully adequate justification of future-oriented egoistic concern, regardless of whether one is a reductionist or a selfist, and for pretty much the same reasons whether one is a reductionist or a selfist, then the problem of justifying egoistic concern is not brought about by reductionism, but only made more visible by it. The root cause of the problem of justifying egoistic concern would then be something else, such as the ubiquity of a certain sort of analytic perspective from which one can ask sensibly on behalf of one's present stage why one should care about one's future stages.

It does not follow from what I've said that future-oriented concern cannot be justified. In my view, it can be justified. My point is only that selfists and reductionists have different, but parallel, resources for answering the challenge posed by the request for a justification of future-oriented egoistic concern. Typically, selfists answer it by appeal to what I have called the me-consideration and by assuming the rationality of self-interest. Reductionists may answer it by appeal to what might be called the *continuer-consideration* and by assuming the rationality of continuer-interest.[19] So far, it would seem, neither response has any advantage over the other. Selfists may seem to have an advantage in that the relevance of the me-consideration and the rationality of self-interest are widely acknowledged, whereas the relevance of the continuer-consideration and the rationality of continuer-interest are not. But that would be a weak reed on which to rest the justification of one's view.

Selfists may also seem to have an advantage in being able to make a temporally neutral appeal to self-interest, that is, to hold that, in calculating one's self-interest, every stage of oneself counts the same. But in the contest between self-interest and continuer-interest, it is not clear why temporal neutrality should be an advantage; and, in any case, reductionists can make their own kind of temporal neutrality appeal: they can say that all continuer continuities that are to the same degree count the same, regardless of when they occur.

Reductionists, on the other hand, may have two advantages of their own: first, they do not have to suppose that, except as a linguistic convention, anything exists that there is no reason to suppose exists; and, second, at least for those who take a three-dimensional view of persons, certain hypothetical examples, especially fission examples, seem to support the view that personal identity is not primarily what matters in survival and, hence, that egoistic concern, rather than being basic, is actually derivative.[20] If either of these two reasons is accepted, then the reductionist has the more serious advantage.

Some philosophers, in addressing this sort of reductionist response to the challenge posed by the extreme claim, seem to assume that continuer-interest must be based on relation R in the way that Parfit understood it, that is, as psychological connectedness and continuity with any cause. On this view, the proponent of continuer-interest as the justification of future-oriented egoistic concern would be saddled with unintuitive consequences, such as those that emerge from Parfit's branch-line case and, to a lesser degree, from teleportation examples. So, one needs to remember that, so far as reductionism is concerned, continuer-interest need not be understood in terms of psychological connectedness and continuity with any cause. It is open to a reductionist to understand continuer-interest in terms of bodily continuity or in terms of psychological connectedness and continuity with its normal cause, both of which would give the reductionist different resources on which to draw in defending the rationality of future-oriented egoistic concern. The important point is that the reductionist who takes herself to see through—at least, intellectually—the illusion of self and therefore on these grounds might be thought plausibly to challenge the rationality of future-oriented *self*-interest does not thereby challenge the rationality of any sort of future-oriented interest. In particular, she does not thereby challenge the rationality of future-oriented continuer-interest. On the face of it, it's rationally permissible for a reductionist to be continuer-interested about herself—that is, about her continuers—in the future.

Ironic Engagement

According to Mādhyamika Buddhists, commitment to the reality of the self in the way in which almost everyone is committed to it is both rationally unjustified (since it's not ultimately true that selves exist) and a source of suffering. The remedy is to remove that sort of commitment to the reality of the self. Of course, one does not need to travel through Buddhism to get to this conclusion. Many contemporary non-Buddhist Western philosophers seem to think that commitment to the reality of the self in the way in which almost everyone is committed to it is not rationally justified. According to Parfit, for instance, that sort of commitment to the reality of the self is not only unjustified but, in his own case at least, is a source of suffering. His suffering, he says, is caused by his feeling alienated from others and by his fear of death.[21]

If one reaches—via any route—the conclusion that commitment to the reality of the self in the way in which almost everyone is committed to it is both rationally unjustified and a source of suffering and then tries to remove that sort of commitment, what, if any, part of that former commitment should one try to retain? In Parfit's view, perhaps none. In much of what he says, he seems to be an eliminativist of sorts about the self in the sense that he doesn't recommend that one leave any more in place of one's former commitment to the self than one has to leave in place. In contrast to Parfit, some contemporary Buddhist commentators recommend that we replace our former (or current) commitment to the self with a similar commitment, but with this difference: we should not be fully engaged, but only *ironically engaged*, with society's personhood conventions.

What does it mean to be ironically engaged with society's personhood conventions? Part of what it means, it seems, is that, to whatever extent we continue to adopt society's personhood conventions, we do so in full awareness of the fact that they are at best only useful fictions, and hence are not true or at least not deeply true descriptions of the way things really are. If one is a reductionist, it is hard to argue with this much of how we should regard our usual personhood conventions. But should we be more engaged with them than that? It seems to me that, regardless of how we answer this question, there is an atavistic but persistent belief in the self that is resistant to intellectual arguments that expose it as a mistake. Since this belief is so resistant to intellectual dissolution, there is not much that one should do—since there is not much that one can do—to remove it. And there is an additional concession that one should make to becoming entangled in society's personhood conventions. It is the recognition that, for practical purposes, such as straightening out with the airlines a confusion about when you originally ordered a ticket, it may be convenient *to talk as if you believe* in the reality of the self. Engaging in this sort of talk does not commit you in any way to actually believing in the reality of the self, except perhaps to believing in it as a convenient fiction.

Is there anything more to being optimally ironically engaged with our normal personhood conventions? Not, it seems, if one is an eliminativist about the self. But some contemporary Buddhist philosophers claim that there is something more to being optimally ironically engaged with our normal personhood conventions. Paul Williams, for instance, argues that, for ethical reasons, one has to acknowledge the conventional existence of "subjects" and of "individual persons." One needs subjects because without them pains would be "free-floating," and it is "incoherent to treat pains as if they are free-floating."[22] One needs individual persons because we have to recognize human individuality in order to help one another. In Williams's words:

> Not only is it incoherent to treat pains as if they are free-floating, but—as anyone who has ever received training in counselling knows—to help others effectively requires *not* that we discount their individuality as the persons they are but actually to focus on that individuality most closely. The good counsellor—dare I say, the good bodhisattva—is someone who can actually discount to an unusually effective extent their own intervening concerns in order to focus on the other *in their uniqueness*. This requires a very vivid awareness of the other as an individual. It is not helped by denying uniqueness to either of us. The pain which we seek to remove is intrinsically embedded in the actual individual in front of us, who is different

> from other individuals and, of course, different from us. However the bodhisattva is going to develop the most effective way to work for the benefit of others. In order to be an effective helper he or she is going to have to recognize and start from the individual person, the fact that each person is an individual with unique circumstances, problems and potential. Anyone who actually works in the caring professions knows that.[23]

But Williams's conclusion does not follow from his premises. One can have subjects and individuality without having selves or persons. Individual human bodies, including their mental states, can function as the unique owners of pain experiences. And, without acknowledging the existence of selves or persons, one can track the careers of individual human bodies. It may be that, to avoid untoward consequences, one has to acknowledge at least the conventional existence of something whose conventional existence some might wish to deny. But nothing that Williams says implies that, to avoid untoward consequences, one has to acknowledge the existence of selves or persons.

To take another example, Mark Siderits recommends that, rather than being an eliminativist about the self, one should concede that it is conventionally true that there are selves. Presumably, this concession, as he understands it, involves something more than simply making use in certain practical contexts, such as dealing with the airlines, of the knowledge that, in our language culture, almost everyone, almost all of the time, not only believes in the reality of the self, but experiences the world as if they believe in the reality of the self. An eliminativist could cheerfully make this concession. Siderits, on the other hand, says that, according to the reductionist:

> [T]he personhood convention prevails because it is more conducive to overall welfare than the readily available alternatives, such as punctualism and the *Weltgeist* convention... [and] utility would be better served if there were some way to combine the virtues of the personhood convention (such as the avoidance of gross imprudence, and the gains in welfare achieved through individual initiative) with a strategy for avoiding existential suffering.[24]

The strategy that he recommends for this purpose is to adopt a certain attitude toward the conventional truth of the reality of the self that enables us to retain some sort of commitment to causal series that have the capacities for self-revision, self-control, and self-scrutiny. In his view, this commitment involves more than what is available to the eliminativist. But it is not clear that it does involve more. An eliminativist about selves or persons can cheerfully admit the existence of causal series that have the capacities for self-revision, self-control, and self-scrutiny. What more might be required?

According to Siderits, the more that's required is something that would allow one to answer what he calls the "alienation objection":

> [This is the objection] that having a life is not the sort of thing one can choose as a means to further some separate end. It would, for instance, be most peculiar for someone to claim as their reason for bestowing love and affection on their spouse and children that this is the best way open to them to contribute to overall welfare. To claim this would seem to show a singular lack of understanding of just what love and affection are, and a person who said this might properly be described as alienated from their feelings of love and affection.[25]

A little later, Siderits adds, "If Reductionism is true, it may also be true that welfare is maximized by our feeling genuinely personal regard for others, and our viewing ourselves as the authors of our own life-narratives. But the belief that Reductionism is true seems to irreparably alienate us from all such person-involving attitudes."[26]

But is it reductionism per se that raises the specter of alienation? Nothing that Siderits says shows that it is. One can feel regard for others without supposing that the others for whom one feels regard are selves or persons. Hence, one can feel regard for others without acknowledging even the conventional existence of selves or persons in any sense that would be unavailable to an eliminativist about selves and persons. I would have thought, à la Parfit, that it is experiencing the world, including oneself, as if one believes in the reality of the self that leads to alienation. It is true that, if one adopts a consistent Parfitian eliminativism, then one has to recast some of the ways in which one feels personal regard for others—say, recast self-regard as continuer-regard. But what reason, in principle, is there to suppose that this will be a problem?[27]

If we become reductionists about persons, we do have to scale back our beliefs. But suppose we scale them back. Should we then ironically engage with our former beliefs, in anything other than the practical way illustrated by my airlines example? I don't see why any sort of fuller engagement is necessary. When, as reductionists, we give up our belief in the reality of the self, we don't give up our belief in the existence of a brain, a body, and a series of interrelated physical and psychological events. Nor do we abandon continuer-interest. What we used to think of as our future selves we still regard, albeit perhaps less robustly, as our future continuers and we may value them as such. We don't value our future selves based on the me-consideration, but we value them—our continuers—based on continuer-interest, and we are free to understand continuer-interest more robustly than Parfit's psychological connectedness and continuity with any cause. Our persistence may be less than we thought, but it is not nothing.

Even so, to give up the me-consideration and value our continuers based merely on continuer-interest, some adjustments will be required. We will have to scale back. But in scaling back, I can't see that we're in any danger of plunging into an abyss. In fact, I can't see that we're in any danger at all. It seems to me that the danger—primarily of alienation—is all on the other side of the equation. There is still the problem of getting ourselves to believe *at all levels of our own psychologies* in the reductionism to which we are committed intellectually. But meditation, not ironic engagement, seems to be the solution to that problem. In sum, to a reductionist, belief in the existence of the self is itself a kind of pretense. To whatever extent one can shed this belief, there is no need to keep on pretending.

Withdrawing one's commitment to the notion of self, and to the normative force of self-interest, and replacing these with the notions of a continuer and continuer-interest involves a sort of scaling back similar to what occurs in other domains in which we also come to philosophy with naive commitments. In the case of free will, for instance, many people initially come to philosophy naively committed to a sort of libertarianism and leave their exposure to philosophy as soft determinists. They still believe in free will, but the free will in which they believe is less robust. So too in the case of the self and related commitments, such as a commitment to the rationality of prudence. What we are left with is not, as the extreme claim would have it, almost nothing, but with continuer beliefs and continuer commitments that are less robust, in a certain way, than the self-beliefs and self-commitments we brought to the table—less robust, but still adequate for every practical purpose worth pursuing. Even so, most of us will not be able to shake an atavistic belief in the reality of the self. Nor will we want to avoid the practical advantages of employing self-talk. Both of these may require the sort of thin ironic engagement that is available to an eliminativist. But that seems to be all that's required.

There remains a final question. If there being no self is not a big deal practically, why have so many people, including so many philosophers, thought that it is a big deal? That, I think, is an interesting question. I would not have time to fully answer it here, even if I knew the answer, which I do not. However, it seems that part of the answer is that ordinary people, as well as many philosophers, have supposed that if the self, or belief in the self, goes, other things of genuine value go with it. As we have seen, some of these things that have been thought to be lost if we relinquish belief in the self are not lost. But there may still be others that are lost. One of these, which has to do with ownership and is an ingredient in Butler's criticism of Locke, has not gotten nearly as much attention in the West as it deserves. It is the possibility that, if there were no selves or persons, then no one would *own*, or be entitled to anticipate *having*, experiences that will be had by "themselves" in the future. If this were a genuine implication of relinquishing belief in the self and if coming to terms with it were required by relinquishing belief in the self, most of us, I think, myself included, would find relinquishing belief in the self to be profoundly challenging.

As we have seen in Candrakīrti's Mādhyamika theory, our everyday conception of self consists in an appropriative act of laying claim to the sorts of elements in the psychophysical aggregate to which Western philosophers, such as Parfit, reduce the self. This may give Candrakīrti an advantage over Western reductionists in explaining the rationality of prudence, which would include such things as the significance of the distinction between the *anticipation* of one's own future pain and the *concern* one feels for the future pain of another. For in Candrakīrti's view, the function of self-talk is not to talk about objects in the world—about selves—or even about the subpersonal parts to which selves may be reduced, but to appropriate experiences, emotions, and bodies. If such appropriation is regarded as rational, as it might well be on many Western views, then concern for whatever is appropriated probably would also be regarded as rational.[28] Candrakīrti, however, uses his account of the appropriative function of self-talk not to make a case for the rationality of special concern for ourselves in the future, but to speak to the idea, which some find suggested by the Buddha, that the concept of self, even correctly understood, is an ill from which we must be cured and, as such, has no place in a properly constituted mental life.[29] If this is right, it would help to explain something that is left obscure in many accounts of Buddhism: how one can subscribe to a no-self view, and thereby align oneself to that extent with the truth, yet nevertheless remain unenlightened. It helps to explain this by pointing out that how one understands self-talk is only one part of aligning with the truth. Another is eliminating the practice of appropriating experiences, emotions, and bodies as one's own. The suggestion that this latter element of aligning with the truth is crucial gives content to the Buddha's saying that "clinging" or "attaching" is the fuel that feeds the fire that is the idea of me and mine. It also explains why properly understanding the nature of the self can go only so far in bringing about enlightenment.

Jonardon Ganeri, in apparent endorsement of Candrakīrti's view, concludes that "learning to think of oneself as a whirlpool of self-appropriating actions" is a remarkable and potentially transformative achievement.[30] He sums up the view that is embedded in this achievement as follows:

> The utterance of "I" serves an appropriative function, to claim possession of, to take something as one's own. The appropriation in question is to be thought of as an *activity* of laying claim to, not the making of an *assertion* of ownership. Grammatical form notwithstanding, the avowal or self-ascription of a mental state, "I have a pain," is not a two-place relation between me and my pain; nor is it like a club's having members, or a tree's having roots.... When I say "I am in pain," I do not *assert* ownership of a particular painful experience; rather, I *lay claim to* the experience within a stream.

Ganeri continues:

> This is a performativist account of the language of self, in which "I" statements are performative utterances, and not assertions, and the function of the term "I" is not to refer. This account has the virtue of elucidating the relation between "I" and the psycho-physical stream, and it clarifies the sense in which the facts of ownership are the "further facts" left out of account by a reductionist theory of self.[31]

But, even if this view about the self is true, it would be one thing to understand it and another to live it. How could one live it? What would be the consequences? Ganeri cites Nāgārjuna and Candrakīrti as answering that it is possible to abandon all activity of self-appropriation of the psychophysical, thereby completely transforming "oneself," and that this would usher in enlightenment and end rebirth. Sounds good, perhaps. But, good or bad, it unquestionably sounds like it would be a big deal practically.

NOTES

Earlier versions of this chapter were read at Cambridge University and at Colgate University. Thanks to people at both of those events, especially Mark Siderits, Ulrich Meyer, and Jay Garfield, for helpful comments. Thanks also to Brad Rives.

1. Siderits 2003: 69.
2. Parfit 1984: 211.
3. Siderits 2003: 69.
4. Butler 1852: 331–332.
5. Including, for instance, Henry Sidgwick and Richard Swinburne. For details, see Parfit 1984: 307–309 and Martin and Barresi 2006: 215–216. For discussion of

the closely related question of whether "nihilism" is depressing, see Olson 2007: 180–210.

6. For discussion of this aspect of Vasubandhu's views, see Ganeri 2007: 166–167.

7. For discussion of what is taken to be Candrakīrti's irrealism about the self, see ibid.: 196–203. For the distinction between irrealism and fictionalism, see Garfield 2006.

8. An interesting thing about this scene, which was known to Plato (*Theaetetus* 152e) and subsequently widely discussed in late antiquity as the "growing argument" (see Sedley 1982), is that both the debtor and the lender have a point. Everyone *is* constantly changing. In a very strict sense of *same person*, every time someone changes, even a little, he or she ceases to exist: so, in this very strict sense of *same person*, the debtor is *not* the same person as the one who borrowed the money, and the lender is *not* the same person as the one who hit the debtor. Obviously, this very strict sense of *same person* is not an everyday notion, but a philosophical term of art. Also obviously, it is not a very useful sense of *same person*—unless you owe someone money! In everyday life, we want to be able to say such things as "I saw you at the play last night," and have what we say be true. If everyone is constantly changing and every change in a person results in his or her ceasing to exist, no such remarks could ever be true. On the assumption that such remarks sometimes are true, there must be a sense of *same person* according to which someone can remain the same person *in spite of changing*. Saying what this sense is or what these senses are is the philosophical problem of *personal identity* (over time).

9. Butler 1852: 332 and 334.

10. In Parfit's view, for instance, it is partly because selves or persons consist solely of brains and bodies, and interrelated physical and mental events, that they are a kind of linguistic fiction. But the subpersonal parts into which persons are reduced are real. See Parfit 1984: 211 and Parfit 1995: 13–45, the latter of which is reprinted in Martin and Barresi 2003: 292–317.

11. For more on these notions and the relations among them, see Horgan 1993, Kim 1998, Gillet and Loewer 2001, and Shoemaker 2001.

12. Johnston 1997 and McDowell 1997.

13. Johnston 1997: 154–156.

14. Parfit 1984: 311.

15. I am borrowing the term "ironic engagement" from Siderits 2003.

16. Strawson 1997; reprinted, with a "Post Script," in Martin and Barresi 2003: 335–377.

17. Perry 1976. For a discussion of Perry's view in connection with the psychological issue of identification, see Martin 1993.

18. Parfit 1984: 327–329.

19. As Parfit pointed out in giving expression to the moderate claim (ibid.: 311–312).

20. So, for instance, it is possible to argue that, in the case of many of us (whether or not we take ourselves to have seen through the illusion of self), our

more fundamental value is continuer-interest and our valuing self-interest is derived from that. These relationships could obtain in a situation of limited options, such as the situations in which humans almost always find themselves, in which continuer-interest and self-interest coincide. In such circumstances, self-interested beings and continuer-interested beings would make the same choices. However, when it comes to certain hypothetical choice situations, they would choose differently, and if continuer-interest were the more fundamental value, then our hypothetical choosers should opt for the choices that express continuer-interest, rather than self-interest.

21. Parfit 1984: 279–280.

22. An interesting discussion of whether the idea of free-floating experiences really is incoherent may be found in Dainton 2008: 244–249.

23. Williams 1998a: 174–175.

24. Siderits 2003: 99–100.

25. Ibid.: 104–105.

26. Ibid.: 105.

27. Siderits' best explanation of his richer notion of ironic engagement is via an analogy:

> Suppose I take pride in the city in which I was born and now live. I am, however, a reductionist about cities (an "urbanist" for short): I know that the existence of a city just consists in the existence of certain buildings and infrastructure in a certain location, and certain people interacting in certain ways. I know that "city" is a mere convenient designator for these more particular entities when related to one another in certain characteristic ways. I know that cities are only conventionally and not ultimately real. Does this knowledge undermine my civic pride?... The suggestion is that it must have a terminally corrosive effect, since one cannot take pride in something one believes to be ultimately unreal. But this need not be true. I am, after all, a reductionist about cities, not an eliminativist. That is, I believe our use of the convenient designator "city" reflects the genuine utility achieved when these more particular elements are related to one another in these characteristically urban ways. Moreover, I may believe that this utility is greatly enhanced when the inhabitants of urban aggregates engage in various kinds of cooperative behavior, and that such behavior is more likely to occur if they feel a sense of attachment to their location. So I may conclude that it is better, all things considered, that city dwellers feel pride in their city; and since I am a city dweller, I should feel pride in my city....
>
> When, for instance, I enthusiastically describe the charms of the place to a visitor, my aim is not to enhance the experiences of all who dwell here. My aim is just to express my pride in the city. True, my pride came about because of my desire that the experiences of the inhabitants be improved. But that hardly makes that desire the motive behind all acts expressive of my pride. To think so is to commit the genetic fallacy. Indeed I can be

> perfectly clear how it is that I came to feel civic pride, yet still have the genuine article. The knowledge will induce a degree of ironic distance—enough to ward off the dangers of civic chauvinism. So as I wax poetic in singing the city's praises to the visitor, I shall also comment wryly on the somewhat hyperbolical character of my account. Still I do wax poetic; I want to share my love of the city with others. I am ironically engaged. (Siderits 2003: 107–108)

But, if I understand Siderits correctly, a problem with his analogy is that he seems to be recommending a kind of pretense in which one does *not* need to engage to have civic pride. In other words, I don't see how urbanism interferes with civic pride. In the case of civic pride, it seems to me, an urbanist can be fully, not just ironically, engaged. Of course, one cannot believe in cities as something over and above "the existence of certain buildings and infrastructure in a certain location, and certain people interacting in certain ways," but I at least don't feel any pull to believe in cities in any such quasi-Hegelian way. In short, in the case of civic pride, there doesn't seem to be any problem to which appeal to ironic engagement might be the solution.

28. See, for instance, Johnston 1997, in Martin and Barresi 2003: 269: "In barest outline, the defense of self-referential concern would be that we find it utterly natural, and that, at least so far, critical and informed reflection on such concern has not made it out to be unreasonable."

29. Ganeri 2007: 159, 185.

30. Ibid.: 204.

31. Ibid.: 202.

10

Svasaṃvitti as Methodological Solipsism: "Narrow Content" and the Problem of Intentionality in Buddhist Philosophy of Mind

Dan Arnold

In the subtitle of an article, Mark Siderits (2001) asks: "Is the Eightfold Path a Program?" What Siderits thus asks is whether persons, on the Buddhist analysis thereof, can be understood as analogous to computers. More generally, Siderits wonders whether Indian Buddhist philosophy might finally be reconcilable with the sort of physicalism currently informed by research programs in the cognitive sciences. This is a large and flourishing field of inquiry comprising various approaches; as Siderits's titular reference to "techno-physicalism" suggests, it is computationalism that he particularly has in mind. What Siderits asks, in any case, is whether the strong dualist tendencies of Indian Buddhist philosophy are really integral to the Buddhist project, or whether, instead, the basic Buddhist commitment to selflessness might be compatible with physicalism. This can be thought a pressing question insofar as contemporary cognitive-scientific iterations of physicalism are often taken to be (as Siderits says) "more difficult to resist" than earlier versions (2001: 307). Siderits argues that the basic Buddhist project is, in fact, compatible with these contemporary physicalist accounts.

The constitutively Buddhist concern to advance a causal-reductionist account of the person surely makes it natural to ask whether Buddhist thought might be compatible with contemporary cognitive-scientific philosophy of mind. Nevertheless, it seems to me that Siderits is wrong to argue that the characteristically Buddhist form of dualism is not really integral to the Buddhist project; the significance of rebirth for that project is surely among several considerations that make it important for Buddhists to refute physicalism.[1] Paul Griffiths is right, I think, to stress "just how radical a dualism" was advanced particularly by the Abhidharma and Yogācāra trajectories of Buddhist thought; physicalism "in any form (identity theory, epiphenomenalism and so forth) is not an option" for this tradition of Buddhist thought (Griffiths 1986: 112).

That is not, however, the claim I want to defend here. My argument here concerns a related but more complex point: while Indian Buddhist thought is not (contra Siderits) reconcilable with physicalism, it is nevertheless the case that the tradition of Buddhist philosophy that originated with the writings of Dignāga (c. 480–540 C.E.) and Dharmakīrti (c. 600–660 C.E.)—a tradition that virtually defined "Buddhist philosophy" for many subsequent generations of Indian philosophers—centrally involves commitments and arguments that are vulnerable to the same kinds of critiques that can be brought to bear against physicalism. Most basically, insofar as they aim for a peculiarly causal account of the mental, these Buddhists share what is arguably the most important presupposition of the contemporary cognitive sciences; for chief among the questions faced by contemporary philosophers of mind, too, is whether it is possible to give an exhaustively causal account of such intentionally describable states or events as *doing something for a reason*.

In this regard, many critiques of cognitive-scientific physicalism focus particularly on a commitment, often thought to be entailed by the physicalist's characteristic emphasis on causation, to what Jerry Fodor has called "methodological solipsism"—a commitment, that is, to the idea that a properly scientific explanation of the mental must finally make reference only to things "inside the head." This is because the causal accounts at which thinkers like Fodor aim really involve only *efficient* causation—only, that is, the constitutively "local" kind of causation paradigmatically exemplified by contact between objects. The idea, then, is that if we are to credit our intentionally describable experience with a real explanatory role, any subjectively experienced *doing of something for a reason*, for example, must be understood to consist in something (such as goings-on in the brain and central nervous system) of the sort that can be causally efficacious; and since the things caused thereby (such as movements of the arms and legs) originate within the body, anything capable of causing these must itself be inside as well.

Among the difficulties with such views is that the content of intentionally described experiences often seems intelligible only with reference to things that are quite external to the subject thereof; a belief, for example, may not be understandable *as the belief that it is* without reference to such things as the conditions under which it would be true, a community of language users who find it intelligible, and so on. One of the things that philosophers such as Fodor have tried to do, then, is explain how the intentional content of thought is derivable from (reducible to, conceptually parasitic upon) something more basic and more proximal than the world we experience—how, that is, we can take our experience to be *about* an objective world, while yet finding that experience fully intelligible without any reference to that world. Fodor does this by arguing that thought must be understood to have "narrow content"—content, that is, which is "determined by the individual's intrinsic properties," where an intrinsic property just is one "that does not depend at all on the individual's environment."[2]

I want to explore here the usefulness of these ideas for understanding what Buddhists like Dignāga and Dharmakīrti meant to advance with their doctrine of *svasaṃvitti*—the doctrine (depending on the dimensions of the idea we want to emphasize with our translation) of "self-awareness," "reflexive awareness," or "apperception."[3] *Svasaṃvitti* is arguably foundational for the epistemological and metaphysical projects of these Buddhists. Unfortunately for those who would understand its foundational significance, though, the very centrality of *svasaṃvitti* is reflected in the fact that it can be quite variously understood; some understanding of *svasaṃvitti* can be thought to be equally important to any of several different ways to take the philosophical project of these thinkers.[4]

Surely, however, the various possible understandings of *svasaṃvitti* all relate to the question—of central concern for traditional interpreters of Dignāga and Dharmakīrti—of whether these thinkers should be taken as finally arguing for idealism. The philosophical texts of both thinkers are, in this regard, traditionally read as alternating between arguments for two kinds of views: a representationalist epistemology of the sort familiar from empiricist sense-datum theories (characterized by later Buddhist commentators as the Sautrāntika perspective) and the metaphysical idealism of the Yogācāra perspective. Adding to the difficulties in understanding the positions here is that the epistemology is arguably the same either way; both views, that is, amount at least to *epistemic* idealism—to the view that what we are immediately aware of is only things somehow intrinsic to cognition. This epistemological claim—which does not by itself commit us to saying that only things intrinsic to cognition *exist*—can be recruited in the same way as the modern foundationalist's appeal to empirical sense data: the one thing we cannot be wrong about is the content of our own cognitions, and this unique certainty provides the basis of all our knowledge. The chief difference between this view and Yogācāra idealism lies only in the metaphysical arguments that, for the idealist, additionally show that only such mental things as sense data *could* be real.[5]

Dignāga and Dharmakīrti's epistemology is, then, compatible with either realism or idealism. Precisely to that extent, their account of our acquaintance with the content of our awareness is fundamentally independent of how things are in the world. This is the sense in which these thinkers are committed to an account of mental content—an account of what thought is *about*—as intelligible with reference only to a subject. I want to suggest that *svasaṃvitti* figures centrally in their arguments to this effect and, more specifically, that the "content" (if it can finally be thought to have any) of Dignāga and Dharmakīrti's *svasaṃvitti* can be understood as "narrow" in the sense elaborated by Fodor.[6] To be sure, the arguments for *svasaṃvitti* also show that the ontological primitives to which persons are reducible will be, for these Buddhists, irreducibly *subjective*; while *svasaṃvitti* surely plays a role in a fundamentally reductionist project, then, we will here see something of the extent to which these Buddhists are committed to opposing physicalism. Nevertheless, my point is to emphasize that the project of Dignāga and Dharmakīrti can be seen to face some of the same problems as Fodor's computational version of physicalism. Whether the particulars to which mental content is reduced be physical or mental, then, both approaches crucially share a commitment to thinking that these are somehow *intrinsic* to the subject. This follows, we will see, given the shared confidence—similarly basic for both philosophical projects—that only things capable of exercising a certain kind of causal efficacy can finally be thought to be *real*. Among the most basic questions here, then, will be whether the intentionality of awareness can be exhaustively explained in terms of the proximate causes thereof.

In elaborating the reading of *svasaṃvitti* that I thus propose, I will especially consider some passages from Jinendrabuddhi's (c. 710–770 C.E.) commentary on Dignāga's *Pramāṇasamuccaya*—in particular, on verses 1.8cd–12 of that text, which constitute the locus classicus for Dignāga's introduction of the doctrine of *svasaṃvitti*. It is useful to take Jinendrabuddhi's text (the original Sanskrit of which was recovered and critically edited in the early twenty-first century) as our main source since this helps to bridge Dignāga and Dharmakīrti; for while Jinendrabuddhi's commentary represents the most faithful of the extant engagements with Dignāga's work, Jinendrabuddhi himself was also much influenced by Dharmakīrti, to whose works he alludes throughout his elaboration of Dignāga.[7] Jinendrabuddhi's text gives us, then, an unusually complete development of the doctrine, replete with something like the full range of arguments relevant to its understanding, in relatively brief scope.

Let us, then, see whether we might understand the doctrine of *svasaṃvitti* as figuring in a philosophical project that, while generally idealist in character, nevertheless shares some of the same intuitions (and faces some of the same problems) as Jerry Fodor's physicalism. We will begin by considering Dignāga's basic statement (as elaborated by Jinendrabuddhi) of the doctrine of *svasaṃvitti*. With a provisional understanding of what Dignāga and Jinendrabuddhi might be saying, we will then elaborate, in conversation with Fodor, an understanding of narrow content. Fodor's idea, we will see, is chiefly motivated by a peculiar concern with the question of mental causation. Among Fodor's arguments for narrow content is one that we might characterize as an argument from introspective access—an argument that Fodor develops in semantic terms. While there are reasons for thinking that semantic considerations are out of place in understanding *svasaṃvitti*, we will then briefly consider how *svasaṃvitti* might nevertheless relate closely to things that Dharmakīrti, in particular, said about semantics. This will also show something of the characteristically Buddhist preoccupation with questions of causation. Finally, we will conclude with some reflection on the problems that can be thought to arise for both of the positions (Fodor's and the Buddhists') here considered. The question here will be whether the *intentionality* of thought can finally be explained, causally, only in terms of narrow content—or whether, instead, an understanding of thought necessarily requires reference to how things are in the world.

Svasaṃvitti as *Pramāṇaphala*

The doctrine of *svasaṃvitti* was first developed in Dignāga's *Pramāṇasamuccaya*, a highly influential text elaborating a characteristically Buddhist epistemology. Central to this text (as to Indian discussions of epistemology more generally) is the category of *pramāṇa*, which we might render as "reliable warrant" or "doxastic practice"—something, at any rate, that picks out its referent's being a *criterion* of knowledge. From around the time of Dignāga, Indian philosophers were generally preoccupied with which doxastic practices (e.g., those involving perception, inference, testimony, comparison) should thus be reckoned as criteria (as *pramāṇas*) and with characterizing the criteria so identified. Dignāga's text famously argued (what would commonly be held by Buddhists writing after him) that only perception and inference have this status. The first chapter is chiefly concerned to characterize perception as constitutively nonconceptual.

In the context of that discussion, Dignāga first elaborates the doctrine of *svasaṃvitti* by way of explaining another claim considered to be characteristic of the school of thought that begins with him: by the word *pramāṇa,* we should really understand ourselves as referring not to any doxastic practice such as we might bring to bear on the independent objects thereof (not, as it were, to the epistemic *instruments* of our awareness), but rather to the cognition that is generally taken to *result* from the exercise thereof—to the *pramāṇaphala* ("result of the *pramāṇa*"). As Dignāga rather strongly puts the point, "a *pramāṇa* is real only as result."[8] It is, he says, only figuratively that the word *pramāṇa* is used as though it picked out something apart from a resultant cognition. And, as Dignāga says in the next verse, this *pramāṇaphala* is *svasaṃvitti.* Insofar, then, as Dignāga has said that a *pramāṇa* is real only as result, and that this result is *svasaṃvitti,* it seems we are to understand that *pramāṇas* themselves are finally to be understood, somehow, as consisting in *svasaṃvitti*—as consisting, that is, simply in self-awareness.

By way of a first approximation of what might motivate the claims made here, let us consider some comments from Brentano regarding what he called *inner perception:*

> [B]esides the fact that it has a special object, inner perception possesses another distinguishing characteristic: its immediate, infallible self-evidence. Of all the types of knowledge of the objects of experience, inner perception alone possesses this characteristic. Consequently, when we say that mental phenomena are those which are apprehended by means of inner perception, we say that their perception is immediately evident. Moreover, inner perception is not merely the only kind of perception which is immediately evident; it is really the only perception in the strict sense of the word.... [This is because] the phenomena of the so-called external perception cannot be proved true and real even by means of indirect demonstration. For this reason, anyone who in good faith has taken them for what they seem to be is being misled by the manner in which the phenomena are connected. Therefore, strictly speaking, so-called external perception is not perception. Mental phenomena, therefore, may be described as the only phenomena of which perception in the strict sense of the word is possible.[9]

Brentano here states an idea that is in play in the epistemologies of thinkers as diverse as Locke and Descartes: the idea that it is uniquely the case for inner perception—for our awareness of the occurrence and contents of our own mental events—that the object of this cognitive act is precisely as it seems to us to be. This is because the "object" of the awareness, in this case—what it is an awareness *of*—just is "how the cognition seems to us." There can thus be said uniquely to obtain, in this case, an identity between the intentional content and the phenomenological character of such cognitions. We might, this idea goes, be wrong in thinking that affairs in the world are just as represented in any particular cognition, but we cannot be wrong about the fact that *that is how it seems to us*, insofar as our being aware—its *seeming* to us that something is thus and so—is finally what we are aware *of*.

We might plausibly suppose that Dignāga similarly means to say that the only thing worth identifying as a criterion of knowledge (as a *pramāṇa*) is, for the same kinds of reasons, simply *the way any cognition seems to us*. It would, though, be more precise to say that Dignāga takes as the criterion the conceptually more basic fact *that* cognition seems some way or another.[10] As he puts it, we may take ourselves to mean by *pramāṇa* the "instrument" of an act of cognizing, but all we are really referring to is the bare fact of a cognition's "being one whose phenomenal content (*ābhāsa*) is an object"[11]—in other words, the bare fact of cognition's seeming to be *about* something.

Here, we can usefully attend to Jinendrabuddhi, who elaborates the elliptical arguments of Dignāga. Jinendrabuddhi discusses the point at issue, typically for Indian philosophical discourse, in the terms of analysis proposed by the Sanskrit grammatical tradition. According to that tradition, any semantically complete expression refers to some *action*, expressible by a verb, whose realization is what the sentence describes; and the parts of a sentence (as denoted by the various affixes whose usage is described by the grammarians) are therefore to be understood in terms of their relations to the verb. On this view, reference to a *pramāṇa*—a word that is formed by an affix denoting instrumentality—must be understood as picking out that factor which is instrumental in realizing an *act of knowing* (*pramiti*).[12]

Insofar, then, as Dignāga wants to say that we are entitled to take the word *pramāṇa* as finally referring only to the fact *that* any cognition seems to be of something or another, it is incumbent upon his commentators to explain why this "seeming" is the best candidate for the status of "instrumental" in realizing an act of cognizing. Jinendrabuddhi explains that, when we thus designate (even if only figuratively) something as instrumental in the realization of any act, we are picking out that factor "immediately" (*avyavadhānena*)[13] because of which the act is realized. The claim, then, is that when it comes to realizing an act of cognizing, the only thing that is thus "immediately" present—the only thing, we might also say, to which we have immediate cognitive access—is the bare fact of the cognition's seeming to represent some object.

Jinendrabuddhi is here exploiting an idea introduced by one of Dharmakīrti's commentators, who similarly thought that the only thing indisputably related to the occurrence of cognition could be something "not separated" (*avyavahita*; the word is from the same root as Jinendrabuddhi's *avyavadhānena*) from it. The point is that the resultant cognition is thus not separated in the very strong sense that goes with its being *identical* with the *pramāṇa* that is typically thought to "produce" it.[14] The position here thus involves an identity of just the sort we noted with reference to Brentano: to have a cognition just is for it to *seem* to a subject that something is the case. Insofar, though, as the one thing that is invariably and indisputably true of awareness is only that it thus *seems* to us to be of something, we have, uniquely, an irrefragable awareness of that "object" which is *how our cognition seems to us*. Here is one of the ways that Jinendrabuddhi develops the point:

> In this regard, with respect to an object such as form, a cognition consisting in resemblance [to that object] must have a nature—the "instrument"—whose essence is experience, *by means of which there is effected an ascertainment of various cognitions as distinct*: "this is a cognition of blue, this is a cognition of yellow." Otherwise, every cognition would be of every object, none would be of just some particular object, because there would be no difference.[15]

As particularly the italicized portion reflects, the point taken to be at issue here is: what is it in virtue of which any cognition *seems* to us, phenomenologically, as it does? And the point is that the only thing that *immediately* (*avyavadhānena*) explains the determinacy of mental content—the one thing in virtue of which we take cognitions to *be* phenomenologically distinct and which we are therefore entitled to characterize as instrumental in the realization of any contentful act of cognizing—is the very fact of the cognition's seeming as it does.[16]

Cognition's seeming to be *about* something is instrumental, then, in the peculiarly strong sense that it is this that constitutes our being aware. This becomes more clear, I think, when Jinendrabuddhi explains why nothing else can thus be thought to be immediately (*avyavadhānena*) related to the occurrence of an act of cognizing. Thus, anticipating the objection that surely there are other things (such as the relative acuity of our sense faculties) to which we might appeal in explaining the determinacy of mental content, Jinendrabuddhi gives a deceptively simple reason that such factors cannot explain what we here want to understand: "because of their not being of the nature of cognition, and because, rather, of their being the *cause* of all cognitions."[17] What is needed, Jinendrabuddhi thus makes clear, is something itself "of the nature of cognition" (*jñānasvabhāva*); nothing that is not itself cognitive or epistemic, nothing that does not itself *seem* to us some way, can explain the phenomenologically distinct character of cognitions. What best explains the determinacy of mental content, we are thus encouraged to suppose, must be the intrinsic properties thereof.

This idea can be recruited for the kind of epistemological role that typifies foundationalism—as is done, I think, when Jinendrabuddhi's notion of immediacy is glossed within the tradition in terms of *necessity*. John Dunne thus summarizes this move: "the unmediated [*avyavahita*] effect is 'distinctive' in that, as [Dharmakīrti's commentator] Śākyabuddhi notes, it 'necessarily occurs.' This is so because the effect is not separated (*avyavahita*) from the instrument; it is, in fact, identical to the instrument itself" (Dunne 2004: 261–262). Nothing, that is, except the bare fact of cognition's seeming some way is immediately (*avyavadhānena*) related to the occurrence of an act of cognizing; for while it can be doubted whether anything else that is proposed as a constraint on the content of cognition is really as it seems, there is in this case alone an identity between the intentional content and the phenomenological character of cognition. Indeed, a cognition's seeming to be of something just is its character *as* a cognition; the immediacy that obtains, then, is of the peculiarly strong sort that goes with *identity*. This, then, is the sense in which our cognitive instrument (*pramāṇa*, only figuratively so called) is finally identical with its result—with the *pramāṇaphala*, which Dignāga has said is all there really is to be referred to here. An intrinsic property of cognition—the simple fact, that is, of a cognition's seeming some way, which just is its identity as a cognition—is thus taken as the only criterion for individuating mental content. And cognition's seeming some way is something regarding which we cannot be wrong.

Svasaṃvitti and Narrow Content

I now want to suggest that Dignāga and Jinendrabuddhi can be understood as thus thinking that the determinacy of mental content can be fully accounted for simply on the basis of what Jerry Fodor has called *narrow content*. We can turn to the elaboration of that idea by way of another passage from Jinendrabuddhi. Thus, continuing the discussion of what is appropriately referred to by the word *pramāṇa*, Jinendrabuddhi entertains various objections to the effect that there are other factors that might more suitably be thought to constrain mental content. Chief among the rival contenders here are positions involving reference to external objects; realist opponents will thus want to argue that the desired explanation must involve reference to something in the objective world—that the determinacy of mental content is explained by the objects that such content is *about*. In the course of entertaining one of several objections to that effect, Jinendrabuddhi says:

> Even if we grant the existence of external objects, nevertheless, a cognitive object is judged only according to awareness [*yathāsaṃvedanam eva*]—hence, that [i.e., cognition] alone makes sense as the result. For there is no experience of an object as it is in itself [*yathāsvabhāvam*]—for in that case it would be ascertained according to the way in which its nature is constituted—since there would be the unwanted consequence that everyone's cognitions would have the same phenomenal aspect [*ekākāra*]. But representations have varying phenomenal aspects [*ākāra*]. That is, with regard just to a single object, many cognitions are apprehended which, owing to differences in the perceivers, are attended by phenomenal aspects of varying vividness, etc.—and a single thing does not itself have multiple aspects, since its multiplicity would follow.[18]

Readers of modern philosophy will surely find some familiar notions suggested by this passage, the principal point of which is to argue that our experience is necessarily mediated by intervening representations, or "aspects" (*ākāra*), and that we can therefore know things only *as they appear to us*, not as they are "in themselves."

Note, though, that the point is not a precisely Kantian one, since the Buddhists are here talking specifically about supposedly immediate, or "non-conceptual" (*kalpanāpoḍha*), acts of cognizing. It is not here suggested, then, that (as for Kant) we experience things only as *conceptually structured*, but rather that we experience them only as *phenomenally represented*. The idea of "representing" here is, then, clearly something more like an empiricist understanding thereof. What might it mean, on such a view, to emphasize that we experience things "only according to awareness" (*yathāsaṃvedanam eva*)? My suggestion is that this can usefully be understood as the claim that we have immediate access only to what Fodor calls narrow content.

The notion of narrow content figures prominently in much of the contemporary literature in philosophy of mind, despite the fact that, as David Chalmers has noted, "it has proven difficult to explicate an acceptable notion of narrow content" (Chalmers 2003: 46). Of the various kinds of arguments that have been developed for the idea, two seem to me to be in play in Fodor's work: arguments having to do with mental causation and those having to do with introspective access.[19] Let us develop these points to see whether they might be comparable to what motivates the Buddhist discussion.

Causal arguments are central to Fodor's whole project (as they are to Dignāga and, especially, Dharmakīrti). Fodor is a physicalist philosopher of mind who claims to be a realist about things like propositional attitudes—his is not, that is, the project of showing things like acts of believing (judging, intending, etc.) to be eliminable in preference to scientifically accredited entities such as brain states; he is, rather, concerned precisely to show how propositional attitudes can be thought to have an explanatory role to play with regard to our behavior. He thinks, however, that such intentionally describable states can only be understood that way insofar as they will admit of an altogether different description. This is because of his characteristically cognitive-scientific understanding of how we must understand "the mental causation of behavior" (Fodor 1982: 277); Fodor's view requires a precise sense in which "it's what the agent has in mind that causes his behavior" (ibid.: 292). In particular, since causation is taken to be local, it must be something proximal—what the agent has in her *brain*—that causes her behavior.

The context for Fodor's commending a computational theory of mind, then, is that of the mind-body problem: given that our bodies are material objects with spatiotemporal identity criteria, a realist understanding of propositional attitudes can be thought to require an understanding of how such attitudes can be causally efficacious with respect to the scientifically describable actions of our bodies. It is, Fodor argues, chiefly the possibility of our understanding how this can be done that has been advanced by the availability, in the late twentieth and early twenty-first centuries, of computer models of representing. Computational processes give us, that is, a model for understanding how a process can be described at the same time in *causal* terms (in terms, e.g., of the conduction of electricity through the circuits of a computer) and in logical or *semantic* terms (in terms that, like the outputs of a computer, track the steps in a calculation). As Fodor puts it:

> I take it that computational processes are both *symbolic* and *formal*. They are symbolic because they are defined over representations, and they are formal because they apply to representations in virtue of (roughly) the *syntax* of the representations. . . . What makes syntactic operations a species of formal operations is that being syntactic is a way of *not* being semantic. Formal operations are the ones that are specified without reference to such semantic properties of representations as, for example, truth, reference, and meaning. . . . formal operations apply in terms of the, as it were, shapes of the objects in their domains.[20]

The idea, then, is that the model of computation gives us a way to understand how things like propositional attitudes—the *semantically* evaluable mental content that we take our thoughts to be about—can at the same time be exhaustively described in terms of the kinds of things (e.g., brain events) that, in virtue of their physical properties (their, "as it were, shapes"), can be understood as causally efficacious with respect to our bodies.

Fodor is thus committed to the view that a propositional attitude's *causing* the behavior in question would be the only way to think it "really" in play at all. There is, however, a real question whether this way of reconciling the two levels of description really counts as *realism* about propositional attitudes. This is because all of the explanatory work, on this picture, is done by mental representations only as formally described; even if the computational model offers a way to understand that these causally efficacious particulars are *also* semantically evaluable, their character *as* meaning something may after all be epiphenomenal.[21] Fodor doesn't say as much, but that conclusion seems to follow from his explanation of why, if we follow the computational model in adopting a formality condition on propositional attitudes, this is "tantamount to a sort of methodological solipsism": "If mental processes are formal, they have access only to the formal properties of such representations of the environment as the senses provide. Hence, they have no access to the *semantic* properties of such representations, including the property of being true, of having referents, or, indeed, the property of being representations *of the environment*" (1982: 283). Among the arguments that can be developed against positions such as Fodor's, accordingly, are those to the effect that mental content cannot, in fact, be individuated without reference to such semantic properties; a belief, for example, cannot be understood *as the belief that it is* without, e.g., some reference to the conditions under which it would be true. Any description of mental content that brackets such considerations will, ipso facto, not be a description *of mental content.*

It is in this regard that Fodor offers something like an argument from "introspective access" for the necessity of supposing there to be narrow content—and indeed, of supposing this is all we *can* be aware of. This argument is cast in the semantic terms of "referential opacity." Thus, Fodor urges that "it is typically under an *opaque* construal that attributions of propositional attitudes to organisms enter into explanations of their behavior" (1982: 286). To attribute a belief under a referentially opaque construal is, on this view, to describe the contents of the belief only in terms of things somehow[22] available to the subject. On a referentially *transparent* construal, in contrast, a propositional attitude is individuated with regard to its *referent.* Fodor (1982: 287) gives a standard example: it makes all the difference for our understanding of the tragedy of Oedipus that we attribute to Oedipus the belief "I want to marry Jocasta" only under a referentially opaque construal; under a referentially transparent construal, that belief would be recognized as equivalent to "I want to marry my mother."

Fodor's idea is that, insofar as we are interested in understanding the "mental causation of behavior," we must attend to what the subject *takes herself to believe* (or desire, intend, etc.)—which of course may be quite independent of facts having to do with what the thought is *of* (its reference). Thus, "when we articulate the generalizations in virtue of which behavior is contingent upon mental states, it is typically an opaque construal of the mental state attributions that does the work; for example, it's a construal under which believing that *a is F* is logically independent from believing *b is F*, even in the case where a = b" (1982: 286). And again: "Ontologically, transparent readings are stronger than opaque ones; for example, the former license existential inferences, which the latter do not. But psychologically, opaque readings are stronger than transparent ones; they tell us more about the character of the mental causes of behavior" (ibid.: 287).

The reason Fodor thus thinks that mental content can be causally efficacious only under a referentially opaque description is that only this way do we have, as causal localism requires, something intrinsic to the subject. Insofar as mental content typically consists in things like acts of believing, there is pressure to refer to things (such as the possible truth or falsity of what is believed) that do not have the kind of identity criteria that go with causal efficacy; it must therefore be, as G. F. Schueler says of views such as Fodor's, "the *things* ('mental states') that *have* these true or false contents that do the explaining."[23] Causally efficacious mental content must, then, be "narrow" insofar as the brain states that ultimately *have* this content are themselves inside the head.

Narrow content is, then, in this sense specifiable simply in terms of the intrinsic properties of awareness; Fodor's is a view on which it makes sense to think of mental events *as contentful* without any reference to *how the world is*. And I suggest that Jinendrabuddhi can be understood as urging something like the same point when he argues that we experience things "only according to experience" (*yathāsaṃvedanam eva*), not "as they are in themselves" (*yathāsvabhāvam*). Recall, in this regard, that Jinendrabuddhi took the absurd consequence of believing otherwise to be that "everyone's cognitions would have the same phenomenal aspects." I am thus suggesting that we can understand this counterfactual idea of everyone's having the same mental content in terms of its being possible for propositional attitudes to be attributed as referentially transparent, such that everyone would know, as it were, what their belief was true *of*. Against this, Jinendrabuddhi can be understood to argue that it is only under referentially opaque construals that mental content can be attributed. The determinacy of mental content—what it is in virtue of which we are aware that we experience something blue on one occasion, something yellow on another—must finally be explained only with reference to something intrinsic to cognition: specifically, the mere fact of its seeming to be about something. All we can be certain of, though, is its *seeming* this way—which must therefore be the basis on which mental content more generally is to be understood.

Svasaṃvitti and Semantics

Now, there is a sense in which the reconstruction here proposed could be thought misleading; for as I noted above, Buddhist discussions of *svasaṃvitti* take this to be constitutively nonconceptual (*kalpanāpoḍha*). The representings (*ākāra*) that concern the Buddhists here are, then, emphatically nondiscursive. But in that case, one might reasonably object, the eminently discursive categories of referential opacity and transparency have no place in reconstructing Jinendrabuddhi's arguments for the decidedly perceptual character of *svasaṃvitti*. Nevertheless, I think there is an account to be given of the centrality of *svasaṃvitti* in addressing precisely these issues—and specifically, of the role that *svasaṃvitti* can be understood to play in grounding the account of linguistic understanding that Dharmakīrti, in particular, offers. This can help to give us, moreover, a sense of the kind of attention to causation that is characteristic of this Buddhist trajectory of thought.

Here, I must be brief,[24] and at points rather speculative (since I have it in mind to connect some dots that aren't, as far as I'm aware, explicitly connected within the tradition); but I want to suggest how we can argue that, on the view to which Dharmakīrti is committed, acts of linguistic expression must (like acts of perceiving) be understood as finally *about* nothing more than subjectively occurrent representations—about, in other words, the narrow content that is identified in arguments for *svasaṃvitti*. And our excursus on Fodor will prove to have been useful insofar as Dharmakīrti's account, like Fodor's, is chiefly guided by a commitment to a narrowly construed sort of causal explanation—and, precisely to that extent, has the effect (like Fodor's project) of taking mental content as fully explicable with reference to its intrinsic properties.

Here, it is pertinent to note something of Dharmakīrti's doctrine of *apoha* ("exclusion"), which represents a basically nominalist attempt to explain linguistic content without reference to really existent universals. This account, as is well known, trades on a certain sort of double negation; on the standard example, the referent of the word *cow* is really to be understood as whatever is "not a non-cow." Less often appreciated is the peculiarly causal spin that Dharmakīrti puts on this: what is thus "excluded" from the range of things to which any word refers is whatever particulars do not produce the same effect.[25] It is easy to imagine how this idea can serve the basic goal of showing linguistic referents to be relative to our interests and goals (and hence, contingently constructed as a function thereof): *what* it is that we exclude when we overlook whatever is a "non-cow" will vary (and the content of the concept will accordingly differ) depending upon whether, e.g., it is milk that we want ("whatever is not productive of the effect that is milk"), or fuel ("whatever is not productive of the effect that is cow manure").

But this picture is complicated by the fact that Dharmakīrti seems ultimately to have in mind a peculiarly narrow understanding of "sameness of effect"; specifically, the "same effects" thus produced by sensible objects consist finally in *the cognitions they cause.* As he says, "cognitions are without difference insofar as they are causes of a single judgment; the individuals in question, too, are without difference, insofar as they cause the same cognitions."[26] There is a very important sense, then, in which what utterances are *about*, for Dharmakīrti, is the phenomenologically comparable cognitions that cause them—which is, I suggest, not conceptually all that different from taking experiences finally to be *about* the brain events that can be thought to cause them.

This idea finds expression in the peculiar form of Dharmakīrti's claim that linguistic cognitions do not count (as, for many other Indian philosophers, they do) as *pramāṇa*s insofar as they are reducible to (one of the two *pramāṇa*s these Buddhists do admit) inference. Specifically, linguistic understanding consists, for Dharmakīrti, in an inference to the effect that some speaker's *intention* has been expressed.[27] What one does in understanding any utterance, on this view, is perform an inference from a particular linguistic item as effect, to a speaker's intention as the cause thereof. Given the aims that motivate the *apoha* doctrine, though, the "intentions" Dharmakīrti thus imagines must of course not be understood as anything like "propositions" (not, that is, as concerning objective states of affairs); they must, rather, themselves be particulars. And that is just what they are; "intentions," more specifically, are here understood as particular *subjectively occurrent representations*: "Language is a reliable warrant in regard to that object which appears in thought [*buddhau prakāśate*], which is the speaker's object of engagement; it is not grounded in the reality of the object itself."[28]

I am suggesting, then, that this fits in with Dharmakīrti's espousing something very much like Fodor's methodological solipsism; for what thus "appears in thought" is, on Dharmakīrti's account, eminently a matter of causally (for Fodor, "formally") describable representations (*ākāra*), whose content can be exhaustively explained without reference to "such semantic properties of representations as, for example, truth, reference, and meaning"—which is to say that the content of thought, on this account, can be fully identified under a referentially opaque construal. And that, as I have suggested, is just what Jinendrabuddhi's argument for *svasaṃvitti* would have us conclude. We now have a picture according to which (in John McDowell's words) "the 'inner' role of [for example] colour concepts is autonomously intelligible, and...[we can] explain their 'outer' role in terms of the idea that for an 'outer' object to fall under a colour concept is for it to be such as to cause the appropriate visual 'inner experience'" (McDowell 1996: 30).

The problem with such an account, though, is that (McDowell continues) "we might manage to externalize at best a propensity to induce the relevant feature of 'inner experience' in us" (1996: 31). Tom Tillemans hints at precisely such a picture, though, when he summarizes Dharmakīrti's "fundamental position" regarding language as one according to which "words are used according to the speaker's wishes and designate anything whatsoever which he might intend. The speaker is thus an authority as to what he is referring to in that he can ascertain his own intention by means of a valid cognition (*pramāṇa*), viz., reflexive awareness (*svasaṃvedana*)" (Tillemans 2000: 163). On the fully elaborated reconstruction that I am suggesting, then, *svasaṃvitti* finally explains the intention that the hearer of any utterance infers from the speech act which is the effect caused thereby; the understanding of an utterance thus consists simply in the hearer's inferring that the speaker has some awareness, and the process is grounded finally in the indubitable character that awareness has for the speaker. On this view, then, the putatively conceptual acts that are linguistic utterances turn out, in a fundamental sense, to be *about* nothing more than the narrow content that constitutes the subject's own mental states.

Conclusion: Methodological Solipsism in Physicalism and in Yogācāra

The foregoing represents, then, the full account I had in mind in proposing that we reconstruct some arguments concerning *svasaṃvitti* in terms of Fodor's methodological solipsism. In the course of explicating Dignāga's concise and sometimes elliptical account of *svasaṃvitti*, Jinendrabuddhi argued that we experience things only according to awareness (*yathāsaṃvedanam eva*) and not as they are in themselves (*yathāsvabhāvam*). I suggested that these Buddhists can be understood thus to argue that experience immediately affords us (in Fodor's words) "no access to the *semantic* properties of [our] representations, including the property of being true, of having referents, or, indeed, the property of being representations *of the environment*."

Having raised the concern that this reference to semantics is out of place in discussing Jinendrabuddhi's arguments concerning the constitutively perceptual—which is to say, for these Buddhists, nonconceptual—character of *svasaṃvitti*, I suggested how we can nevertheless understand the discussion of *svasaṃvitti* as playing a fundamental role in the account that Dharmakīrti, in particular, offers. On Dharmakīrti's development of the *apoha* doctrine, I thus argued, linguistic content (which is what *apoha* aims to explain) is finally explained in terms of individual mental content.[29] In particular, what a speaker is immediately aware of, what *causes* her to utter a sentence—and we know that the intention in question must serve as a cause, since the inference a hearer performs is from utterance as effect to intention as cause—is only the narrow content that is finally all anyone *could* be immediately aware of. The explanatory terminus, on the *apoha* account of linguistic content, is a subject's immediate acquaintance with his or her own mental content. In this way, *svasaṃvitti* is foundational not only for this epistemology, but for Dharmakīrti's semantics as well.

In light of these similarities in the two trajectories of thought, it is reasonable to think we might learn something interesting about their projects by considering the extent to which Dignāga and Dharmakīrti face the same problems as Fodor—and this despite the fact that they are not only not (like Fodor) physicalists, but are dualists if not idealists. Indeed, the arguments for *svasaṃvitti* are surely to be read as central to a case for the view that persons are (as Buddhists are centrally concerned to argue) reducible to ontological primitives that are themselves irreducibly mental; for these Buddhists, all mental events necessarily have prior mental events as their causes.[30] Nevertheless, the causal, internalist accounts of mental content here turn out, I think, to be more conceptually similar than not.

Let us consider, in this regard, an important equivocation in Fodor's case for narrow content. Fodor exploits the idea of referential opacity—which, as in the Oedipus example, amounts simply to the adoption of a first-person epistemic perspective on the truth of any subject's beliefs—to recommend the view that all that any subject could be immediately aware of is things (in Jinendrabuddhi's terms) only as experienced (*yathāsaṃvedanam eva*). The reference to a subject's intrinsic properties is, though, already preferred here on the grounds that only things internal to the subject's head can be causes of behavior—on grounds, that is, having to do with the question of mental causation.

Note, however, that the appeal to referential opacity still represents a basically intentional level of description; narrow content, after all, is still represented as being *content*. Having argued that mental content can only be attributed to a subject under a referentially opaque construal, then, Fodor claims that the items thus picked out can be described, *non*intentionally, in terms of causally efficacious particulars inside the skull. There is, though, no more reason to think that narrow content could explain this move from an intentional to a nonintentional level of description than there is to think that *wide* content could. It is not obvious that narrow content, just because it reflects the subject's own perspective on what she believes, gets us any closer to brain events than wide content does; the fact that we are, as it were, epistemically closer does not by itself tell us anything about what this content essentially consists in.

The problem, then, with thus exploiting an intentional level of description to individuate narrow content is that this still keeps in play what Fodor ultimately thinks he is explaining: the idea that thoughts are *about* something. The content individuated under a referentially opaque attribution would help with Fodor's problem of mental causation, however, only if such content (as contra wide content) uniquely tracks its proximal causes. This would be, in effect, to hold that our beliefs are finally *about* brain events. It is quite unclear, however, that such a picture is (as John McDowell has said in a related context) "entitled to characterize its inner facts in content-involving terms—in terms of its seeming to one that things are thus and so—at all."[31] Fodor must leave behind, then, the idea that narrow content is *contentful* just insofar as he takes it uniquely to explain mental causation.[32]

We can, perhaps counterintuitively, best understand the doctrine of *svasaṃvitti* in similar terms if we briefly consider (what would seem most sharply to divide Dignāga and Dharmakīrti from physicalists like Fodor) what the doctrine of *svasaṃvitti* might look like if it were taken as finally integral to a case for metaphysical idealism—as part of a doctrine, that is, according to which the most fundamental existents are acts of representing that are not, finally, *about* anything but themselves. Fittingly, we can here take our bearings from one of Dharmakīrti's succinct statements to the effect that the criterion of the real is "pragmatic efficacy" or (the different reading of Dharmakīrti's term is significant) "causal efficacy": "Whatever has the capacity for pragmatic—*or*, causal—efficacy [*arthakriyāsamartham*] is said here to be ultimately existent; everything else is conventionally existent. These two [sets consist, respectively, in] unique particulars and abstractions."[33]

The use of (what is among Dharmakīrti's principal terms of art) the word *arthakriyā* here is pivotal, for this idea will admit of either a teleological or an efficient causal reading, depending on which of two lexically possible senses we take *artha* to have.[34] Dharmakīrti's term can, on one hand, plausibly be taken to refer to the eminently teleological idea of action (*kriyā*) with respect to a goal (*artha*). On such an understanding, his claim—that only those particulars that have the capacity for facilitating this should be judged to be real—would recommend the commonsensical view that whatever can advance our purposeful interventions in the world is "real."

Dharmakīrti's term can, on the other hand, also be taken to refer to the efficient causal idea of the action of a thing (*artha*). On this understanding, the claim could just as well be understood as attributing causal efficacy to existents of a very different sort than the medium-sized dry goods that figure in our everyday activity. While John Dunne (2004: 260) is, I think, right to note that Dharmakīrti's works don't decisively settle things in favor of one or the other of these understandings, both of which are clearly in play at various points, it seems clear that the general trend in Dharmakīrti's thought is finally away from the teleological reading—and that the extent of Dharmakīrti's exclusive focus finally on something like efficient causation is a source of philosophical problems similar to those that Fodor's project faces.

The centrality of *svasaṃvitti* is important to seeing this. John Dunne recognizes as much when he ventures a "speculative interpretation" according to which it is particularly in the doctrine of *svasaṃvitti* that the efficient causal reading of *arthakriyā* is to the fore; it is, Dunne thus says, especially in the case of *svasaṃvitti* that "the notion of *arthakriyā* may be applicable only in terms of sheer causal efficiency, since it is difficult to see how practical action (*vyavahāra*) makes sense within this context" (2004: 260). Consider, in this regard, that Dignāga and Dharmakīrti alike take only perception to have really existent things as its object; on the view that *really existent* means causally efficacious, this means (as Dharmakīrti characteristically emphasizes) that perceptual cognitions are *caused* by their objects. Dignāga said, though (and I think Dharmakīrti agrees), that "a *pramāṇa* is real only as result," and this result is *svasaṃvitti*; *pramāṇa*s, it seems we are thus encouraged to conclude, are themselves finally to be understood as consisting simply in "self-awareness." Jinendrabuddhi suggests as much when he urges that *svasaṃvitti* is, in the final analysis, the only "ultimately real" (*pāramārthikaṃ*) *pramāṇa*, as opposed to the merely "conventionally" valid (*vyāvahārika*) *pramāṇa*s that go with the commonsense view of the mental.[35] And the ultimacy of *svasaṃvitti* consists in the fact that (in Dunne's words) "it reveals the mere fact of experience, which is the same as saying that it reveals the mere causal efficiency (*arthakriyā*) of awareness" (2004: 276). And Dunne is surely right that "it is difficult to see how practical action (*vyavahāra*) makes sense within this context."

The point, as we could also put it, is that it is only under a nonsemantic, nonintentional description that an act of cognizing can be thought to disclose nothing more than the bare fact of its own causally describable occurrence. Of course, insofar as cognitions to this effect can be thought to have the uniquely indubitable status that goes with the *identity* between their intentional content and their phenomenological character, something like this minimal sort of cognitive disclosure has been taken by many philosophers to provide the surest foundations for our knowledge. Fodor's methodological solipsism amounts to the similarly Cartesian[36] confidence that a full account of mental content can be elaborated on the basis only of the narrow content that can be individuated with reference to its intrinsic properties; what thought is *about*, that is, can finally be explained from a perspective that brackets from consideration the semantic properties (to revisit Fodor's words) of "being true, of having referents, or, indeed, the property of being representations *of the environment*." But despite the evident appeal of this idea to some epistemologists, the difficulty in understanding "how practical action makes sense within this context" reflects the difficulty of thus bracketing reference to the possible truth or referents of our propositional attitudes. We still do not have, on this kind of account, an explanation of how to get from a nonintentional level of description—the one at which "the mere causal efficiency of awareness" is discharged—to the intentional level of description at which *someone has a thought*.

On the view to which (I take it) these Buddhists are ultimately committed, though, the bare, causally describable occurrence of awareness is finally all there is for any cognition *to* be about; on the Yogācāra account that I take these Buddhists finally to endorse, the whole point they would finally have us understand is that everything about our ordinary, practical action is illusory: all that exists is causally describable arisings of awareness, which are finally to be understood as not being *about* anything at all.[37] Thus, to say, with Dunne, that *svasaṃvitti* "reveals the mere causal efficiency of awareness" is to say that it reveals all that could really *be* revealed; it reveals, that is, *what* there is that appears. And the very problem to be overcome by Buddhist practice, on this view, is described in terms of *how* that is typically taken to appear: viz., in Yogācāra terms, as *parikalpita*, erroneously "imagined" as consisting in a discrete subject's grasping of constitutively distinct objects.[38] What we are to realize (if it makes sense to think of any "realization" here) in getting beyond this merely imagined character, then, is that cognition is not finally intentional at all. Surely, it is reasonable to think that this is the view that Jinendrabuddhi, for one, endorses when he says that *svasaṃvitti* is the only "ultimately real" *pramāṇa*.

Here, then, is the problem that our brief consideration of Fodor has helped us characterize even with respect to the fully elaborated Buddhist idealism to which *svasaṃvitti* may be most central: if Fodor's account of narrow content is problematic as an attempt to salvage an explanatory role for our propositional attitudes, and if Dignāga and Dharmakīrti take *svasaṃvitti* as a criterion for distinguishing the phenomenological content of cognitions that are thought ultimately to have no content, the reasons for the problems may be fundamentally the same: "Content in general, not just the focusing of thoughts on objects, requires directedness towards reality.... Cognitive space incorporates the relevant portions of the 'external' world."[39] Perhaps, that is, it is just not possible to give an account of thought without reference to such semantic properties as truth, reference, and meaning—which is, in effect, to say that a non-intentional account of intentionality cannot finally work. To the extent that is right, it is a point that counts not only against Fodor, but also, in just the same way (and despite their significant differences from him), against Buddhist philosophers in the tradition of Dignāga and Dharmakīrti.

NOTES

In working through much of the material considered here, I particularly benefited from the comments and suggestions of my students Tupac Cruz, Sonam Kachru, and Pierre-Julien Harter. Thanks, as well, to Rick Nance, Charles Goodman, and the editors of this volume (especially Mario D'Amato), all of whom made helpful suggestions regarding earlier drafts.

1. A well-known elaboration of such arguments (developed precisely in the context of arguing for rebirth) comes in chapter 2 of Dharmakīrti's *Pramāṇavārttika*; for a useful point of access to some of these arguments, see Taber 2003.

2. This is the formulation of Curtis Brown (2007), who provides an illuminating overview of the various understandings of (and arguments for) narrow content in the contemporary literature.

3. The word *svasaṃvitti* (like the semantically equivalent *svasaṃvedana*) is formed from the reflexive pronominal prefix *sva-* and a nominal form of the verbal root *saṃ-√vid* ("to be aware"). I will generally leave it untranslated, allowing my engagement with the considered passages to do the work of showing its significance.

4. The vexed status of *svasaṃvitti* can be readily appreciated by attending to the apparent tensions between any number of things that both traditional and modern interpreters have said about it. In first arguing for the doctrine, for example, Dignāga maintained that it is only by invoking *svasaṃvitti* that one can stop the infinite regress that otherwise will result from any attempt to distinguish, phenomenologically, first- from second-order cognitions—and yet traditional critics of the doctrine charged that it is precisely the appeal to *svasaṃvitti* that opens a regress. There is, as well, considerable question whether *svasaṃvitti* identifies a specifiable act of

cognizing or whether, instead, it picks out something like the defining characteristic of any such act—whether, that is, *svasaṃvitti* is the idea of an intentional, reflective awareness that *accompanies* other cognitions or the idea of the reflexive dimension *of* any awareness. On these and other basic issues, see, inter alia, Arnold 2005b, MacKenzie 2007, and Williams 1998b.

5. I have particularly elaborated these points (also apropos of a study of Dharmakīrti's doctrine of *svasaṃvitti*) in Arnold 2008a.

6. Jay Garfield has similarly found it useful to consider some developments in Buddhist thought vis-à-vis Fodor; see Garfield 2002a, where the Madhyamaka trajectory of Buddhist philosophy is considered as constitutively refusing views much like Fodor's. For Garfield, too, the salient point about Fodor's project is the attempt to show that "*all* scientific taxonomy is individualistic—that science never does, and must never, identify phenomena for theoretical purposes *qua* relational, because all such taxonomy depends upon the causal powers of the phenomena to be classified, and because causal powers are always local" (2002a: 14). While it is not my point to do so here, I have also tried (see, e.g., Arnold 2005a) to understand Madhyamaka as having elaborated Buddhist commitments in ways opposed to the philosophical tradition of Dignāga and Dharmakīrti—a tradition, I will be arguing, that is committed to views such as Garfield here characterizes.

7. Much scholarship (e.g., Hayes 1988) has emphasized the differences between Dignāga and Dharmakīrti, who surely have been too often taken to exemplify a monolithic school. For present purposes, though, I am inclined to follow Dreyfus and Lindtner in taking some of the works of these Buddhist thinkers (especially insofar as they concern *svasaṃvitti*) as "products of a unified intention" (1989: 27). The edition of Jinendrabuddhi's commentary is that of Steinkellner et al. 2005; all translations from this edition are my own. Many earlier discussions of *svasaṃvitti* (e.g., Ganeri 1999 and Matilal 1986: 148–160) were based only on Hattori's translation (1968) from the Tibetan translations of Dignāga.

8. *Pramāṇasamuccaya* 1.8d. All translations from Dignāga are my own and are made from the Sanskrit text reconstructed by Steinkellner et al. 2005.

9. Brentano 1973: 91. The fairly radical character of Brentano's point here is better appreciated if one bears in mind that he means to distinguish our awareness of mental phenomena not from that of physical *objects*, per se, but of physical *phenomena*. In considering, that is, what distinguishes our awareness of the mental from that of the physical, Brentano is in both cases considering only (what he thinks we can understand independently of an external world) *what appears to us in thought*.

10. This is important to note since, on the view to which (I take it) Dignāga and Dharmakīrti are ultimately committed, *how* cognition seems is, finally, deeply mistaken (indeed, it is just this that Buddhist practice would have us realize); but to say this is not to deny *that* there is some cognition that mistakenly appears. See note 38, below.

11. *Pramāṇasamuccaya* 1.9cd.

12. On the significance, for Indian epistemology, of the Sanskrit grammarians' *kāraka* analysis of sentences, see Dunne (2004: 17–20ff.). On a standard example

of this kind of analysis (that of an act of cutting wood), the axe would fill this instrumental role, with the woodcutter as nominative agent.

13. Literally, "without interval."

14. See Dunne (2004: 261–262, 269), who is considering arguments made by the commentator Devendrabuddhi.

15. Translated from Steinkellner et al. 2005: 66.7–10; emphasis added.

16. Dunne (2004: 272) effectively shows that Devendrabuddhi, too, takes Dharmakīrti to make this point.

17. Translated from Steinkellner et al. 2005: 66.11–67.1.

18. Translated from ibid.: 68.12–69.3.

19. See Brown 2007 for a useful survey of the range of arguments for narrow content.

20. Fodor 1982: 279. It should be noted that Fodor's thinking on the subject has evolved. In Fodor 1994, for example, he suggested that his project does not depend on arguments from narrow content (though he emphasized that this is not to say he has abandoned the idea that there is such a thing).

21. Fodor is not unaware of this objection, which is (in his words) one to the effect that "it is the computational roles of mental states, and *not* their content, that are doing all the work in psychological explanation"; given this, it looks "as though *content* per se drops out of psychological explanations" (1994: 49–50). See ibid.: 49–54 for one attempt by Fodor to frame and meet this objection.

22. Epistemically, one might suppose—or else perhaps only in the sense of *internal to the subject's head.* See the discussion in the conclusion of this chapter of Fodor's equivocation on a couple of different ways of being "available to the subject," and his here presupposing the intentional kind of description that he means to explain.

23. This is G. F. Schueler's (2003: 58) characterization of one of the main intuitions driving this line of thinking.

24. I have, however, developed parts of this picture at considerable length in Arnold 2006.

25. See Dunne 2004: 119–126.

26. From Dharmakīrti's autocommentary on *Pramāṇavārttika* 1.109; see Arnold 2006: 437n52.

27. Here, of course, the sense of *intention* is different from the sense of *intentionality* that has so far been in play. Dharmakīrti's reference to a "speaker's intention" involves the garden-variety sense of someone's intending to express some point or another; what has hitherto been in play, however, is chiefly the philosophically technical sense (deriving from Brentano) of intentionality as picking out the *aboutness* that characterizes thought—the fact of thought's having some content. It is possibly confusing, but also revealing, that these two senses are not, after all, so far apart, for the garden-variety sense of *intending* to do something is itself an instance of an intentionally describable act, in the philosophical sense. That is, to intend to do something is itself to have a thought that is directed toward some content. Moreover, the sense of a speaker's intention, in particular, turns out

to be quite close to the Brentano sense of intentionality. Thus, if the problem of intentionality is (as Lynne Rudder Baker has put it) the problem of understanding "how one thing (some mental item) *can mean or represent or be about* some other thing" (Baker 1987: 9; emphasis added), it turns out that language may be deeply implicated in the problem; for linguistic items (sentences, stories, claims) can also "mean or represent or be about" states of affairs. See note 29 for one expression of the relation between these issues.

28. *Pramāṇavārttika* 2.2; see Arnold 2006: 438n53.

29. Indeed, one of the questions that can be understood to animate Indian philosophical debate (between, e.g., these Buddhists and some Brahmanical rivals, especially the Mīmāṃsakas) is the same as what Roderick Chisholm, on reading Wilfrid Sellars's "Empiricism and the Philosophy of Mind," took to be at issue between him and Sellars: "Can we explicate the intentional character of believing and of other psychological attitudes by reference to certain features of language; or... must we explicate the intentional characteristics of language by reference to believing and to other psychological attitudes?" (Chisholm and Sellars 1972: 215). I am here taking *svasaṃvitti* to figure importantly in an argument for something like the latter position; when, e.g., Mīmāṃsakas argue against *svasaṃvitti*—and argue, as well, for the irreducible reality of such linguistic abstractions as the referents of words—they can be understood as arguing for something like the former.

30. This (perhaps without the reference to what is *necessarily* the case) is one of Dharmakīrti's arguments for rebirth; see note 1, above.

31. McDowell 1998: 242–243. McDowell is here speaking of the kind of "fully Cartesian" picture that he takes to be in play in Russell's appeal to singular propositions—where the kind of internalism exemplified by Fodor (and not the Cartesian idealism that Fodor surely rejects) is the salient point of such a picture. What is "Cartesian" here, that is, is the two-component view of mindedness, according to which there is one component—Fodor's narrow content is an example—that is autonomously intelligible. McDowell notes that

> [i]n the physicalistic modern version of the insistence on autonomy, the self-standingness of the inner realm suffices to exclude intrinsic involvement with the world, without any need for an appeal to phenomenology. And in the most clear-sighted form of the position, the darkness of the interior is institutionalized. The intrinsic nature of inner states and events, on this view, is a matter of their position in an internal network of causal potentialities, in principle within the reach of an explanatory theory that would not need to advert to relations between the individual and the external world. (ibid.: 250)

Thus, for example, McDowell says of Daniel Dennett's "hetero-phenomenology" that, like Fodor's approach:

> [It] generates the appearance that we can find (narrow) content-bearing states in the interior considered by itself. But the idea looks deceptive. If we are not concerned with the point of view of the cognitive system itself (if,

indeed, we conceive it in such a way that it has no point of view), there is no justification for regarding the enterprise as any kind of phenomenology at all. (ibid.: 256n)

32. Arguments broadly to this effect (that is, that avowedly nonintentional accounts of intentionality invariably turn out to presuppose what they aim to explain) have figured prominently in critiques of projects such as Fodor's; see, e.g., Baker 1987: 113–174 and Garfield 1988: 109–127. I have briefly developed a case for such arguments as fundamentally Kantian in Arnold 2008b.

33. *Pramāṇavārttika* 3.3; see Arnold 2006: 435n46.

34. I here follow Dunne 2004: 256–260, who partly follows Nagatomi 1967–1968.

35. Cf. Steinkellner et al. 2005: 75.1–3. Dharmakīrti's commentator Śākyabuddhi, too, makes this point; see Dunne 2004: 317, 406–408.

36. See note 31, above.

37. Proponents of Yogācāra characteristically put this point by arguing that cognition (*vijñāna*) should be understood ultimately to lack the subject-object structure (the duality, that is, of *grāhakākāra* and *grāhyākāra*, "apprehending aspect" and "aspect to be apprehended") that is typically taken to characterize awareness.

38. I have here presented a basically Yogācāra picture by paraphrasing the first few verses of Vasubandhu's *Trisvabhāvanirdeśa* (for a translation of which, see Garfield 2002b). Reference to this is recommended by several passages in Jinendrabuddhi where he alludes to precisely this doctrine by referring to the third "nature" that Yogācāra philosophers take to be real: the "perfected" (*pariniṣpanna*) reality that consists simply in the "dependent" as no longer distorted by our conceptual activity. See Steinkellner et al. 2005: 75.5–6, 76.12–13, for passages in which, I take it, Jinendrabuddhi is thus showing his Yogācāra credentials.

39. McDowell (1998: 257–258). I take McDowell's scare quotes here not to query or bracket the external world, but to question the idea of its being definable as constitutively external *to* our supposedly internal cognitive space.

Bibliography

Ames, William. 1995. "Bhāvaviveka's *Prajñāpradīpa*: A Translation of Chapter Two." *Journal of Indian Philosophy* 23.3: 295–365.

App, Urs. 1994. *Master Yunmen: From the Record of the Chan Teacher "Gate of the Clouds."* New York: Kodansha.

Arnold, Dan. 2005a. *Buddhists, Brahmins, and Belief: Epistemology in South Asian Philosophy of Religion.* New York: Columbia University Press.

———. 2005b. "Is *Svasaṃvitti* Transcendental? A Tentative Reconstruction following Śāntarakṣita." *Asian Philosophy* 15.1: 77–111.

———. 2006. "On Semantics and *Saṃketa*: Thoughts on a Neglected Problem with Buddhist *Apoha* Doctrine." *Journal of Indian Philosophy* 34.5: 415–478.

———. 2008a. "Buddhist Idealism, Epistemic and Otherwise: Thoughts on the Alternating Perspectives of Dharmakīrti." *Sophia* 47.1: 3–28.

———. 2008b. "Transcendental Arguments and Practical Reason in Indian Philosophy." *Argumentation* 22.1: 135–147.

Baker, Lynne Rudder. 1987. *Saving Belief: A Critique of Physicalism.* Princeton, NJ: Princeton University Press.

Bhattacharya, Kamaleswar. 1977. "On the Relationship between the *Vigrahavyāvartanī* and the *Nyāyasūtras.*" *Journal of Indo-European Studies* 5.2–3: 265–273.

———. 1999. "Nāgārjuna's *Vigrahavyāvartanī.*" In *Encyclopedia of Indian Philosophies*, vol. 8, ed. Karl Potter: 124–133. Delhi: Motilal Banarsidass.

Brentano, Franz. 1973. *Psychology from an Empirical Standpoint*, ed. Oskar Kraus and trans. Antos C. Rancurello, D. B. Terrell, and Linda L. McAlister. London: Routledge and Kegan Paul.

Brown, Curtis. 2007. "Narrow Mental Content." *Stanford Encyclopedia of Philosophy*. http://plato.stanford.edu/entries/content-narrow (accessed May 22, 2007).

Butler, Joseph. 1852. *The Analogy of Religion: Natural and Revealed.* London: Bohn.

Cabezón, José Ignacio. 1997. "Rong ston Shākya rgyal mtshan on Mādhyamika Thesislessness." In *Tibetan Studies: Proceedings of the 7th Seminar of the International Association for Tibetan Studies,* vol. 1, ed. Helmut Krasser: 97–105. Wien: Verlag der Österreichischen Akademie der Wissenschaften.

Candrakīrti. 2003. *Prasannapadā,* ed. Gelugpa Student Welfare Committee. Sarnath: Central Institute of Higher Tibetan Studies.

Canfield, John. 1975. "Wittgenstein and Zen." *Philosophy* 50.194: 383–408.

Chadwick, David. 1999. *Crooked Cucumber: The Life and Zen Teaching of Shunryu Suzuki.* London: Thorsons.

Chalmers, David J. 2003. "The Nature of Narrow Content." *Philosophical Issues* 13: 46–66.

Chisholm, Roderick M. 1976. *Person and Object.* LaSalle, IL: Open Court.

Chisholm, Roderick M., and Wilfrid Sellars. 1972. "The Chisholm-Sellars Correspondence on Intentionality." In *Intentionality, Mind, and Language,* ed. Ausonio Marras: 214–248. Urbana: University of Illinois Press.

Conant, James. 1989. "Must We Show What We Cannot Say?" In *The Senses of Stanley Cavell,* ed. Richard Flemming and Michael Payne: 242–283. Lewisburg, PA: Bucknell University Press.

———. 1992. "Kierkegaard, Wittgenstein, and Nonsense." In *Pursuits of Reason,* ed. Ted Cohen, Paul Guyer, and Hilary Putnam: 195–224. Lubbock: Texas Tech University Press.

———. 1995. "Putting Two and Two Together: Kierkegaard, Wittgenstein, and the Point of View for Their Work as Authors." In *Philosophy and the Grammar of Religious Belief,* ed. Timothy Tessin and Mario von der Ruhr: 248–331. New York: St. Martin's.

———. 1997. "How to Pass from Latent to Patent Nonsense: Kierkegaard's *Postscript* and Wittgenstein's *Tractatus.*" *Wittgenstein Studies* diskette 1, 11-2-97, TXT.

Conze, Edward, ed. and trans. 1957. *Vajracchedikā Prajñāpāramitā.* Rome: Istituto Italiano per il Medio ed Estremo Oriente.

Crary, Alice, and Rupert Read, eds. 2000. *The New Wittgenstein.* London: Routledge.

Dainton, Barry. 2008. *The Phenomenal Self.* Oxford: Oxford University Press.

D'Amato, Mario. 2000. "The Mahāyāna-Hīnayāna Distinction in the *Mahāyānasūtrālaṃkāra*: A Terminological Analysis." Ph.D. diss., University of Chicago.

———. 2003. "The Semiotics of Signlessness: A Buddhist Doctrine of Signs." *Semiotica* 147.1–4: 185–207.

Dancy, Jonathan, ed. 1997. *Reading Parfit.* Oxford: Blackwell.

Davidson, Donald. 1984. "On the Very Idea of a Conceptual Scheme." In Davidson, *Inquiries into Truth and Interpretation*: 183–198. Oxford: Clarendon.

———. 2001. "Foreword." In *Two Roads to Wisdom? Chinese and Analytic Philosophical Traditions,* ed. Bo Mou: ix. LaSalle, IL: Open Court.

de Jong, J. W. 1972. "The Problem of the Absolute in the Madhyamaka School." *Journal of Indian Philosophy* 2: 1–6.

———. 1978. "Textcritical Notes on the *Prasannapadā*." *Indo-Iranian Journal* 20: 25–59, 217–252.

———, ed. 1977. *Nāgārjuna's Mūlamadhyamakakārikā Prajñā Nāma*. Revised by Christian Lindtner. Chennai: Adyar Library and Research Center.

Demiéville, Paul. 1987. "The Mirror of the Mind," trans. Neal Donner. In *Sudden and Gradual*, ed. Peter N. Gregory: 13–40. Honolulu: University of Hawaii Press.

Diamond, Cora. 1991. *The Realistic Spirit*. Cambridge, MA: MIT Press.

Dogen, Eihei. 1985. *Moon in a Dewdrop: Writings of Zen Master Dogen*, trans. Kazuaki Tanahashi. New York: North Point.

Dreyfus, Georges. 1997. *Recognizing Reality: Dharmakīrti's Philosophy and Its Tibetan Interpretations*. Albany: State University of New York Press.

Dreyfus, Georges, and Christian Lindtner. 1989. "The Yogācāra Philosophy of Dignāga and Dharmakīrti." *Studies in Central and East Asian Religions* 2: 27–52.

D'Sa, Francis X. 1980. *Śabdaprāmāṇyam in Śabara and Kumārila: Towards a Study of the Mīmāṃsā Experience of Language*. Vienna: Indologisches Institut der Universität Wien.

Dunne, John D. 1996. "Thoughtless Buddha, Passionate Buddha." *Journal of the American Academy of Religion* 64.3: 525–556.

———. 2004. *Foundations of Dharmakīrti's Philosophy*. Boston: Wisdom.

Dutt, Nalinaksha, ed. 1978. *Bodhisattvabhūmi*. Patna: Jayaswal Research Institute.

Etchemendy, John. 1990. *The Concept of Logical Consequence*. Cambridge, MA: Harvard University Press.

Finnigan, Bronwyn. 2005. "A Challenge to the Ontological Commitments of Parfit's Reductionism and Indeterminacy Thesis." M.A. thesis, University of Sydney.

Fodor, Jerry. 1981. "Imagistic Representation." In *Imagery*, ed. Ned Block: 63–88. Boston: MIT Press.

———. 1982. "Methodological Solipsism Considered as a Research Strategy in Cognitive Psychology." In *Husserl, Intentionality, and Cognitive Science*, ed. Hubert L. Dreyfus: 277–303. Cambridge, MA: MIT Press.

———. 1994. *The Elm and the Expert: Mentalese and Its Semantics*. Cambridge, MA: MIT Press.

Frege, Gottlob. 1884. *Die Grundlagen der Arithmetik, eine logisch mathematische Untersuchung über den Begriff der Zahl*. Breslau: W. Koebner.

———. 1891. *Funktion und Begriff*. Jena: H. Pohle.

Funahashi, Naoya, ed. 1985. *Mahāyānasūtrālaṃkāra (Chapters I, II, III, IX, X): Revised on the Basis of Nepalese Manuscripts*. Tokyo: Kokushokankokai.

Galloway, Brian. 1989. "Some Logical Issues in Madhyamaka Thought." *Journal of Indian Philosophy* 17: 1–35.

Ganeri, Jonardon. 1999. "Self-Intimation, Memory, and Personal Identity." *Journal of Indian Philosophy* 27.5: 469–483.

———. 2007. *The Concealed Art of the Soul: Theories of Self and Practices of Truth in Indian Ethics and Epistemology*. Oxford: Oxford University Press.

Garfield, Jay L. 1988. *Belief in Psychology: A Study in the Ontology of Mind*. Cambridge, MA: MIT Press.

Garfield, Jay L. 1995. *The Fundamental Wisdom of the Middle Way: Nāgārjuna's Mūlamadhyamakakārikā*. New York: Oxford University Press.

———. 1996. "Emptiness and Positionlessness: Do the Mādhyamika Relinquish All Views?" *Journal of Indian Philosophy and Religion* 1: 1–34.

———. 2002a. "Epochē and Śūnyatā: Scepticism East and West." In Garfield, *Empty Words: Buddhist Philosophy and Cross-Cultural Interpretation*: 3–23. New York: Oxford University Press.

———. 2002b. "Vasubandhu's Treatise on the Three Natures: A Translation and Commentary." In Garfield, *Empty Words: Buddhist Philosophy and Cross-Cultural Interpretation*: 128–151. New York: Oxford University Press.

———. 2002c. *Empty Words: Buddhist Philosophy and Cross-Cultural Interpretation*. New York: Oxford University Press.

———. 2006. "Reductionism and Fictionalism: Comments on Siderits's *Personal Identity and Buddhist Philosophy*." *APA Newsletter on Asian and Asian-American Philosophers and Philosophies* 66.1: 1–7.

Garfield, Jay L., and Graham Priest. 2003. "Nāgārjuna and the Limits of Thought." *Philosophy East and West* 53.1: 1–21.

Gillet, Carl, and Barry Loewer, eds. 2001. *Physicalism and Its Discontents*. Cambridge: Cambridge University Press.

Gomez, Luis O. 1976. "Proto-Mādhyamika in the Pāli Canon." *Philosophy East and West* 26.2: 137–165.

Goodman, Charles. 2005. "Vaibhāṣika Metaphoricalism." *Philosophy East and West* 55.3: 377–393.

Goodman, Nelson. 1968. *Languages of Art*. Indianapolis, IN: Bobbs-Merrill.

Go rams pa bSod nams seng ge. 1988. *lTa ba'i shan 'byed*. Sarnath: Sakya Students' Union.

Griffiths, Paul J. 1986. *On Being Mindless: Buddhist Meditation and the Mind-Body Problem*. LaSalle, IL: Open Court.

———. 1990. "Pure Consciousness and Indian Buddhism." In *The Problem of Pure Consciousness*, ed. Robert K. C. Forman: 71–97. New York: Oxford University Press.

———. 1994. *On Being Buddha*. Albany: State University of New York Press.

Gyatso, Lobsang. 2005. *The Harmony of Emptiness and Dependent-Arising*. Dharamsala: Library of Tibetan Works and Archives.

Haack, Susan. 1978. *Philosophy of Logics*. Cambridge: Cambridge University Press.

Hacker, Peter. 2000. "Was He Trying to Whistle It?" In *The New Wittgenstein*, ed. Alice Crary and Rupert Read: 353–388. London: Routledge.

Hakamaya, Noriaki. 1971. "Asvabhāva's Commentary on the *Mahāyānasūtrālaṃkāra* IX.56–76." *Journal of Indian and Buddhist Studies* 20.1: 473–465.

Harvey, Peter. 1990. *An Introduction to Buddhism*. Cambridge: Cambridge University Press.

Hattori, Masaaki. 1968. *Dignāga on Perception: Being the Pratyakṣapariccheda of Dignāga's Pramāṇasamuccaya from the Sanskrit Fragments and the Tibetan Versions*. Cambridge, MA: Harvard University Press.

Hayes, Richard P. 1988. *Dignāga on the Interpretation of Signs*. Dordrecht: Kluwer.

———. 1994. "Nāgārjuna's Appeal." *Journal of Indian Philosophy* 22.4: 299–378.
Hopkins, Jeffrey. 1983. *Meditation on Emptiness*. London: Wisdom.
Horgan, Terence. 1993. "From Supervenience to Superdupervenience." *Mind* 102.408: 555–586.
Hutchinson, Phil, and Rupert Read. 2005. "Whose Wittgenstein?" *Philosophy* 80.313: 432–455.
———. 2006. "The Elucidatory Reading of Wittgenstein's *Tractatus*." *International Journal of Philosophical Studies* 14.1: 1–29.
———. 2008. "Toward a Perspicuous Presentation of 'Perspicuous Presentation.'" *Philosophical Investigations* 31.2: 141–160
Ingalls, Daniel. 1951. *Materials for the Study of Navya-Nyāya Logic*. Cambridge, MA: Harvard University Press.
Jackson, David. 1987. *The Entrance Gate for the Wise (Section III): Sa-skya Paṇḍita on Indian and Tibetan Traditions of Pramāṇa and Philosophical Debate*. Wien: Wiener Studien zur Tibetologie und Buddhismuskunde.
Jackson, Frank. 1982. "Epiphenomenal Qualia." *The Philosophical Quarterly* 32.127: 127–136.
Jaimini. 1916. *The Pūrva Mīmāṃsā Sūtra of Jaimini*. Allahabad, India: Sudhidranath Vasu.
Johnston, E. H., Arnold Kunst, and Kamaleswar Bhattacharya, eds. and trans. 1978. *The Dialectical Method of Nāgārjuna*. Delhi: Motilal Banarsidass.
Johnston, Mark. 1997. "Human Concerns without Superlative Selves." In *Reading Parfit*, ed. Jonathan Dancy: 149–179. Oxford: Blackwell.
Kalupahana, David. 1976. *Buddhist Philosophy: A Historical Analysis*. Honolulu: University of Hawaii Press.
Kamalaśīla. 1994. *Āryaprajñāpāramitāvajracchedikāṭīkā*. Sarnath: Central Institute of Higher Tibetan Studies.
Katagiri, Dainin. 2000. *You Have to Say Something*. Boston: Shambhala.
Keenan, John Peter. 1980. "A Study of the *Buddhabhūmyupadeśa*." Ph.D. diss., University of Wisconsin, Madison.
Keira, Ryusei. 2004. *Mādhyamika and Epistemology: A Study of Kamalaśīla's Method for Proving the Voidness of All Dharmas*. Vienna: Arbeitskreis für Tibetische und Buddhistische Studien.
Kim, Jaegwon. 1998. *Mind in a Physical World*. Cambridge: Cambridge University Press.
La Vallée Poussin, Louis de, ed. 1903–1913. *Mūlamadhyamakakārikās (Mādhyamikasūtras) de Nāgārjuna, avec la Prasannapadā Commentaire de Candrakīrti*. St. Petersburg: Académie Impériale des Sciences.
———, trans. 1937. *Documents d'Abhidharma: les deux, les quatre, les trois vérités*. Bruges, Belgium: Imprimerie Sainte Catherine.
Lévi, Sylvain, ed. 1907. *Mahāyāna-Sūtrālaṃkāra*. Paris: Librairie Honoré Champion.
Lindtner, Christian. 1982. *Nagarjuniana: Studies in the Writings and Philosophy of Nāgārjuna*. Copenhagen: Akademisk Forlag.
Lopez, Donald. 1994. "dGe 'dun chos 'phel's Position on *Vigrahavyāvartanī* 29." *Buddhist Forum* 3: 161–185.

Lopez, Donald. 2005. *The Madman's Middle Way: Reflections on Reality of the Tibetan Monk Gendun Chopel*. Chicago: University of Chicago Press.

Mabbett, Ian. 1996. "Is There a Devadatta in the House? Nāgārjuna's *Vigrahavyāvartanī* and the Liar Paradox." *Journal of Indian Philosophy* 24.3: 295–320.

MacDonald, Anne. 2007. "Revisiting the *Mūlamadhyamakakārikā*: Text-Critical Proposals and Problems." *Studies in Indian Philosophy and Buddhism* 14: 25–55.

MacKenzie, Matthew. 2007. "The Illumination of Consciousness: Approaches to Self-Awareness in the Indian and Western Traditions." *Philosophy East and West* 57.1: 40–62.

Magee, William. 1999. *The Nature of Things: Emptiness and Essence in the Geluk World*. Ithaca, NY: Snow Lion.

Makransky, John J. 1997. *Buddhahood Embodied*. Albany: State University of New York Press.

Martin, Raymond. 1993. "'Having' the Experience: The Next Best Thing to Being There." *Philosophical Studies* 70.3: 305–321.

———. 1998. *Self-Concern: An Experiential Approach to What Matters in Survival*. Cambridge: Cambridge University Press.

Martin, Raymond, and John Barresi. 2006. *The Rise and Fall of Soul and Self*. New York: Columbia University Press.

———, eds. 2003. *Personal Identity*. Oxford: Blackwell.

Matilal, Bimal Krishna. 1985. *Logic, Language, and Reality*. Delhi: Motilal Banarsidass.

———. 1986. *Perception: An Essay on Classical Indian Theories of Knowledge*. Oxford: Clarendon.

McDowell, John. 1996. *Mind and World: With a New Introduction*. Cambridge, MA: Harvard University Press.

———. 1997. "Reductionism and the First Person." In *Reading Parfit*, ed. Jonathan Dancy: 230–250. Oxford: Blackwell.

———. 1998. "Singular Thought and the Extent of Inner Space." In McDowell, *Meaning, Knowledge, and Reality*: 228–259. Cambridge, MA: Harvard University Press.

Merricks, Trenton. 2002. *Objects and Persons*. New York: Oxford University Press.

Meuthrath, Annette. 1999. *Die Nāgārjuna zugeschriebene Vigrahavyāvartanī und die Nyāyasūtras: Eine Untersuchung des Verhältnisses beider Texte zueinander*. Reinbek, Germany: Dr. Inge Wezler Verlag für Orientalistische Fachpublikationen.

Mortensen, Chris. 1989. "Mental Images: Should Cognitive Science Learn from Neurophysiology?" In *Computers, Brains, and Minds: Essays in Cognitive Science*, ed. P. Slezack and W. Albury: 123–136. Dordrecht: Kluwer.

———. 2002. "Paradoxes Inside and Outside Language." *Language and Communication* 22.3: 53–62.

Nagatomi, Masatoshi. 1967–1968. "*Arthakriyā*." *Adyar Library Bulletin* 31.2: 52–72.

Nanjio, Bunyiu, ed. 1923. *The Laṅkāvatāra Sūtra*. Kyoto: Otani University Press.

Nguyen, Cuong Tu. 1990. "Sthiramati's Interpretation of Buddhology and Soteriology." Ph.D. diss., Harvard University.

Nishijima, G., and C. Cross, trans. 1996. *Master Dōgen's Shōbōgenzō*, bk. 2. London: Windbell.

Noonan, Harold. 2003. *Personal Identity*. London: Routledge.

Oberhammer, Gerhard. 1963. "Ein Beitrag zu den Vāda-Traditionen Indiens." *Wiener Zeitschrift für die Kunde Süd- und Ostasiens und Archiv für Indische Philosophie* 7: 63–103.

Oetke, Claus. 1996. "Ancient Indian Logic as a Theory of Non-Monotonic Reasoning." *Journal of Indian Philosophy* 24.5: 447–539.

———. 2003. "Some Remarks on Theses and Philosophical Positions in Early Madhyamaka." *Journal of Indian Philosophy* 31.4: 449–478.

Olson, Eric. 2007. *What Are We? A Study in Personal Ontology*. Oxford: Oxford University Press.

Parfit, Derek. 1984. *Reasons and Persons*. Oxford: Oxford University Press.

———. 1995. "The Unimportance of Identity." In *Identity*, ed. H. Harris: 13–45. Oxford: Oxford University Press.

Peirce, Charles Sanders. 1992. *The Essential Peirce*, vol. 1, ed. Nathan Houser and Christian Kloesel. Bloomington: Indiana University Press.

Perry, John. 1976. "The Importance of Being Identical." In *The Identities of Persons*, ed. Amélie Oksenberg Rorty: 67–90. Berkeley: University of California Press.

Phillips, D. Z. 1977. "On Wanting to Compare Wittgenstein and Zen." *Philosophy* 52.201: 338–343.

Priest, Graham. 2001. *Introduction to Non-Classical Logic*. Cambridge: Cambridge University Press.

———. 2002. *Beyond the Limits of Thought*, 2nd (extended) ed. Oxford: Oxford University Press.

Priest, Graham, and Jay L. Garfield. 2002. "Nāgārjuna and the Limits of Thought." In Priest, *Beyond the Limits of Thought*, 2nd (extended) ed.: 249–270. Oxford: Oxford University Press.

Priest, Graham, and Richard Routley. 1989. "First Historical Introduction: A Preliminary History of Paraconsistent and Dialetheic Approaches." In *Paraconsistent Logic: Essays on the Inconsistent*, ed. Graham Priest, Richard Routley, and Jean Norman: 3–75. Munich: Philosophia Verlag.

Putnam, Hilary. 1982. "Why There Isn't a Ready-Made World." *Synthese* 51: 141–168.

Quine, W. V. O. 1969. *Ontological Relativity and Other Essays*. New York: Columbia University Press.

Ramsey, F. P. 1931. *The Foundations of Mathematics and Other Logical Essays*. London: Routledge and Kegan Paul.

Read, Rupert. 1995. "The *Real* Philosophical Discovery." *Philosophical Investigations* 18.4: 362–369.

———. 2002. "Marx and Wittgenstein on Vampires and Parasites." In *Marx and Wittgenstein*, ed. Gavin Kitching and Nigel Pleasants: 254–281. London: Routledge.

———. 2004. "Throwing Away 'the Bedrock.'" *Proceedings of the Aristotelian Society* 105.1: 81–98.

Read, Rupert. 2005. "Just in Time: Notes for the Meeting of Wittgenstein and Zen." *UEA Papers in Philosophy* 16: 32–44.

———. 2006. "A No-Theory?" *Philosophical Investigations* 29.1: 73–81.

———. 2008. "The 'Hard' Problem of Consciousness Is Continually Reproduced and Made Harder by All Attempts to Solve It." *Theory, Culture, and Society* 25.2: 51–86.

Read, Rupert, and Rob Deans. 2003. "Nothing Is Shown." *Philosophical Investigations* 26.3: 239–268.

Reps, Paul, and Nyogen Senzaki. 1998. *Zen Flesh, Zen Bones*. Boston: Tuttle.

Rescher, Nicholas. 2001. *Paradoxes: Their Roots, Range, and Resolution*. LaSalle, IL: Open Court.

Rescher, Nicholas, and Robert Brandom. 1980. *The Logic of Inconsistency*. Oxford: Basil Blackwell.

Rorty, Amélie Oksenberg, ed. 1976. *The Identities of Persons*. Berkeley: University of California Press.

Ruegg, David Seyfort. 1977. "The Uses of the Four Positions of the *Catuṣkoṭi* and the Problem of the Description of Reality in Mahāyāna Buddhism." *Journal of Indian Philosophy* 5: 1–71.

———. 1983. "On the Thesis and Assertion in the Madhyamaka/dBu ma." In *Contributions on Tibetan and Buddhist Religion and Philosophy*, ed. Ernst Steinkellner and Helmut Tauscher: 205–241. Wien: Arbeitskreis für Tibetische und Buddhistische Studien.

———. 1986. "Does the Mādhyamika Have a Thesis and Philosophical Position?" In *Buddhist Logic and Epistemology*, ed. Bimal Krishna Matilal: 229–237. Dordrecht: Reidel.

———. 2000. *Three Studies in the History of Indian and Tibetan Madhyamaka Philosophy*. Wien: Arbeitskreis für Tibetische und Buddhistische Studien.

———. 2002. *Two Prolegomena to Madhyamaka Philosophy*. Wien: Arbeitskreis für Tibetische und Buddhistische Studien.

Ryle, Gilbert. 1984. *The Concept of Mind*. Chicago: University of Chicago Press.

Sagal, Paul T. 1992. "Nāgārjuna's Paradox." *American Philosophical Quarterly* 29.1: 79–85.

Schueler, G. F. 2003. *Reasons and Purposes: Human Rationality and the Teleological Explanation of Action*. Oxford: Clarendon.

Sedley, David. 1982. "The Stoic Criterion of Identity." *Phronesis* 27: 255–275.

Sharma, Chandradhar. 1960. *A Critical Survey of Indian Philosophy*. Delhi: Motilal Banarsidass.

Shaw, J. L. 1978. "Negation and the Buddhist Theory of Meaning." *Journal of Indian Philosophy* 6: 59–77.

Shoemaker, Sydney. 2001. "Realization and Mental Causation." In *Physicalism and Its Discontents*, ed. Carl Gillet and Barry Loewer: 74–98. Cambridge: Cambridge University Press.

Sider, Theodore. 1999. "Presentism and Ontological Commitment." *Journal of Philosophy* 96.7: 325–347.

Siderits, Mark. 1991. *Indian Philosophy of Language: Studies in Selected Issues*. Dordrecht: Kluwer.

———. 1997. "Buddhist Reductionism." *Philosophy East and West* 47.4: 455–478.

———. 2001. "Buddhism and Techno-Physicalism: Is the Eightfold Path a Program?" *Philosophy East and West* 51.3: 307–314.

———. 2003. *Personal Identity and Buddhist Philosophy: Empty Persons*. Burlington, VT: Ashgate.

———. 2007. *Buddhism as Philosophy: An Introduction*. Indianapolis, IN: Ashgate/ Hackett.

———. 2008. "Paleo-Compatibilism and Buddhist Reductionism." *Sophia* 47.1: 29–42.

Stanley, Jason. 2001. "Hermeneutic Fictionalism." In *Midwestern Studies in Philosophy*, vol. 25: *Figurative Language*, ed. Peter A. French and Howard K. Wettstein: 36–71. Boston: Blackwell.

Steinkellner, Ernst. 2005. "Dignāga's *Pramāṇasamuccaya*, Chapter 1." www.oeaw.ac.at/ias/Mat/dignaga_PS_1.pdf (accessed June 2, 2005).

Steinkellner, Ernst, Helmut Krasser, and Horst Lasic, eds. 2005. *Jinendrabuddhi's Viśālāmalavatī Pramāṇasamuccayaṭīkā: Chapter 1, Part I: Critical Edition*. Beijing and Vienna: China Tibetology Publishing House, Austrian Academy of Sciences Press.

Stone, Martin. 2000. "Wittgenstein on Deconstruction." In *The New Wittgenstein*, ed. Alice Crary and Rupert Read: 83–117. London: Routledge.

Strawson, Galen. 1997. "The Self." *Journal of Consciousness Studies* 4: 405–428.

Suzuki, Shunryu. 2002. *Not Always So: Practicing the True Spirit of Zen*, ed. Edward Espe Brown. New York: HarperCollins.

Taber, John. 2003. "Dharmakīrti against Physicalism." *Journal of Indian Philosophy* 31.4: 479–502.

Takahashi Hisao, Maeda Takashi, Yonezawa Yoshiyasu, Taki Eikan, Nagashima Jundō, Matsunami Yasuo, Kouda Ryōshū, Yoshizawa Hidetoshi, and Nishino Midori, eds. 2006. *Vimalakīrtinirdeśa: A Sanskrit Edition Based upon the Manuscript Newly Found at the Potala Palace*. Tokyo: Taisho University Press.

Tanaka, Koji. 2003. "Three Schools of Paraconsistency." *Australasian Journal of Logic* 1: 28–42.

———. 2006. "Davidson and Chinese Conceptual Scheme." In *Davidson's Philosophy and Chinese Philosophy*, ed. Bo Mou: 55–71. Leiden: Brill.

———. 2007. "In Defence of Priest: A Rejoinder to Mortensen." *Philosophy East and West* 57.2: 257–259.

Thera, Nyanaponika, and Bhikkhu Bodhi, trans. 1999. *Aṅguttara Nikāya: Numerical Discourses of the Buddha*. Walnut Creek, CA: AltaMira.

Thich Nhat Hanh. 2002. *Anger*. New York: River Trade.

Tillemans, Tom J. F. 1992. "Note liminaire." In *Etudes bouddhiques offertes à Jacques May*, ed. Johannes Bronkhorst, Katsumi Mimaki, and Tom J. F. Tillemans. *Asiatische Studien/Etudes Asiatiques* 46.1: 9–12.

———. 1999. *Scripture, Logic, Language: Essays on Dharmakīrti and His Tibetan Successors*. Boston: Wisdom.

———. 2000. *Dharmakīrti's Pramāṇavārttika: An Annotated Translation of the Fourth Chapter (parārthānumāna)*, vol. 1 (k. 1–148). Wien: Verlag der Österreichischen Akademie der Wissenschaften.

Tillemans, Tom J. F. 2001. "Trying to Be Fair to Mādhyamika Buddhism." *The Numata Yehan Lecture in Buddhism, Winter 2001*. Calgary: Religious Studies Department, University of Calgary.

———. 2003. "Metaphysics for Mādhyamikas." In *The Svātantrika-Prāsaṅgika Distinction*, ed. Georges Dreyfus and Sara McClintock: 93–123. Boston: Wisdom.

———. 2004. "What Are Mādhyamikas Refuting? Śāntarakṣita, Kamalaśīla, *et alii* on Superimpositions (*samāropa*)." In *Three Mountains and Seven Rivers: Prof. Musashi Tachikawa's Felicitation Volume*, ed. S. Hino and T. Wada: 225–237. Delhi: Motilal Banarsidass.

Tola, Fernando, and Carmen Dragonetti. 1998. "Against the Attribution of the *Vigrahavyāvartanī* to Nāgārjuna." *Wiener Zeitschrift für die Kunde Südasiens und Archiv für Indische Philosophie* 42: 151–166.

Tsong kha pa. 1973. *rTsa shes ṭīk chen*. Sarnath: Pleasure of Elegant Sayings Press.

———. 2000–2004. *The Great Treatise of the Stages of the Path to Enlightenment*. Ithaca, NY: Snow Lion.

———. 2006. *Ocean of Reasoning: A Great Commentary on Nāgārjuna's Mūlamadhyamakakārikā*, trans. Ngawang Samten and Jay L. Garfield. New York: Oxford University Press.

Uddyotakara. 1936. *Nyāyavārttika*, ed. Taranatha Nyaya-tarkatirtha and Amarendramohan Tarkatirtha. Calcutta: Calcutta Sanskrit Series.

Vose, Kevin Alan. 2005. "The Birth of Prāsaṅgika: A Buddhist Movement in India and Tibet." Ph.D. diss., University of Virginia.

Walton, Kendall. 1990. *Mimesis as Make-Believe*. Cambridge, MA: Harvard University Press.

Wayman, Alex. 1971. "The Mirror-Like Knowledge in Mahāyāna Buddhist Literature." *Asiatische Studien* 25: 353–363.

Williams, Paul. 1980. "Some Aspects of Language and Construction in the Madhyamaka." *Journal of Indian Philosophy* 8: 1–45.

———. 1998a. *Altruism and Reality: Studies in the Philosophy of the Bodhicaryāvatāra*. Surrey, England: Curzon.

———. 1998b. *The Reflexive Nature of Awareness: A Tibetan Madhyamaka Defence*. London: Curzon.

Wittgenstein, Ludwig. 1922. *Tractatus Logico-Philosophicus*, trans. C. K. Ogden. London: Routledge.

———. 1958. *Philosophical Investigations*. London: Macmillan.

———. 1998. *Culture and Value*, ed. George Henrik von Wright and trans. Peter Winch. Oxford: Blackwell.

Wright, Crispin. 1997. "Language Mastery and the Sorites Paradox." In *Vagueness: A Reader*, ed. Rosanna Keefe and Peter Smith: 151–173. Cambridge, MA: MIT Press.

Yablo, Stephen. 2001. "Go Figure: A Path through Fictionalism." In *Midwestern Studies in Philosophy*, vol. 25: *Figurative Language*, ed. Peter A. French and Howard K. Wettstein: 72–102. Boston: Blackwell.

Index